DEVELOPING COUNTRIES IN THE GATT LEGAL SYSTEM

In this reissued edition of *Developing Countries in the GATT Legal System*, the seminal impact of the late Robert E. Hudec's work on the situation of developing countries within the international trade system is once again available. Robert Hudec is regarded as one of the most prominent commentators on the evolution of the current international trade regime. This book offers his analysis of the dynamics playing out between developed and developing nations. This analysis, insightful when the book was first published, continues to serve as a thoughtful guide to how future trade policy must consider the demands of the developing world.

This edition includes a new introduction by J. Michael Finger that reviews Hudec's work to understand how the General Agreement on Tariffs and Trade (GATT) got into its current historical-institutional predicament. It also examines the lasting impact of Hudec's work on current research on international trade systems.

The late Robert E. Hudec was the Melvin E. Steen Professor of Law at the University of Minnesota. He was a leading authority on trade law and the GATT. During the early stages of the Kennedy Round of multilateral trade negotiations, conducted under the auspices of the GATT, he was Assistant General Counsel to the Special Representative for Trade Negotiations (STR) in the Executive Office of the President of the United States (1963–65), later known as the Executive Office of the President. Professor Hudec wrote many articles in professional journals on the law of international economic affairs. He was the author of *Adjudication of International Trade Disputes* (1977) and *The GATT Legal System and World Trade Diplomacy* (1975).

Developing Countries in the GATT Legal System

ROBERT E. HUDEC

With an Introduction by
J. Michael Finger

CAMBRIDGE
UNIVERSITY PRESS

CAMBRIDGE UNIVERSITY PRESS
Cambridge, New York, Melbourne, Madrid, Cape Town, Singapore,
São Paulo, Delhi, Dubai, Tokyo, Mexico City

Cambridge University Press
32 Avenue of the Americas, New York, NY 10013-2473, USA

www.cambridge.org
Information on this title: www.cambridge.org/9781107003293

First published by Gower Publishing Company Limited 1987
New edition with Introduction by J. Michael Finger published 2011

Printed in the United States of America

A catalog record for this publication is available from the British Library.

Library of Congress Cataloging in Publication data

Hudec, Robert E.
Developing countries in the GATT legal system / Robert E. Hudec ; [foreword by] Joseph
Michael Finger.
    p. cm.
Includes bibliographical references and index.
ISBN 978-1-107-00329-3 (hardback)
1. Tariff – Law and legislation – Developing countries.   2. Foreign trade regulation –
Developing countries.   3. Tariff – Law and legislation.   4. Foreign trade regulation.
5. General Agreement on Tariffs and Trade (Organization)   I. Title.
K4609.5.H83   2010
343.172405′6–dc22   2010040099

ISBN 978-1-107-00329-3 Hardback

In memory of Jan Tumlir

Contents

Foreword

RELATIONS between developed and developing countries in the international trading system, whose norms, rules and procedures are set out in the General Agreement on Tariffs and Trade (GATT), have been reaching an *impasse*. For a quarter of a century, the developed countries have been allowing, or encouraging, the developing countries to become contracting parties to the GATT without requiring them to abide by the more important obligations of membership. What is more, they have acquiesced in the formal derogation from the principle of non-discrimination, which is the keystone of the GATT, to permit the Generalized System of Preferences (GSP) in favor of developing countries to be established and maintained.

At the same time, developing countries – especially the more advanced ones – have been faced with discriminatory protection against them whenever their exports have been uncomfortably successful in the markets of developed countries, with such protection often taking the form of export-restraint arrangements negotiated "outside" the framework of GATT norms, rules and procedures.

The costs to developing countries of limitations on their access to the markets of developed countries are not so much offset as multiplied by their more or less complete freedom to establish and maintain trade regimes which are highly protectionist and Byzantine in their complexity.

By the early 1980s, it was clear that the role of developing countries in the international trading system was bound to attract increasing attention, especially if a new "round" of multilateral trade negotiations under GATT auspices was to be undertaken. Accordingly, the Trade Policy Research Centre, with the help of a grant from the Leverhulme Trust in London, embarked in 1983 on a major program of studies on the Participation of Developing Countries in the International Trading System, supervised by Martin Wolf, the Centre's Director of Studies.

The purpose of the program has been to clarify, for public discussion and policy formation, the underlying reasons for the current difficulties in relations between developed and developing countries in the GATT system. The program focuses on both economic and legal issues in the GATT system *per se* and on impediments to trade liberalization in individual developing countries. The emphasis on the latter derived from the perception that the GATT framework of norms, rules and procedures can be no more than the "handmaiden" of trade liberalization. Liberalization will not be brought about, however, unless there is a consensus in the countries concerned on both its feasibility and its value in promoting their economic growth and development. The domestic impediments to trade liberalization have to be understood if they are to be overcome.

It is true for all countries that multilateral negotiations are a means more of achieving the trade liberalization that is already widely understood to be in each country's own interests than of liberalizing when no such benefit is seen. In other words, reciprocal bargaining is a way of overcoming domestic resistance to the trade liberalization that is strongly desired by prevailing forces in each country, both in government and in society at large. A desire to liberalize, almost irrespective of what happens elsewhere, is particularly significant in small countries. The smaller the country, the less effective is its international bargaining power and, therefore, the less persuasive is the argument that improved access to markets abroad depends on the liberalization of access to its own market. For this reason, smaller countries usually liberalize only if there is a strong domestic consensus that such liberalization is in their own interests, such a consensus having been long established in countries like Sweden, Switzerland and Singapore.

In developing the program of studies it was clear that both the trade policies of developing countries and the role of those countries in the international trading system reflect economic ideas that have found legal expression in the GATT and associated codes. In particular, developing countries have consistently denied the relevance to themselves of the twin GATT concepts of "equal treatment" and reciprocal trade liberalization. Arguing that "equal treatment of unequals is unfair", developing countries have demanded discrimination in their favor under the general rubric of "special and differential treatment" or, more recently, "differential and more favorable treatment". Arguing that reliance on the market thwarts economic development, developing countries have insisted on their need to introduce protection at home while receiving market access and preferential treatment abroad.

Drafts of the papers arising from the Centre's program of studies were presented at a three-day research meeting at Wiston House, near Steyning, in the United Kingdom, attended by those engaged on the program and a number of other scholars and officials. The meeting was immediately preceded by a two-day meeting, also at Wiston House, of a study group which is drawing together the conclusions of the program of studies. This meeting, too, was attended by a number of officials. The two international meetings were funded by a grant from the Ford Foundation in New York. As mentioned earlier, the program of studies, as a whole, has been funded by the Leverhulme Trust in London.

As usual, it has to be stressed that the views expressed in this book do not necessarily represent those of members of the Council or those of the staff and associates of the Trade Policy Research Centre which, having general terms of reference, does not represent a consensus of opinion on any particular issue. The purpose of the Centre is to promote independent analysis and public discussion of international economic policy issues.

HUGH CORBET
Director
Trade Policy Research Centre
London
May 1987

Acknowledgments

THE IDEA for this study was conceived by Martin Wolf, Director of Studies at the Trade Policy Research Centre, as part of a program of studies on the Participation of Developing Countries in the International Trading System. An early draft of the study, along with drafts of other studies in the program, was presented at an international conference of scholars and senior officials which the Centre held at Wiston House, near Steyning, West Sussex, England, in October 1984. During the two years it took to bring the study from its Wiston House version to the more ambitious first edition form, Martin functioned as principal editor, critic and motivation coach. With all this assistance came a completely free hand to pursue the issues as I saw fit. To say that I am grateful to Martin and to the Centre would be to state the obvious.

Colleagues who read and commented on earlier typescripts include J. Michael Finger and Robert E. Baldwin at the Wiston House conference, Frieder Roessler and Richard Blackhurst at the GATT Secretariat, and Dan Farber and Dan Gifford at the Minnesota Law School. I am indebted to each of them.

I owe a very special debt to the late Jan Tumlir, the former Director of Economic Research and Analysis of the GATT Secretariat. For almost a decade, Jan was a teacher, a friend and a model of what it means to have integrity in this business. His last words to me were about this study – a typically gruff complaint that I was avoiding several hard issues, coupled with an expression of his personal conviction that I would have something worthwhile to say about them. This study is dedicated to Jan's memory.

ROBERT E. HUDEC
Minneapolis
June 1987

DEVELOPING COUNTRIES IN THE GATT LEGAL SYSTEM

Introduction to the New Edition

J. Michael Finger

The history of GATT's relationship with developing countries began with what Robert E. Hudec describes as "a legal relationship based essentially on parity of obligation" {24}.[1] Yet as the GATT system evolved it increasingly left developing countries outside of the momentum towards liberalization that the negotiations built up among developed countries and exempted them from the general though imperfect sense of discipline that developed countries came to accept. From GATT's beginning through the mid-1980s – the period Hudec studied – the identity of developing countries in the system became almost entirely a matter of their demanding non-reciprocal and preferential treatment and developed countries responding grudgingly to those demands.

The result was a relationship that Hudec describes as "form without substance" {99}.

In form, the relationship was extensively elaborated:

> After years of debate and of gradual compromising, all the key ideas advanced by developing countries – non-reciprocity, preferences, special and differential treatment – were accepted at the formal level during the 1970s. They now appear in several GATT legal texts and in countless declarations. {155}

These expressions did not, however, have the force of international law obligation. The commitments were compromised by language such as "The developed countries shall to the fullest extent possible – that is, except where compelling reasons, which may include legal reasons, make it impossible, . . ."[2]

This is almost a mirror image of the "diplomat's jurisprudence" that Hudec in other investigations found to exist among developed countries.[3] This "diplomat's jurisprudence" was a compromise between jurisprudence as understood by lawyers and the reality of the limited influence trade negotiators had over national trade policy decisions. In an era in which there was sometimes a greater sense of shared objective among trade negotiators than between these negotiators and government officials at home, not pinning down trade differences with legal precision could allow the working out of a mutually acceptable solution before the matter reached domestic politics.

If the system did not ask for reciprocity from developing countries in exchange for what they wanted, for example, better access to developed country markets, then how did it attempt to motivate developed countries to provide such concessions?

Hudec's answer: appeal to "the welfare obligation".

> The power to govern usually brings with it, according to most twentieth-century political norms, a duty to take care of the disadvantaged members of the group being governed. For example, it would not have been possible to create governing power in the European Community unless the Community undertook a responsibility to do something for the depressed areas within its domain. {31}[4]

Not reciprocity but rather the welfare obligation of the rich to assist the poor came increasingly to be the motive that the system called on to stimulate developed countries response to the demands of developing countries.

Hudec moves on to ask if further appeal to the welfare obligation – or to an alternative strategy in which developing countries' offered reciprocity – might be effective (a) to discipline developed country restrictions of particular relevance to developing country exports and (b) to support policies within developing countries that would help them to better use international trade as a vehicle for development.

As to influencing developed country liberalization, he concludes that the gradual pace of developed country liberalization is likely to continue but would not be significantly affected by either strategy. Likewise – writing in the mid-1980s – he saw neither strategy as likely to discipline the growing use of "voluntary" quantitative restrictions where developing countries were enjoying particular export success. The moral force of the welfare obligation had been spent and, so far as trade is concerned, refocused on the poor at home. As for reciprocity, developing countries did not have the economic size or power for it to provide them great leverage.

The one source of power the system might provide is the most-favored nation (MFN) principle:

> [T]he MFN obligation is, above all else, a legal substitute for economic power on behalf of smaller countries. {180}

But the MFN obligation, particularly with regard to developing countries, had been compromised. The institutionalization of special and differential treatment for developing countries has been part of the general erosion of this principle.[5] What developing countries have gained from the granting of discriminatory treatment in their favor has been overwhelmed by this systemic erosion.

From this followed Hudec's first recommendation:

> [D]eveloping countries should re-direct their long-term objectives to the strengthening of the GATT's MFN obligation in all respects. {189}

His second recommendation was that:

> GATT's legal policy towards developing countries should change and . . . the Contracting Parties should instead establish a regime of developing country legal obligations that would provide support for governments of developing countries in opposing unwanted protectionist policies at home. {190}

"Unwanted protectionist policies" does not necessarily mean *all* protectionist policies. Hudec admitted the possibility that while some import restrictions will be wasteful, others could be constructive. Developing countries, like developed ones, would benefit from the support the system can provide to sort one from the other.

However, for the system to provide such support, developing countries would have to change their attitude towards it. Even on application and reform of GATT provisions such as Article XVIII's infant-industry protection provisions, the developing country stance had been simply to broaden what the provisions allow rather than to work for an effective differentiation of constructive from wasteful trade interventions. The system Hudec saw was about more latitude to intervene versus less, not about good intervention versus bad.

CONTENT OF THE INTRODUCTION

In the following parts of this introduction, I summarize the arguments behind these conclusions and recommendations – in a way that I hope will be a stimulus to read the book rather than a substitute for such a reading. I also report what I have learned from an examination of the citations the book has received in other published works.

The summary has been significantly influenced by what I learned from the citations. When I first read the book I interpreted it as a skilled example of what in my undergraduate days had been called "institutional economics" and has come since to be called "the new institutional economics".[6] However, I found when I examined the citations that hardly anyone else had read the book as an application of institutional economics.

Readers have cited Hudec's historical-institutional analysis as "expert testimony" that special and differential treatment has been an unproductive strategy, but have not taken up the reasoning he brought to the issue. Its conclusions but not its logic have been added to the more familiar comparative static and econometric analysis of the impact of this policy or that, for example, of infant-industry protection or the General System of Preferences (GSP). This overlooks Hudec's work to understand how the GATT got into the historical-institutional rut he identified and wastes the insights this analysis might provide to move it to a more productive relationship. I therefore precede my summary with a brief note on institutional economics.

In the last section I speculate on an extension of Hudec's analysis to cover the extensive liberalization by developing countries and their growing role in the international trading system. Hudec's story line was to ask how developing countries remained outside of the momentum toward liberalization that the GATT legal system created among developed countries. I suggest that the new story line is how – and influenced by what – they created their own momentum and how this momentum has interacted with the momentum of the GATT/World Trade Organization (WTO) system. Analyzing the evolution of developing country trade policy as either application of or resistance to the GATT/WTO system would miss a lot of what has gone on.

HUDEC AND INSTITUTIONALISM

David Palmeter (2003), in a perceptive tribute to Robert Hudec, pointed out that much of Hudec's work is grounded in a mode of thought Palmeter identifies as "American legal realism", whose counterpart in economics he points out is institutionalism.[7]

Institutionalism studies how organizations and their formalities (rules, procedures, etc.) evolve from the intersection of the customs, traditions, values and perceptions of reality (e.g., the science or economics) of the persons and groups who are prominent in the events that make up this evolution. A key precept here is that organizations and their formalities *evolve* rather than *are created*. They are shaped by repetitions (experiences) perhaps more than by design.

One of the key findings of institutional economics is that institutions such as the WTO – evolving as they do from their principal actors' limited perceptions of the relevant science and the varied if not conflicting objectives they bring to the issues taken up – often turn out not to be socially or economically efficient. Douglass North, whose work has earned a Nobel Prize in economics, separates successful examples of economic development from unsuccessful ones according to how the institutions for ownership, use and exchange of economic resources have developed.[8] Walton H. Hamilton, in the *Encyclopaedia of the Social Sciences* that first appeared in 1932, phrased the point well: "An institution is an imperfect agent of order and of purpose.... Intent and chance alike share in its creation" (1963, p. 89).

The issues that institutions take on and the procedures they evolve to deal with these issues feed back to reshape values and perceptions of reality. The quip, "When we put on our GATT hats, we put on our GATT minds," captures something of the meaning here. Drawing again on Walton Hamilton's graceful phrasing, "Institutions and human actions, complements and antitheses, are forever remaking each other in the endless drama of the social process" (1963, p. 89).

THE EVOLUTION OF THE RELATIONSHIP

The GATT began as part of the plan among post–Second World War Western leaders to establish a safer and more stable (Western) world than they had inherited. Linking countries into a web of commerce and shared prosperity would help to free them from the power diplomacy and every second-generation cycle of war in which Europe-based civilization had been trapped.

The evolution of developing countries' position in the GATT system, as Hudec explained it, is a matter of the ethics and the economics that the major actors brought to the issues they took up within the GATT and how these were applied in the repetitions that fixed them into policies, regulations and procedures.

Developing countries at the ITO and GATT negotiations demanded a commitment from developed countries to provide significant resource transfers. They also wanted freedom from the general idea of discipline that the arrangements were trying to impose on others. In the latter regard, their position was hardly different from that of developed countries, acting individually {29–31}.

However, the GATT as adopted in 1948 made few concessions to the developing country position. How then, Hudec asked, did developing countries' position in the system become increasingly a demand for unreciprocated trade concessions and the developed countries' reluctant response to these pleas?

The Path of Least Resistance

Part of the answer is the values that the system embodied. As high politics, the GATT was collective action: *individual sacrifice for the common good*. As low politics it was mercantilism — the benefit was access to foreign markets, but this had to be paid for by giving access to one's own.

Another element in the ethics of the system was the welfare obligation. The moral obligation of the rich to assist the poor came increasingly to be what the system called on to motivate developed countries to respond to the demands of developing countries.

As to economics, the mercantilist virtue of import restrictions and the (individual) sacrifice of giving them up was driven home by the developed countries' insistence on retaining some of theirs. Europeans were more sympathetic to the infant-industry (and reconstruction) argument for protection than were US leaders, but the US position on discipline had its own exceptions, including quantitative restrictions on agricultural imports, escape clauses and antidumping provisions.

The ethics and the economics came together in a way that Hudec described as follows:

> This theoretical contradiction was fundamental. In an avowedly welfare relationship, where the needy have a recognized claim to unilateral payments, the strong cannot make a principled demand for liberal trade policies by the needy when, in the same breath, they define trade liberalization as a "payment". {34}

Within such a conception, developing country leaders can enhance their status by demanding exemption from discipline over trade restrictions; developed countries' trade officials find it easier to acquiesce in these demands than to convince their governments to reduce import barriers. This is a principal-agent problem in the making:

> Once it has been conceded, as a matter of principle, that legal freedom constitutes "help" to developing countries, the future was virtually fixed. . . . When other kinds of "help" were not enough (which was almost invariably the case), there was always the possibility of doing something more on the legal side. {35}

> The policy of non-reciprocity has flourished primarily because, for both sides, it has been **the path of least resistance**. . . . It has been the easy way out for diplomats from developing countries, for it has allowed them to maintain the posture of vigorous representation without ever having to ask home governments to take difficult decisions. Finally, and perhaps most important, it has been the easy way out for the governments of developed countries and for their diplomats. Relaxation of legal discipline has always been the cost-free answer — the concession that developed countries could make without having to go through the unpleasant business of asking legislatures for real trade

liberalization [or real resources]. Like penny gin, it was an inexpensive way to keep the peace by pandering to the other side's worst instincts. {190–91, emphasis added}

Not about Developing Country Policies but about How Developed Countries Treat Them

Within GATT's first decade, pressure waned on developing countries to give concessions in the tariff negotiations, and rules that regulated restrictions by developing countries were relaxed. What this came to was that:

> From about 1958 onwards, developing countries seized the initiative and persuaded the GATT to concentrate on the behavior of developed countries towards them, rather than on their own behavior. {46}

The GATT response to the Haberler Report of 1958[9] was an early indication that the GATT was about the behavior of developed, not developing, countries. It concluded that existing arrangements were relatively unfavorable to primary producing countries, but it also concluded that progress depends on both developing and developed countries reducing their restrictions. The Action Program that followed took up only the need for change in developed country policies.

The formality of the legal relationship between developed and developing countries disguised its lack of substance. By the mid-1950s, a large share of GATT's developed as well as of its developing contracting parties had balance-of-payments measures in place, and legal reviews were as rigorous for developing countries as for developed. The difference was that developed countries were pressed to remove such measures – through the GATT reviews and other relationships such as the International Monetary Fund (IMF) and the Organization for European Economic Co-operation. In contrast,

> The developing country reviews became increasingly pro forma as their balance of payments problems remained drearily the same. Waivers for surcharges were routinely given. {44}

And soon:

> With developing countries, legal form is all there is to the relationship. Setting aside the formalities . . . they [developed and developing countries] would have nothing else to say to each other. {46}

In contrast, the relationship among developed countries was less formal but more substantive. A "diplomat's jurisprudence"[10] among developed countries avoided clear legal decisions so as to allow developed country governments to adjust towards shared objectives in ways that their understandings of domestic politics indicated would be most effective.

The GATT-UNCTAD Rivalry

The Cold War rivalry for developing countries' loyalties played an important role in shaping the place of developing countries in the GATT system. United Nations agencies, in documents such as the Declaration of a New International Economic Order and the Charter of Economic Rights and Duties of States, provided general voice for the claim of developing countries to non-reciprocal and preferential treatment {77–78}. The United Nations Conference on Trade and Development (UNCTAD), created in 1964, became a trade-specific venue for this competition, and in the rivalry between GATT and UNCTAD to "staff out" the concern to promote developing country interests, UNCTAD achieved several important victories.

One of these victories concerned the attachment of negative connotations to the way in which the normal GATT mode of reducing trade barriers would provide improved access for developing country exporters – even when the improved access was provided without reciprocity from developing countries. Let me give an example. Suppose that in negotiations with each other, Australia and New Zealand agree that each will reduce its MFN tariff rates on products on which each imports $1,000 worth from the other and $500 worth from a developing country. Australia and New Zealand have each reduced their tariff on $500 of imports from a developing country and have done so without a reciprocal concession from the developing country.

The formula UNCTAD applied in its evaluation of the Kennedy Round, however, would not grant Australia and New Zealand credit for affirmative action. UNCTAD's calculations would compare the amount of developed country exports covered by the agreed concessions ($2,000, in this example) with the amount of developing country exports covered (only $1,000) and use the comparison as a basis to criticize Australia and New Zealand's treatment of developing countries rather than to acknowledge the non-reciprocal market access they had provided.

The UNCTAD formula detached the traditional GATT mode of trade liberalization – exchanging reciprocal concessions, extended to all through the MFN principle – from the earning of any affirmative action credits. It focused attention on the lower coverage of "products of export interest to developing countries," and it became quickly the accepted approach, adopted even by the GATT Secretariat in its assessment of the Tokyo Round.

Hudec described that assessment as follows:

It was written quickly (but very thoroughly) in order to preempt the kind of negative evaluation that UNCTAD had made after the Kennedy Round. . . . It celebrated all the "victories" achieved by the Group of 77. . . . [A] central element of the "victories" was all the new legal freedoms developing countries had won, especially those which involved discriminatory special and differential treatment. . . . The year was 1979. Here was the GATT, still thoroughly preoccupied with holding the allegiance of developing countries and still making a virtue of the fact that GATT rules do not apply to developing countries. {90}

If the Kennedy and Tokyo Rounds were the two halves of a GATT-UNCTAD soccer match, one could say that the score was UNCTAD 2, GATT 0; the second goal being an own-goal.

Form without Substance

The last chapter in Hudec's history of the legal relationship bears the sub-title "Form without Substance". The GATT system, as it evolved, came to include an increasing number of expressions of the role of special and differential treatment in the system and an increasing use of legal language in these expressions. To the extent that the expressions had legal force, such as the Framework Agreements of 1979, they relaxed obligations that would otherwise have prevented discriminatory action such as tariff preferences in favor of developing countries. They also relaxed certain disciplines on developing countries such as those on infant-industry protection.

To the extent that the expressions were about obligating developed countries to provide special treatment for developing countries, they stopped short of making such into obligations. The "commitments" language of GATT Part IV, for example, states that "developed countries shall to the fullest extent possible – that is, except where compelling reasons, which may include legal reasons, make it impossible . . ." (GATT Article XXXVII, paragraph 1).

MAKING SPECIAL AND DIFFERENTIAL TREATMENT AN INTERNATIONAL LAW OBLIGATION

The many repetitions of the special and differential treatment obligation bring forward a key question: Will the non-reciprocity principle ever take on the nature of an international law obligation? As Hudec posed the issue:

[T]he effort in recent years to define a new "international law of economic development" has included, as one of the new obligations to be recognized, a duty of preferential and non-reciprocal treatment towards developing countries. If such a duty were recognized as an obligation of customary international law, binding on all governments, this would obviously make a major contribution to the success of the non-reciprocity policy. {158–59}

In his review of the legal discussion, Hudec noted that

[T]he number of quasi-commitments has already persuaded many legal scholars to characterize the welfare concept as a sort of quasi-law, using various labels such as "soft law", "legal principle", "law-in-the-making" and "obligation of good faith". {159}

He concluded, however, that "this is as far as the legal force of the welfare obligation can ever go" {159} and quoted in support a United Nations review of the development of such legal principles {100–01}. He also examined the form that the "have versus have-not obligation" has taken in national laws and points out that:

The examples of redistributive justice found in national tax and welfare laws do not ... create citizen-to-citizen rights and duties. They are always structured as public law; the extra duties of the rich (for example, paying higher taxes) are owed to the sovereign rather than to particular deserving claimants; the rights of the deserving poor (for example, rights to welfare payments) are recognized as an obligation owed by the sovereign, rather than by any individual taxpayer. {159}

Creating in contemporary law an obligation or right to non-reciprocal and preferential treatment is not in the cards, even though, Hudec pointed out, feudal law "was able to enforce status-defined rights and duties"[11] {159}.

Hudec concluded that "the emerging international law of economic development will not be able to add any legal force to the demand of developing countries for non-reciprocal liberalization by developed countries" {160}.

Even so, the repetition of demands and acknowledgements might have some effect: It could influence actions by the developed countries without going so far as to regulate them. Ever the institutionalist, Hudec concluded that "[t]ime has also endowed GATT obligations with a quality of law in the institutional sense, so that GATT obligations now possess a certain amount of respect-for-law force independent of their substance" {161}.

BETTER SUPPORT FOR TRADE AS A VEHICLE FOR DEVELOPMENT

In the second half of the book Hudec turned his attention to how developing country governments might influence the GATT system to buttress their use of trade as a vehicle for development. I summarize first his analysis of how the system might better support the choice between constructive and wasteful trade policies and in the following sub-section the matter of maintaining and expanding their access to developed country markets.

Support for Good Developing Country Trade Policies

As to the best trade policy, Hudec accepted that "the theoretical case for infant-industry protection is certainly a respectable one" {129}. Consequently, he takes up the impact of GATT's no-obligations policy towards developing countries under the assumption that intervention policies are both harmful and, alternatively, that they are helpful.

When intervention policies are assumed to be harmful, the case against the no-obligations policy is familiar. The key flaws are that (a) it insulates the decisions taken with regard to protecting domestic production from the export sector's interests and (b) it leaves protection as a politically attractive though economically costly solution to problems that might be more effectively addressed by "domestic" policies.

In this case the GATT system might provide developing country governments the same assistance to overcome these flaws as it has provided to developed: "[I]n most developing countries, the governments wishing to follow a liberal trade policy have essentially the same internal needs for political assistance that governments of developed countries have . . ." {147}.

When Hudec posited that some trade interventions might be economically beneficial, the challenge he examined is how the GATT system might guide governments towards such policies and away from harmful interventions, that is, ordinary protection. He began this analysis by pointing out that there is nothing in the infant-industry argument to suggest that only industries with unrealized comparative advantage will come forward for protection. The question is whether acceptance of GATT obligations would help a developing country government to separate beneficial interventions from ordinary protection {147}.

Hudec was skeptical. His review of government as economic manager led him to conclude that "the theoretical case for intervention becomes less persuasive when the capacity of governments to operate such a policy is examined" {129}. He suggested that Article XVIII procedures might help to discipline application of balance of payments and infant-industry protection to constructive applications, but concluded that developing country governments have not attempted to use the instruments in this way. The changes of these provisions they have supported, he found, have been towards general relaxation of discipline rather than towards better focus on constructive use {150}. He concluded that "the GATT's current policy is harming developing countries more than it is helping them, even under the assumption that developing countries can be helped by infant-industry policies" {139}.

He ended this analysis pessimistically, acknowledging that Article XVIII procedures might be more constructively used, but offering no suggestions on how such provisions might be rewritten.

Access to Developed Country Markets

Before looking into how voluntary export restraints (VERs) aimed at developing country export successes might be disciplined, Hudec reviewed briefly the general trend of developed country liberalization. He acknowledged that there were substantial forces in developed countries that would continue their long-term trend of liberalization {188} and that the non-reciprocated access that developing countries had gained would likely be maintained:

> the non-reciprocity doctrine of the GATT's current policy has demonstrated a considerable degree of political effectiveness in assembling support within developed countries for liberal trade policies towards developing countries. {169–70}

Hudec concluded that developing country reciprocity would add little to the trend of developed country liberalization. Developing country markets were at the time small, and the long history of trade-related crises in developing countries had left developed country governments unsure that GATT bindings would effectively restrain developing country restrictions. Moreover, "most developing countries already import as much as their foreign exchange earnings permit, without any legal commitments at all" {164}.

Summing this up in Hudec's words, "none of the legal strategies currently available to developing countries appears to offer much help in improving the behavior of developed countries towards them" {188}.

Disciplining VERs

Hudec recognized that restrictions on trade in agricultural products and on some labor-intensive products were continuing problems, but pointed out as "the most ominous barriers on the industrial side" {156} the growing use of "voluntary" quantitative restrictions where developing countries were enjoying particular export success. For the reasons taken up earlier, neither appeal to the welfare obligation nor developing country reciprocity was likely to limit such actions.

Hudec saw this protection as particularly ominous because targeting the few "disruptive" suppliers from developing countries (the new guys) made traditional suppliers into beneficiaries from the restrictions. "Discrimination thus permits the building of a nice coalition of interested parties, all in favor of restricting trade" {180}.

Developing country reciprocity or appeal to the welfare principle would be no more effective here than in changing the general trend of developed country policies. The obvious policy logic is that if GATT contracting parties had to apply all restrictions on an MFN basis, then third-party exporters would be losers, too. They would have an incentive to resist rather than to support a restriction {179–81}.

RECOMMENDATIONS

In the last chapter, titled "First Steps Towards a Better Legal Policy," Hudec presented two recommendations:

- Developing country governments and other contracting parties should direct their efforts towards strengthening the MFN principle.
- The contracting parties should establish and developing country contracting parties accept a legal regime that would support developing country governments in opposing wasteful protectionist policies at home.

Neither objective, he acknowledged, would be easy to achieve.[12] He saw widespread acceptance by developing countries of legal obligations as a particularly messy business, achieved perhaps "through the decisions of individual developing countries to 'cave in' to pressure from developed countries"[13] {193}. As to restoring the MFN principle, Hudec pointed out that an overwhelming number of interests are benefiting from regional arrangements and other forms of discrimination {182–83}. Piecemeal reform would face the multiple beneficiaries of whatever was in the docket. Discrimination, like ordinary protection, can be immediate and personal; non-discrimination is systemic and cold. Compared with the individual-sacrifice-for-the-common-good courage needed to put the GATT system in place, discrimination is the easy way out.

ANALYSIS OF CITATIONS TO DEVELOPING COUNTRIES
IN THE GATT LEGAL SYSTEM

The "Google Scholar" section of the Google search engine allows one to search for the citations to a particular book or article. I used this search facility to identify citations to each of Robert E. Hudec's publications – working from the Hudec bibliography provided by Daniel Kennedy and James Southwick in the festschrift that they edited (2002, pp. 667–71).[14] The screenings identified a total of almost 1,000 books, published papers and working papers that cited Hudec publications.

Citations to All of Hudec's Publications

Table 1 provides a summary of my tabulation of citations to all of Robert Hudec's published works. My guiding principle in this tabulation was to determine how many other works cited Hudec's books and papers; hence I counted only once a publication in which Hudec might have been cited several times. I screened as best I could for duplications such as a working paper and a published article with the same title by the same author, but included in the count "working papers" for which I could not identify a published version.

As one might expect, the tally indicates that almost two-thirds of the citations are to Hudec's work on dispute settlement. Including the publications that I have classified in the table as "dispute-settlement related" (e.g., on US "Section 301" and on "fairness") increases the total to three-fourths of the citations. Hudec's work on developing countries in the GATT system received 15 percent of the citations I was able to identify.

I did not undertake to sort citations as "in a law publication" versus "in an economics or public policy publication," but I have the impression that a significantly larger percentage of the citations to his work on developing countries in the GATT is in economics or policy publications. There are two bases for this impression, the first being the content of the references to the work on developing countries, which I discuss later. The second is my tabulation of the references to Hudec's work in the festschrift edited by Kennedy and Southwick (2002). When I counted the Hudec publications cited in its footnotes or in references listed at the ends of chapters,[15] I found thirty-four references to Hudec publications, all except two to his work on dispute settlement. The other two were to the book *Developing Countries in the GATT Legal System*. They were by Sylvia Ostry and by me; both of us are economists or policy analysts rather than legal scholars.

TABLE 1. *Summary of Google academic search identification of works that cite Robert Hudec's publications*

	Number	Percentage of Total
Dispute Settlement	602	63
Book: *Enforcing International Trade Law: The Evolution of the Modern GATT Legal System*	205	21
Book: *The GATT Legal System and World Trade Diplomacy*	117	12
Book: *Adjudication of International Trade Disputes*	14	1
Articles, monographs, and addresses	266	28
Dispute-Settlement Related	111	12
Articles, etc. on		0
Trade remedies	11	1
Environmental law and trade	56	6
Section 301 and fairness	44	5
Developing Countries in the GATT	147	15
Book: *Developing Countries in the GATT Legal System*	127	13
Articles, monographs and addresses	20	2
Other	98	10
Books	57	6
Articles, monographs and addresses	41	4
Totals	958	100

Source: Google Academic Search accessed 13 March, 2009.

Citations to Developing Countries in the GATT Legal System

My screening with Google Scholar identified 127 books, published papers, and working papers that contained references to the book. From resources available at the World Bank–IMF library or through the Internet I was able to obtain copies of almost all of these works, and I examined each to determine to what effect it had cited the book. In this tabulation, when a book, article, or paper cited *Developing Countries* more than once, I took account of the citations separately. Here, the objective was to identify the points on which *Developing Countries* was cited as source or authority rather than the number of publications that had cited the book.

About 15 percent of the citations were to the book as a general source on GATT history or developing countries in the GATT system – for example, "for a detailed review of developing countries in GATT see...." I did not include these in Table 2.

TABLE 2. *Conclusions, facts and recommendations for which* Developing
Countries in the GATT Legal System *is cited as source or support*

Conclusion, Information or Recommendation	Percentage
Conclusions	67
Special and differential treatment has not been a productive strategy.	20
An MFN regime is the only substitute for economic power.	11
DC reciprocity would not buy better market access from developed countries.	9
GATT's BoP and infant-industry provisions allow measures that do economic harm to the country applying them.	5
Participation in reciprocal negotiations would win more market access than asking for preferences.	
Preferences have been of limited value to developing countries.	
SDT is bad economics for DCs (this point different from it being a bad strategy for achieving good economic results).	
Seeking preferences diminishes the capacity of developing country governments to overcome domestic pressures for protection.	
Seeking preferences diminishes the incentive for domestic liberalization.	
Seeking preferences is not an effective strategy for changing developed country policies in a way constructive for DCs.	
Special and differential treatment came to dominate the GATT conception of trade and development.	
Special and differential treatment cannot be made a GATT/WTO legal obligation.	
The MFN system is critical to defending DC interests.	
Negotiators recognized that special and differential treatment of DCs was justified.	
DCs' small size prevented their lawsuits from having impact in GATT.	
The many developed country trade restrictions GATT accepted endorse trade restrictions as a legitimate instrument of development.	
There is a theoretical case for infant-industry protection.	
DC strategy has been to seek special and differential treatment.	
GATT in the 1960s displayed an anti-legalistic trend.	
Part IV, etc., constitute hortatory, not legal, obligations.	
Uruguay achieved little with its 1961 GATT suit against 15 developed countries.	
Information	31
Colonial experience was one in which developed country metropoles applied many restrictions.	
Conduct of DCs in GATT procedures.	
Content and structure of negotiations.	
Content of a GATT procedure.	
Content of US Reciprocal Trade Agreements.	

Conclusion, Information or Recommendation	Percentage
Content or outcome of a GATT dispute.	
DC position in the negotiations.	
GATT 1954–55 review outcome.	
GATT legal structure.	
History of GATT and of negotiations.	
Positions taken or accepted by negotiators.	
Result of a GATT procedure.	
Recommendations	2
DC governments and other GATT contracting parties should accept reciprocity and non-discrimination as the basis for the GATT system's relationship within DCs.	
DC interests should have priority in MFN negotiations.	

Note: None of the individual facts or reasons for which no percentage is given accounted for more than 3 percent of the citations. SDT: special and differential treatment; BoP: balance of payments; DC: developing countries.

My tally of the other citations to *Developing Countries* is presented in Table 2. About two-thirds of the hits cite the book in support of a particular conclusion, and the other third cite it as a source of information – for example, a secondary source on the content of the GATT or of a GATT Working Group report. Although many of the articles and books that cite this book present policy recommendations, these are almost always presented as the author's own recommendations rather than as Hudec's. Hudec is instead cited among the sources of information from which the author crafts his or her own recommendation.

Again, as one might expect, the conclusion most often cited is what most would agree is a major theme of the book: that special and differential treatment has not been a productive strategy. A related point, that preferences granted by developed countries have been of limited value to developing countries, was also frequently cited.[16]

A second observation is that in none of the references did I find the author arguing that Hudec was wrong – disputing his facts or conclusions. All citers I was able to locate take Hudec's point as given and go on to incorporate it into their own analysis.[17]

A third observation overlaps with the previous one. It relates to the question: Is Hudec more often cited in writings that conclude in sympathy with or averse to special and differential treatment? I do not have a precise count on this point, but I did observe that many authors whose general thrust was favorable to special and differential treatment or infant-industry protection drew support from the book. Some, for example, cite Hudec's acceptance that there could be a theoretical case for infant-industry protection and then elaborate their own suggestions as to how to make such protection productive. A number of writings cite in similar vein Hudec's conclusion that because developing country markets are too small to be of value to developed country exporters, reciprocity from developing countries would have little effect on developed countries' policies. The conclusion that GSP preferences have been of limited value is sometimes the beginning of an argument that developed countries should give more; Hudec's conclusion on special and differential treatment is the take-off for an argument that, if suitably tweaked, it would be productive.

It surprised me to find how few of the works that cite the book take up Hudec's historical/institutional reasoning and interpret it simply as an analysis of the effectiveness of special and differential treatment. Special and differential treatment is not, after all, the *subject* of the historical analysis; it is the *conclusion*. The subject, as the book's title informs, is *developing countries in the GATT legal system*. Hudec's insights on how the GATT system got into the institutional rut in which he found it are not questioned, and they are not brought to bear on how it might get out.

Unaware that institutional analysis often finds human institutions to have evolved in forms that are neither socially nor economically efficient, some citers have passed off Hudec's conclusions about the GATT as "overly cynical" or "a dark vision". Some of the conflict here might be discomfort with ideas not expressed in academic jargon. If explained as "maximizing behavior", with perhaps a footnote to a scholarly article on the principle-agent problem, Hudec's stating simply that officials have taken the easy way out is no longer cynicism. It becomes science.

David Palmeter (2003) has accurately described Hudec's mode of analysis as "realistic, functional, fact-focused and anti-conceptual" (p. 705). I found particularly troubling articles that offered little more than an attempt to translate Hudec's analysis into contemporary jargon. Such attempts purported to complement Hudec by doing so, but they have the opposite effect. Working from, say, "the analytical framework of the contemporary law of global space", they end up pointing out mostly things that Hudec does not elaborate. The illusion is that Hudec left things out; the substance is that what he left out was academic flourish not needed to make his points. More complementary and more productive would be an effort to translate that analytical framework into the realistic, functional, fact-focused and anti-conceptual mode that Hudec employed.

EXTENDING HUDEC'S ANALYSIS

It is tempting as I close this introduction to speculate on what an update of Hudec's analysis might contain or to suggest from the analysis of citations what research the trade policy community might take on. I have resisted both of these urges, for reasons I set out in these closing paragraphs.

As to the first temptation, speculating about an update is difficult because the story line that brought dramatic tension to Hudec's analysis seems inappropriate for what has happened since.[18]

That story line was to ask how developing countries remained outside of the momentum towards liberalization that the GATT legal system created among developed countries. A straightforward extension would be inappropriate because – as we all know – the positions of developing countries in the world trading system and in the GATT/WTO legal system have changed dramatically since the period Hudec studied. They now account for significant shares of world imports as well as world exports. Concurrent with the growth of their trade, a number of developing countries have undertaken extensive economic reforms, including exchange rate reform and trade liberalization.

However, it would be inappropriate to interpret what happened in developing countries as eventual acceptance of the GATT point of view or absorption into "the GATT system". In contrast with the mercantilist rationale that had been important in developed country liberalization – give up your own restrictions in exchange for access to foreign markets – developing country liberalization has been, in large part, unilateral. As to what motivated those reforms, the Asian example enjoyed considerable influence, and it was heavily proselytized by the Bretton Woods institutions (and others) in the 1970s and 1980s. Key concepts in this view of trade restrictions were "domestic resource cost" and "effective protection", concepts that highlight the burden a country's import restrictions place on its own industries.

This suggests that the new story line is not how developing countries got taken up in the momentum the GATT system had created. Rather, it is how – and influenced by what – they created their own momentum, and how this momentum has interacted with the momentum of the GATT/WTO system. It might be possible to argue that the increasing consistency of developing country trade policies with the general line espoused by the GATT and the growing influence of developing countries in the GATT system have been the result rather than the cause of their changed economic policies. Analyzing the evolution of developing country trade policy as either application of or resistance to the GATT/WTO system would miss a lot of what has gone on.

As to suggesting what research the trade policy community might take on – it would seem to me very un-Hudecian to do so. In pointing out that a number of readers have overlooked the institutionalist tradition in which I find it productive to interpret Hudec, I am defending Hudec's analysis against what I take to be unjustified criticism. I am not suggesting that everyone become an institutionalist. Robert Hudec led the intellectual community by example, not by fiat. I cannot envisage him stating a priori that institutionalism rather than legal formalism, or research on these topics rather than on those, would be more productive. In what I experienced of Hudec as a conference participant and as a commenter on my own work, he sorted by quality rather than by category.

NOTES

1. Numbers in curly brackets, {}, indicate page numbers in this reissue of the 1987 book.
2. GATT Part IV, Article XXXVII, paragraph 1.
3. Particularly in Hudec 1970 and generally in Hudec 1975 and Hudec 1978.
4. This is a key concept in Hudec's analysis. The words "welfare obligation", "welfare concept", or "welfare idea" appear more than twenty times. They refer, Hudec explained, "to the idea that rich countries have a moral duty (and possibly a legal duty) to assist the development of poorer countries" {155}.
5. Hudec gave full weight to other contributions to this erosion, such as the acceptance of preferential arrangements, particularly the European Common Market, and the incorporation into the system of the discriminatory Multi-fiber Arrangement.
6. I first met Robert Hudec in 1985 at a seminar organized by Martin Wolf, then Director of Studies at the Trade Policy Research Center (TPRC). The seminar format was that each paper was presented by a discussant rather than the author; Martin honored me by inviting me to present Hudec's paper – an early draft of *Developing Countries in the GATT Legal System*, which the TPRC published in 1987. Beginning then, my work has been much influenced by Hudec's ideas. Indeed, I have taken many of them so to heart that I am no longer willing to ask if they are his ideas or mine.
7. Palmeter adds, "If ever there was an international organization that lent itself to analysis from these perspectives, that organization is the WTO" (2003, p. 706).
8. Examples are North (1981) and (1993).
9. Campos et al. (1958).
10. Hudec 1970.
11. Hudec, in another part of the book, is critical of legal reasoning that has gone farther, to conclude not only that the equality principle (equal cases should be treated equally, unequal cases unequally) deserves to be called law, but also that the acts of government used as precedent for the new principle – in this case, GATT's one-sided legal relationship – likewise take on the status of legal obligation. If, as much economic analysis indicates, he continued, "the legal freedom to use trade distortions might actually be harmful to developing countries, then GATT legal

policy may be a gross perversion of the equality principle being cited to sustain it. ... If the GATT's history is viewed through the lens of the contrary economic assumption, there are some rather striking parallels between GATT's developing country policy and penny gin" {125}.

12. Both fit more comfortably into the "building up over many repetitions" logic of institutional economics than into the "shift this parameter to achieve that result" logic of much contemporary analysis.

13. While this phrase might describe some of what happened at the Uruguay Round, Hudec seemed not to have foreseen how developing countries would use the taking on of GATT/WTO commitments to buttress their unilateral liberalizations.

14. Robert Hudec and his work have received a number of tributes. Among them are the festschrift volume edited by Daniel L. Kennedy and James D. Southwick (2002); the book of essays edited by Chantal Thomas and Joel P. Trachtman (2009); a 2003 issue of the *Journal of World Trade* (volume 37, number 4) and a 2005 issue of the *World Trade Review* (volume 5, number 1). The Society of International Economic Law inaugurated at its 2008 meeting a "Robert Hudec Lecture", to be delivered at each biennial meeting by a noted academic or practitioner.

15. Some chapters were formatted in the style of social science works with lists of references at the end, others in the format of legal works with citations fully described in the footnotes and without lists of references at the end. For the chapters with lists of references, I counted the Hudec publications listed. For the other chapters, I counted the Hudec publications cited in the footnotes. I did not double-count within chapters; if one Hudec publication was cited in more than one footnote in a chapter, I counted it only once for that chapter. There is double counting across chapters; I did not tally how many times a particular Hudec publication was cited in the book.

16. The number of citations to this point is perhaps disproportional to the number of pages the book devotes to the issue. This conclusion is usually cited as introduction to a paper providing further research on the question rather than as the final word on the subject.

17. Many of the citations do not quote a statement from Hudec or even cite a particular page number. While most of the citations seem to be consistent with what the book says, I have not attempted to determine whether each point attributed to Hudec is in fact made by Hudec.

18. No doubt my view is influenced by having worked on developing country trade issues for many years as a World Bank staff member. The points I make in this section confirm my suspicion that no one could produce an "unbiased" extension of Hudec's analysis.

REFERENCES

Campos, Roberto de Oliveira, Gottfried von Haberler, James Meade, and Jan Tinbergen. 1958. *Trends in International Trade*, Geneva, GATT.

Hamilton, Walton H. 1963. "Institution", in Edwin R. A. Seligman and Alvin Johnson, eds., *Encyclopaedia of the Social Sciences*, Macmillan, volume 8, pp. 84–89.

Hudec, Robert E. 1970. "The GATT Legal System, a Diplomat's Jurisprudence", *Journal of World Trade Law*, volume 4, pp. 615–65.

_____. 1975. *The GATT Legal System and World Trade Diplomacy*, New York, Praeger (399 pp.). Second edition, Salem, NH, Butterworth, 1990 (376 pp.).

_____. 1978. *Adjudication of International Trade Disputes*, Thames Essay No. 16, London, Trade Policy Research Center (86 pp.).

Kennedy, Daniel L., and James D. Southwick, eds. 2002. *The Political Economy of International Trade Law: Essays in Honor of Robert E. Hudec*, New York, Cambridge University Press.

North, Douglass C. 1981. *Structure and Change in Economic History*, New York, Norton.

_____. 1993. "Economic Performance through Time", The Sveriges Riksbank Prize in Economic Sciences in Memory of Alfred Nobel Lecture 1993, at http://nobelprize .org/nobel_prizes/economics/laureates/1993/north-lecture.html, last accessed 9 May 2010.

Palmeter, David. 2003. "Robert E. Hudec – A Practitioner's Appreciation", *Journal of World Trade Law*, volume 37, number 4, pp. 703–17.

Thomas, Chantal, and Joel P. Trachtman, eds. 2009. *Developing Countries in the WTO Legal System*, Oxford, Oxford University Press.

PART I

A HISTORY OF THE LEGAL RELATIONSHIP

INTRODUCTION

ON 30 OCTOBER 1947, governments of twenty-three countries signed the Final Act of the General Agreement on Tariffs and Trade (GATT). The General Agreement created a legal framework for a mutual reduction in tariffs negotiated between the signatory governments. It contained, first, each government's commitment to reduce tariffs (called its Schedule of Concessions) and, second, a code of behavior regulating other forms of government interference with international trade.

The GATT code of behavior rested on three central principles. The first was that while governments would not be prohibited from protecting domestic industries against foreign competition, all such protection should be in the form of tariffs. Under this first principle, governments accepted the obligation to eliminate the many other kinds of non-tariff measures affecting trade that had become common in the pre-war years – above all, restrictions limiting the quantity of imports allowed. The second principle was that while there would be no a priori limits on tariff levels, governments would participate in periodic negotiations aimed at gradually reducing existing levels. The third was the most-favored-nation (MFN) principle, requiring governments to treat the trade of all other GATT countries equally. Under the MFN principle, any advantage given to one GATT country had to be given immediately, and unconditionally, to every other GATT country.

The trade-policy discipline required by these three principles was rather modest – a far cry from free trade. Moreover, the actual code of behavior adopted in 1947 contained a substantial number of exceptions. Nevertheless, the rules of the General Agreement did represent a coherent discipline requiring gradual trade liberalization. Working within these rules, the developed-country governments within the GATT achieved a very substantial reduction of trade barriers during the 20 years from 1947 to 1967, most of which still remains in place.

The developing-country members of the GATT have never agreed to accept the same discipline. They began by seeking to be excepted from the obligations in the GATT's code of behavior. Later on, they added requests for special and more favorable treatment, both from each other and from developed countries. The history of the GATT's legal relationship with developing countries is primarily the history of these demands for special status.

The history begins with a legal relationship based essentially on parity of obligation, with only very limited, almost token, exceptions. Over the years the relationship has gravitated, in seemingly inexorable fashion, toward the one-sided welfare relationship demanded by the developing countries. This relationship is one in which developing countries are excused from legal discipline while developed countries are asked to recognize a series of unilateral obligations, based on economic need, to promote the exports of developing countries. In the 1970s, a counter-reaction of sorts began under the name "graduation" – the idea that advanced developing countries should begin to move back towards a parity of obligations and privileges. As the 1970s came to a close, however, the graduation claim, having gained some degree of formal recognition, seemed to come to a standstill in the face of more forceful demands to enlarge the area of special treatment still further.

This study examines the GATT's legal relationship with developing countries. Part I describes the history of that relationship. It begins with a brief look at the years before World War II; then it takes up the story in earnest, starting with the post-war negotiations that created the GATT. It then describes each of the major developments in the legal relationship, from 1947 until the mid-1980s.

Part II of the study examines the legal policy issues raised by the GATT's current policy towards developing countries. The central issue is whether the current welfare-based legal policy can provide effective protection of developing-country interests or whether developing countries would do better by accepting the same GATT discipline as everyone else.

An initial word of caution about real and imagined bias is in order. It is difficult to find a vocabulary for the GATT's legal history that does not imply normative judgments about the way things are going. Expressions like "one-sided" can be read to suggest disapproval of developing-country positions; so can terms like "legal discipline", which sound like something that should be beneficial to moral and spiritual health. Alternatively, it is just as easy to make developed-country positions look rapacious or insensitive, or to make GATT obligations resemble Anatole France's law that prohibits rich as well as poor from sleeping under bridges.

A reading of the entire study will show that the author does have biases, but that the biases are not the ones indicated by the vocabulary just described. The author does believe that the GATT legal policy towards developing countries has been wrong and harmful. The author also believes, however, that the standard arguments on both sides of the debate – from "one-sidedness" to "sleeping under bridges" – rest on fundamentally wrong perceptions about the economic and legal character of these relationships. The author's main purpose in preparing this study is to try to present the issues in a way that is not distorted by these misperceptions.

It would be tedious to have to disavow this or that value judgment every time a potentially value-laden term is used. It is hoped that this initial disclaimer will serve until the true content of the author's biases makes itself clear.

1

Post-war Negotiations on Trade Liberalization

GATT LEGAL policy towards developing countries owes nothing to the past. There was no Golden Age that pointed the way. Before 1939, the organizing principle for rich-poor relationships had been colonialism. Most of the countries in Africa and Asia were colonies *de jure*. A goodly portion of those in Central and South America were colonies de facto. This colonial past was not what the post-1945 world was looking for. The world required a clean start – a completely new departure.

Policy in the United States before 1939 stood apart from the explicitly colonial policies of the other major powers. The United States had few *de jure* colonies. Although its economic and political relationship with most Latin American countries was de facto colonial, its formal legal relationship with those countries consisted of conventional sovereign-to-sovereign dealings, with very few of the preferential qualities found in the typical colonial relationship. In the years 1934–42, the United States negotiated reciprocal trade agreements with twenty-seven countries, including the following sixteen developing countries: Cuba, Haiti, Brazil, Honduras, Colombia, Guatemala, Nicaragua, El Salvador, Costa Rica, Ecuador, Turkey, Venezuela, Argentina, Peru, Uruguay and Mexico.[1] Each agreement contained a reciprocal exchange of tariff reductions and a framework of other GATT-like obligations to protect the commercial value of the tariff reductions. None of these agreements called for special treatment because of developing-country status.[2] Indeed, the chief distinguishing feature of the sixteen developing-country agreements was that they tended to contain fewer special derogations than did the agreements with developed countries such as France.[3] The 1942 agreement with Mexico is generally regarded as the model used by the United States for the initial draft of the GATT, which it submitted in 1946.[4]

There is little evidence, however, that the "equal treatment" policy followed by the United States during the 1930s represented a considered response to any sort of developing country demand for preferential treatment. The issue was simply never presented. The United States Administration was having enough difficulty lowering trade barriers as things were, for at this time even the idea of reciprocal trade liberalization, based on full payment, by the other party, was a daring new idea in the politics of the United States. The relative novelty of the developing-country problem should be borne in mind when viewing its evolution during the next 40 years. Not only was there no Golden Age to point towards as a goal but, perhaps more important, there had been no past failures that could serve as a lesson about what *not* to do – nothing resembling the lesson that developed countries had been taught by the beggar-thy-neighbor policies of the 1930s. Individual governments no doubt had ideas – even convictions – about what would work and what would not work, but there was no collective experience. If the years that followed exhibited a propensity towards expedient short-run compromise, part of the reason may lie here.

INITIAL POSITIONS OF DEVELOPED COUNTRIES

The design of international trade policy after World War II was laid down in a series of international negotiations, conducted from 1946 to 1948, that produced (i) the never-ratified Charter of the International Trade Organization (ITO) and (ii) the supposedly provisional General Agreement on Tariffs and Trade (GATT). The negotiations began with war-time planning discussions between the United States and the United Kingdom. The major landmarks are well-known. In the Atlantic Charter of August 1941, the United States and the United Kingdom agreed to the general objectives of the post-war economic order. The specific details of this new order were then developed, in stages, through the negotiations that produced the United States–United Kingdom Lend-Lease Agreement of February 1942, the International Monetary Fund (IMF) Agreement of July 1944 and the United States "Proposed Charter" of December 1945.

The documents produced by the United States–United Kingdom planning process give no hint that developing countries should be accorded any "special and differential treatment" in the commercial-policy field. The Atlantic Charter pledged to seek "the enjoyment by all states, great and small, victors and vanquished, of access, on equal terms, to the trade and raw materials of the world which are needed for their prosperity".[5] Article VII of the Lend-Lease Agreement spoke in similarly universal terms.[6] The IMF Agreement was also rigorously neutral; although it had weighted voting and other provisions that worked differently on rich and poor, the criteria were all objective and there were no separate classes of members.[7]

The early drafting of the post-war rules on trade policy were likewise based on the idea of one set of rules for all countries. On the United Kingdom's side, James Meade produced a plan for an "international commercial union" in late 1942; the plan had no special provisions for developing countries.[8] On the United States' side, the first draft of the ITO Charter – the Proposed Charter of December 1945 – also contained one set of rules for all members.[9] There were no provisions on economic development, nor were there any special rules or exceptions for developing countries. The United States explained the absence of developing-country provisions in the Proposed Charter by saying that the special needs of developing countries would be addressed in the Economic Development Sub-commission of the United Nations and Social Council and by institutions such as the World Bank.[10] In other words, special attention may have been needed, but not in the trade-policy rules.

The United States continued to follow this approach in the draft resolution it submitted asking the Economic and Social Council to convene the ITO negotiations. Once again, no mention was made of any special rules for developing countries. Interestingly, when the Economic and Social Council responded to the United States' proposal, it voted an amendment to the draft resolution that called for the ITO negotiations to

> . . . take into account the special conditions which prevail in countries whose manufacturing industry is still in the initial stages of development . . .[11]

The United States politely ignored the suggestion. When several months later it published a more detailed text, called the "Suggested Charter", the text still contained no special provisions for developing countries.[12]

This initial position of the United States rested on the view that the key to industrial development was capital investment, especially private investment, coupled with an open international market for exports. The United States was unsympathetic to the infant-industry argument on conventional economic grounds – infant-industry protection would merely promote the creation of inefficient local industries, thereby wasting resources.[13] These positions were drawn from, and reinforced by, a global economic and political policy that had two main objectives:

(a) The desire to reduce trade protection generally, so that the world would not repeat the destabilizing economic situation created by the protectionism of the 1930s.

(b) The desire to eliminate discrimination – partly for the same economic reasons, but also because the United States wanted to eradicate the colonial system.

To be sure, this global policy also served somewhat narrower visions of self-interest. Under the mercantilist perceptions of national advantage that tended to prevail in these calculations, the over-powering dominance of the United States' economy during this period made it appear that the United States had the most to gain from an open world market for exports.

The major objectives of the United States did not have the complete support of either the United Kingdom or France. Both countries wanted the United States tariff reduced and so they were willing to subscribe to the general design of the United States. But both countries wished to retain their preferential tariff regimes. And both wished to have as much freedom as possible to use protection and discrimination to foster the process of post-war economic reconstruction.[14]

The desire of Britain and France to retain their existing preferences revealed a rather sharp difference with the United States, particularly over policy towards developing countries. At the level of principle, Britain and France were advocating the view that market distortions were needed to help the poor countries. This was hardly surprising, for they were taking the same position with regard to their own welfare needs, insisting that the rules should permit countries in Western Europe to give each other preferred treatment to foster post-war reconstruction. In terms of narrower economic interests, Britain and France also seemed to be looking at things in mercantilist terms which, from their perspective, appeared to counsel special bilateral relationships with favored developing countries as a way of protecting their export markets from competition by the United States.

This policy disagreement in the developed-country camp was never to be resolved. Once Western Europe was freed from dependence on the United States, its support for the position of the United States would ultimately be withdrawn.

POSITIONS OF DEVELOPING COUNTRIES

The substance of the developing-country positions during the ITO negotiations was described by Clair Wilcox, the vice-chairman of the United States delegation, as follows:

> Some eight hundred amendments were presented [at the final Havana Conference], among them as many as two hundred that would have destroyed the very foundations of the enterprise.[15]

Later, in the same account, he wrote:

> Some of the proposals advanced in the name of economic development have to be seen to be believed.[16]

Developing countries tabled a wide range of proposals, many calling for positive transfers of resources. In the field of trade policy, their demands were focused on securing freedom from the Charter's legal obligations. They wished to protect infant industries with measures not otherwise permitted; they wished to be permitted to receive new tariff preferences from other developed or developing countries; they wanted the right to benefit from developed-country tariff concessions without having to offer equivalent tariff concessions of their own. In related areas, they wanted a similarly wide freedom to control foreign investment, and they wanted developed countries to accept the cartel-type discipline of commodity agreements in order to sustain "remunerative" prices for developing-country commodity exports.[17]

About the only major element of the recent developing-country proposals for a New International Economic Order[18] that did not appear during the GATT-ITO negotiations was the call for systematic tariff preferences by the developed countries – the idea now embodied in the Generalized System of Preferences (GSP).[19] There were demands that the ITO rules should permit the granting of such preferences, but there was no demand for a legal obligation requiring developed countries to do so. Apparently, the intensity of the opposition to voluntary preferences pre-empted any initiative for mandatory ones.

The developing-country position came to the fore very promptly as soon as the United States announced its proposals in late 1945.[20] It appears to have arisen as almost a reflex response. The author has found no evidence of any serious difference of opinion within the developing-country group at this time.

This almost spontaneous rejection of the policy goals of the United States was no doubt primarily due to the trade-policy education which developing countries had received from developed countries in the past. Those that had been colonies had been taught by their parent countries that economic benefit was maximized by controlling trade and suppressing competition from alternative suppliers. This lesson had even been given to the United Kingdom's colonies and former colonies when, in 1932, it had abandoned its long-standing free trade policies by enacting both a general tariff and a systematic and reciprocal program of tariff preferences called the Imperial (later Commonwealth) Preference System. Those who traded with the United States had been taught a similar lesson when, in 1930, the United States had chosen to protect itself by enacting what was believed to be the highest tariff in its history – the infamous Smoot-Hawley tariff.

It is possible that the design of the ITO enterprise may itself have encouraged this preference for market-distorting solutions. The ITO represented a new idea in international economic affairs – the idea that the governments of the world, by acting together in concerted rule-making activity, could shape the international trade environment in which their economies would operate. Although the sponsors of this "architectonic"[21] enterprise were actually seeking to diminish government activity in the market place, rule-making institutions tend to encourage just the opposite instincts – the urge to improve on nature by writing rules about how it should function. The existence of the institution tends to affirm the efficacy of the work it does.

In addition, the fact that the ITO would be playing a "governmental" role probably helped to add a welfare perspective that further reinforced the belief in market-distorting measures. The power to govern usually brings with it, according to most twentieth-century political norms, a duty to take care of the disadvantaged members of the group being governed. For example, it would not have been possible to create governing power in the European Community unless the Community undertook a responsibility to do something for the depressed areas within its domain. The ITO was to govern an even larger "community", and so it was natural for the disadvantaged members of that community to feel that the community must "do something" to help them. The ITO had no money to give, only rules. Thus rule assistance was naturally the help that was sought.

RESULTS OF THE ITO NEGOTIATIONS

It is fair to say that the GATT-ITO negotiations ended, as they had begun, with no basic consensus on the trade-policy rules that should apply to developing countries. The negotiating process was essentially one of compromise between the views of the developing countries, on one side, and those of the United States (usually supported by some developed countries), on the other. The final texts consisted of carefully negotiated substantive terms containing some of each position and, then, carefully negotiated procedural provisions seeking to limit the ways in which the other side's substantive criteria were to be applied. Procedure was often the key to the compromise. The developing countries usually obtained some recognition of the principle that "economic development" could be a legitimate reason for using trade-distorting measures prohibited by the Charter. The United States usually obtained additional substantive criteria limiting the scope of the exceptions and procedural conditions and requirements designed to limit application of the exception to only the very clear cases.

In terms of the results of the negotiations alone, the United States could have claimed a victory for its point of view. The central trade-policy issue at stake was the right to protect infant industries by using trade restrictions that were otherwise prohibited – (i) by raising "bound" tariffs,[22] (ii) by imposing quantitative import restrictions or (iii) by securing preferential tariffs from other developed or developing countries. The Charter recognized a right to each of the three exceptional measures, but each was made subject to prior approval of the Organization. In the case of bound tariffs, the substantial agreement of countries having contractual rights in the concession was also required.[23] These procedural requirements were far more restrictive than the requirements attached to other exceptions wanted by the developed countries – that is, the balance-of-payments exception, the "escape clause" (or "safeguards") exception for "serious injury" to a domestic industry, the exception allowing quantitative restrictions on certain agricultural imports or the exception permitting export subsidies on primary products.[24] In none of these "developed-country" exceptions was prior approval required; nor were any subject to a veto by interested countries. The comparison made the economic-development exceptions look like very grudging exceptions at best and quite possibly no more than token exceptions in practice.

NARROWER CONCESSIONS IN THE GATT

The ITO Charter was completed at the Havana Conference in early 1948, but it was rejected by the United States Congress and so never came into force.[25] The trade-policy rules of the Charter did survive, however, in the form of a separate agreement that had been negotiated in the autumn of 1947 – the General Agreement on Tariffs and Trade.[26] The General Agreement was intended to serve as a trade agreement to implement an early round of tariff reductions before the ITO Charter came into force. Its rules were drawn from the trade-policy provisions of the draft ITO Charter as they then stood. When it came to the "economic development" exceptions, however, the GATT governments were unwilling to incorporate all the concessions that had been made in the draft ITO Charter. The GATT did incorporate the ITO Charter's infant-industry exceptions for tariffs and quantitative import restrictions (ITO Article 13), but, in spite of vigorous protests, the United States refused to agree to include the ITO provision permitting new preferences (ITO Article 15). The United States viewed this provision as one of its major concessions and was unwilling to grant the concession without the quid pro quo of the entire ITO Charter.[27]

When the ITO Charter died for want of ratification, so did the more extensive legal privileges developing countries had gained in that document. The final product was the more limited 1947–48 GATT, an agreement even closer to the original United States point of view.

WEAKNESSES IN THE POSITION OF THE UNITED STATES

The victory of the United States in the GATT-ITO negotiations proved to be temporary. Over the next four decades, the legal discipline applicable to developing countries all but disappeared. One of the ways to shed some light on the present situation is to ask why the United States' victory was not sustained. Although this question properly belongs at the end of the story, it is useful to anticipate the question here by looking for other elements in the GATT-ITO negotiations that foreshadowed the eventual outcome.

In the first place, it should be noted that, however much they gave up on procedure, the developing countries did succeed in gaining recognition for the legitimacy of their basic premise – that the special position of developing countries justified some dispensation from the GATT-ITO legal discipline. This principle was recognized from the very beginning of the drafting process. The opposing view, implicitly stated in the no-exceptions rules of the United States Proposals and Suggested Charter, never commanded enough negotiating support to be considered a serious alternative. The United States itself retreated almost immediately, offering a draft Economic Development chapter during the first Preparatory Committee meeting in London in late 1946.[28] This was a major concession, for it shifted the basic premise of all further debate. From then on the question was no longer "whether" but "how much".

Why did the initial position of the United States give way so quickly? The weakness was not that the United States was rejecting the duty to help developing countries. The United States accepted that obligation. What it wanted to argue was that the special treatment developing countries were asking for – more legal freedom – would not give them any extra "help" or "assistance". The United States was insisting that freedom to distort market forces was not an advantage; on the contrary, it was a disadvantage.

This position had several inherent weaknesses. The first might be called "diplomatic". It is very difficult to convene an enterprise involving rich and poor without having some welfare dimension to the work. There must be something to "give" in order to satisfy demands for welfare assistance. In the position taken by the United States, there was nothing to "give". There were welfare concessions to be made in other areas, but diplomats at one meeting always want to bring home some achievement of their own. Although it may be difficult to believe that such factors exert undue influence, it is the author's view that inability to resist this need to "give something" has been a constant factor in the dynamics of GATT legal policy.

Second, the position of the United States was full of internal contradictions. Although they and other countries might say that market distortions do not "help" in the long run, from the very beginning their own conduct belied this message. The GATT and the ITO Charter contained a very large number of exceptions written for the benefit of developed-country producers. The United States had to ask for two glaring exceptions of this kind – the right to use quantitative import restrictions on agricultural imports and the right to use export subsidies. The United States had also given in to Britain and France on their demands for the right to retain tariff preferences with colonies and ex-colonies, as well as the right to use discriminatory restrictions in coping with balance-of-payments difficulties. Even the "escape clause" seemed to testify to a developed-country view that trade protection could "help" weak industries. This contradiction has also been a constant in the GATT's legal history and is as true today as it was in 1947.

In addition, the theory of the United States legal design made it very hard to argue that freedom from GATT legal obligations was not a valuable good that developing countries ought to seek. The dominant message of that theory was "reciprocity". The fixation with reciprocity, expressed a clear mercantilist view of international trade: "Reductions in our own trade barriers hurt us by permitting more imports; they must be paid for, therefore, by reductions in your trade barriers, which will help us by increasing our exports." In short, the theory was saying that higher trade barriers were better than lower trade barriers. While it was possible to rationalize the insistence on reciprocity in non-mercantilist terms – "It's for your own good", or "The gains from trade are maximized this way", or even "We need it for political reasons back home"[29] – most developed-country governments behaved otherwise.

This theoretical contradiction was fundamental. In an avowedly welfare relationship, where the needy have a recognized claim to unilateral payments, the strong cannot make a principled demand for liberal trade policies by the needy when, in the same breath, they define trade liberalization as a "payment".

Apart from these substantive weaknesses, there was also a major weakness in the bargaining posture of the United States. While the United States clearly wanted an open and non-discriminatory trading system, it also wanted to establish an organization that had more or less universal membership. Once it became clear that developing countries did not share its trade-policy goals, the United States was confronted with a choice. If it refused to compromise, it would risk losing the participation of many developing countries. If it agreed to compromise, on the other hand, it would put its trade-policy objectives at risk.

The United States chose to compromise. It did so with the expectation that concessions to the developing-country viewpoint could be contained and that an effective legal discipline could nonetheless be achieved. Being members of the ITO would at least expose developing countries to some pressure to apply the correct policies and, over time, some of the ground lost in the negotiations might even be regained.

The "participation" objective began to surface fairly quickly in GATT affairs, even in the unyielding atmosphere of the early discussions. While the United States was not prepared to accept Article 15 on new preferences from the ITO Charter, it did make several other concessions to encourage the accession of developing countries. For example, the United States agreed to adopt the somewhat more flexible ITO Charter text on exceptions for infant industries, expressly justifying the concession as necessary to encourage the accession of developing countries to the new GATT.[30]

Once it had been conceded, as a matter of principle, that legal freedom constitutes "help" to developing countries, the future was virtually fixed. Things might conceivably have been different if developing countries had been able to improve the economic welfare of their citizens as much as they felt was needed. But, of course, that did not happen. As a consequence, developed-developing country relations for the next forty years began and ended on the same note – "more help is needed". When other kinds of "help" were not enough (which was invariably the case), there was always the possibility of doing something more on the legal side. Granting legal freedom to other countries is an easy concession to give, for it requires neither domestic legislation nor the use of other legal powers by the grantor countries. It is possible to "give" merely by agreeing to do nothing. Governments on both sides of the issue would find such concessions an easy way to maintain the appearance of progress.

NOTES AND REFERENCES

1. The 1934–42 program is reviewed in detail in *Hearings on the Extension of the Trade Agreements Act Before the House Ways and Means Committee*, 79th Congress, 1st Session at 636, 837–38, 932–33 (1945).
2. The trade agreement with Cuba contained reciprocal tariff preferences but these were vestiges of a preferential colonial relationship rather than welfare assistance. See Articles II–III, *Reciprocal Trade Agreement between the United States and Cuba*, 24 August 1934, 49 Statutes at Large 3559, Executive Agreement Series (EAS) No. 67. Likewise, although the concentration on negotiating agreements with Latin America was no doubt motivated by a policy of regional assistance, the form was rigorously MFN and reciprocal.
3. Compare, for example, *Reciprocal Trade Agreement between the United States and France*, 6 May 1936, 53 Statutes at Large 2236, EAS No. 146, with *Reciprocal Trade*

Agreement between the United States and Mexico, 23 December 1942, 57 Statutes at Large 833, EAS No. 311.

4. The Mexican Agreement, cited in the previous footnote, was the last and most refined of the trade agreements negotiated under the 1934 trade agreements legislation. On its place in drafting the post-war agreements, see William Adams Brown, *The United States and the Restoration of World Trade: an Analysis and Appraisal of the ITO Charter and the General Agreement on Tariffs and Trade* (Washington: Brookings Institution, 1950) pp. 20–22.

5. *United States Department of State Bulletin*, Washington, Vol. V, 1941, p. 125. The best general work on the war-time and post-war negotiations is Richard N. Gardner, *Sterling-Dollar Diplomacy* (Oxford: Clarendon Press, 1956). The standard works in English on the general history, law and policy of GATT itself are, in order of publication: Gerard Curzon, *Multilateral Commercial Diplomacy: the General Agreement on Tariffs and Trade and Its Impact on National Commercial Policies and Techniques* (London: Michael Joseph, 1965); John H. Jackson, *World Trade and the Law of GATT: A Legal Analysis of the General Agreement on Tariffs and Trade* (Indianapolis: Bobbs-Merrill, 1969); Karin Kock, *International Trade Policy and the GATT 1947–1967* (Stockholm: Almqvist & Wiksell, 1969); Kenneth W. Dam, *The GATT: Law and International Economic Organization* (Chicago and London: University of Chicago Press, 1970); Robert E. Hudec, *The GATT Legal System and World Trade Diplomacy* (New York: Praeger, 1975); Olivier Long, *Law and its Limitations in the GATT Multilateral Trade System* (Dordrecht: Martinus Nijhoff, 1985); Edmond McGovern, *International Trade Regulation: GATT, the United States and the European Community*, 2nd edition (Exeter: Globefield Press, 1986).

6. *United States Department of State Bulletin*, Vol. VI, 1942, p. 192.

7. *Articles of Agreement of the International Monetary Fund*, formulated 1–22 July 1944, opened for signature 27 December 1945, 2 United Nations Treaty Series (UNTS) 29.

8. See Ernest F. Penrose, *Economic Planning for Peace* (Princeton: Princeton University Press, 1953) pp. 89–90.

9. *Proposals for Consideration by an International Conference on Trade and Employment*, Publication No. 2411, Commercial Policy Series No. 79 (Washington: United States Department of State, 1945).

10. Clair Wilcox, *A Charter for World Trade* (New York: Macmillan, 1949) p. 141. Clair Wilcox served as chairman or vice-chairman of the United States delegation to the various GATT-ITO negotiating conferences in 1946–48.

11. The history of the United Nations Economic and Social Council resolution is recounted in Brown, *The United States and the Restoration of World Trade*, op. cit., pp. 57–60.

12. *Suggested Charter for an International Trade Organization of the United Nations*, Publication No. 2598, Commercial Policy Series No. 98 (Washington: United States Department of State, 1946).

13. See Wilcox, *A Charter for World Trade*, op. cit., pp. 30–31 and 143.

14. The best account of the conflicts between the positions of the United States, Britain and France is given in Gardner, *Sterling-Dollar Diplomacy*, op. cit., pp. 145–161, 269–86 and 348–80.

15. Wilcox, *A Charter for World Trade*, op. cit., p. 47.
16. Ibid., p. 142.
17. The best systematic account of the developing-country positions taken at various stages of the negotiations is given in Brown, *The United States and the Restoration of World Trade*, op. cit., pp. 97–104, 152–60, 178–80 and 203–11. See also Wilcox, *A Charter for World Trade*, op. cit., pp. 47–49 and 140–152.
18. The term New International Economic Order (or NIEO) refers to a number of economic reform proposals made by developing countries in the 1970s, calling for what some referred to as a fundamental re-ordering of the world economy. The United Nations documents collecting the proposals are *Declaration on the Establishment of a New International Economic Order*, and *Programme of Action on the Establishment of a New International Economic Order*, United Nations Documents, General Assembly Resolutions 3201 and 3202 (S-IV), 1 May 1974.
19. Adoption of the GSP is discussed in Chapter 3.
20. Brown, *The United States and the Restoration of World Trade*, op. cit., p. 59.
21. "Architectonic" is Kenneth Dam's term for a regulatory model based on detailed rules of conduct, a model of which both GATT-ITO and the 1944 IMF Agreement were examples. Damn, *The Rules of the Game: Reform and Evolution in the International Monetary System* (Chicago and London: University of Chicago Press, 1982) p. 212.
22. When a government "binds" a tariff it undertakes a legal obligation not to exceed a maximum rate. The GATT was designed to encourage the reduction and binding of tariff rates through negotiation; maintenance of such binding obligations was central to the enterprise.
23. See *ITO Charter*, Article 13 (economic development) and Article 15 (preferences). The official title of the ITO Charter is *Havana Charter for an International Trade Organization*. The official text of the never-ratified instrument is contained in United Nations Document E/Conf. 2/78 (24 March 1948). The text was reprinted in Cmd 7375 (London: Her Majesty's Stationery Office, 1948) and in Publication No. 3206, Commercial Policy Series No. 114 (Washington: United States Department of State, 1948).
24. See *ITO Charter*, Articles 21 and 23 (balance-of-payments restrictions), Article 40 (escape clause), Article 20(2) (agricultural quantitative import restrictions) and Article 27 (export subsidies).
25. All governments waited for the United States to ratify the ITO Charter. The Congress balked, partly because an anti-internationalist mood had set in by 1948 and partly because the many substantive compromises in the Charter managed to offend both sides – too liberal for protectionists and too exception-ridden for advocates of free trade. After seeking Congressional ratification for more than two years, the Administration gave up late in 1950 and withdrew the Charter from further consideration. See William T. Diebold, *The End of the ITO*, Princeton Essays in International Finance No. 16 (Princeton: Princeton University, 1952).
26. The General Agreement was concluded on 30 October 1947. Its formal citation is 55 UNTS 194.
27. See Brown, *The United States and the Restoration of World Trade*, op. cit., p. 242. The GATT met twice in March and September of 1948 to consider making its October 1947 text conform to the final text of the ITO, which had been concluded

in Havana in March of 1948. The final rejection occurred in September; see GATT Document GATT/CP.2/SR/20 (7 September 1948).

28. Brown, *The United States and the Restoration of World Trade*, op. cit., pp. 68, 97 and 99.

29. For an analysis of the various non-mercantilist arguments in favor of a reciprocity requirement, see Frieder Roessler, "The Rationale for Reciprocity in Trade Negotiations under Floating Currencies", *Kyklos*, Basle, Vol. 31, No. 2, 1978, pp. 258–74. See also Richard Blackhurst, "Reciprocity in Trade Negotiations under Flexible Exchange Rates", in John P. Martin and Alasdair Smith (eds), *Trade and Payments Adjustment under Flexible Exchange Rates* (London: Macmillan, for the Trade Policy Research Centre, 1979) pp. 212–44.

30. Brown, *The United States and the Restoration of World Trade*, op. cit., p. 242.

2

First Decade of the GATT – 1948–1957

OF THE ORIGINAL twenty-three contracting parties of the GATT, ten were developing countries: Brazil, Burma, China, Ceylon, Chile, Cuba, India, Pakistan, Syria and Lebanon. Within the first few years China (by then the Taiwan government), Lebanon and Syria withdrew. Four more developing countries acceded in the Annecy negotiations in 1949: the Dominican Republic, Haiti, Nicaragua and Uruguay. Indonesia became a contracting party in 1950 on achieving independence; Peru and Turkey negotiated their entry during the Torquay Round negotiations of 1951. By the end of the Torquay Round negotiations, the total developing-country membership stood at fourteen. The developed-country membership had risen to twenty and included all the major developed countries except Japan, which joined in 1955, and Switzerland, which joined in 1966.[1]

EVOLUTION OF DEVELOPING-COUNTRY MEMBERSHIP

Developing-country membership remained virtually unchanged during the rest of the 1950s. Only Ghana and Malaysia acceded, both entering in 1957 under special procedures that allowed newly independent territories to succeed to the rights and obligations of their parent countries. In the late 1950s, the situation began to change when a number of newly independent developing countries began to establish provisional contacts with the GATT. By the end of the decade, however, the total membership of the GATT stood at only thirty-seven, and developed countries still held a twenty-one to sixteen majority.[2]

The 1960s produced a sharp change in the numerical balance. The developed-country membership grew by only four during this period, with Iceland, Ireland, Poland and Switzerland acceding. Developing-country membership increased by thirty-six. Seven commercially important developing countries gained admission by negotiating tariff concessions: Argentina, Israel, Korea, Portugal, Spain,[3] the United Arab Republic and Yugoslavia. Twenty-eight others gained admission via the special procedures for newly independent territories, mainly African and Caribbean states that had been colonies of France and Britain. Nigeria and Jamaica were the most prominent countries in this group.

As of May 1970, there were seventy-seven contracting parties to the GATT – twenty-five developed countries and fifty-two developing countries. One other country, Tunisia, had acceded provisionally, and another thirteen developing countries had declared that they were applying the GATT on a de facto basis. This latter group also participated, in varying degrees, in the work of the GATT.[4]

In the sixteen years from 1970 to 1987, the number of contracting parties continued to grow, from seventy-seven to ninety-five. The character of the GATT changed very little. With the exception, possibly, of Hungary and Romania, the new members were all developing countries. The number of additional countries applying the GATT provisionally or de facto rose to thirty.[5]

GATT OPERATIONS BEFORE THE REVIEW SESSION

In the first seven years of GATT operations, the policy towards developing countries adhered fairly closely to the policy defined in the GATT-ITO negotiations.

Balance-of-payments restrictions were a major presence during this period, reducing the need for, and the significance of, other forms of protection. As of 1 January 1954, sixteen of the twenty developed-country members were restricting imports for balance-of-payments reasons and nine of the fourteen developing countries were doing likewise. The five developing countries not under restriction were Western Hemisphere countries, namely Cuba, the Dominican Republic, Haiti, Nicaragua and Peru. The four developed countries were Belgium, Luxembourg, Canada and the United States. Of the twenty-five countries applying balance-of-payments restrictions, twenty-three were applying them in a discriminatory manner. West European countries were discriminating not only against the United States, but also against Latin America and Asia.[6]

Resort to the infant-industry exceptions in Article XVIII was limited, but what activity there was treated with some importance. In 1949 and 1950, Cuba, Haiti, and India each received approval for quotas on a single product. Ceylon, having passed major development legislation, obtained releases for a wide variety of products during the same period[7] and returned for further releases in 1952.[8] In each case, a GATT working party reviewed the proposals carefully, often attached specific conditions and, in Ceylon's case, persuaded the applicant to withdraw a number of its original requests.[9] According to a 1954 statement by the delegation of Ceylon, the review procedure under Article XVIII was so strict that "it practically destroys the benefits that it professes to confer".[10] The statement seemed to frighten away every other developing country except Ceylon. The only country ever to use Article XVIII after 1954 was, oddly enough, Ceylon.[11]

The same "by-the-book" approach was taken towards other aspects of rule compliance by developing countries. Four of the first five legal complaints filed in the GATT were complaints by developed countries against violations of the rules by developing countries.[12] Balance-of-payments reviews were carried out with careful scrutiny. Developing countries acceding to the Agreement were expected to negotiate meaningful tariff concessions as a payment for the legal right to benefit from the tariff concessions of other GATT members.

AMENDMENTS OF THE 1954–1955 REVIEW SESSION

In 1954 the Contracting Parties decided to consider the long-term future of the GATT. The ITO was dead[13] and the GATT had to prepare itself for the role of a permanent organization. An extraordinary session of the Contracting Parties (the Review Session) was called to conduct a comprehensive review of the operation of the General Agreement. The Contracting Parties tried once again to create a formal international organization, this time the "Organization for Trade Cooperation" (OTC), but once again the organization's charter was rejected by the United States Congress.[14] The GATT governments also conducted a fairly thorough review of the General Agreement's substantive provisions,[15] and here they did accomplish some changes.

The Review Session provided an occasion for developing countries to renegotiate the GATT-ITO compromises on legal policy towards developing countries. Developing countries did not make a serious effort to reintroduce the highly controversial ITO provision authorizing new tariff preferences. They did, however, renew demands for greater legal freedom to create new protective trade barriers for infant-industry protection; they also wanted less pressure to be applied in negotiations for reciprocal tariff concessions.

The negotiating setting in 1954–55 was different from that in the ITO. In certain respects, the developing countries had lost some leverage because it is always harder for a government to walk out of an organization than it is to refuse to join. On the other hand, much of the Third World was still outside the GATT and the United States still wanted a universal organization.

"Cold War" competition for influence in the Third World had begun, giving added weight to this goal. Developing countries within the GATT were thus in a position to do serious damage by declaring the GATT unsatisfactory.

The Review Session agreed to a slight loosening of the original GATT-ITO rules. Three basic changes were made. First, governments agreed to rewrite the infant-industry exceptions in Article XVIII. The introduction to Article XVIII was revised and expanded to give a more positive tone to the protective measures which the Article authorized. The new introduction stated that economic development furthers the objectives of the General Agreement, thus making clear that the trade barriers authorized by Article XVIII were not derogations from GATT policy but, instead, were entirely legitimate measures in complete harmony with GATT policy. In the same spirit, the draftsmen deleted a tough-minded sentence in the original text warning that unwise use of such measures would harm both the applicant country and others. The cosmetic changes to the preamble were more significant than the changes made to the substance of the infant-industry provisions, which were relaxed only slightly. The need to obtain prior approval was retained, but a provision granting an absolute veto to certain affected countries was removed; the standard for using quantitative import restrictions on infant-industry grounds was made easier to satisfy.

Second, the Review Session relaxed the requirements that developing countries had to satisfy in order to use quantitative restrictions to limit imports in times of serious balance-of-payments disequilibrium. The Contracting Parties wrote a separate provision on balance-of-payments restrictions for developing countries, placing it in Article XVIII(B). The new provision permitted restrictions whenever monetary reserves were inadequate in terms of a country's development program. Since developing countries have an almost infinite need for additional development resources, the new test made it possible to justify almost any restrictions.

Third, governments agreed to a rather vague relaxation of the "reciprocity" principle. A new Article XXVIII(*bis*), setting out procedures for tariff negotiations, asked contracting parties to take account, when calculating reciprocity, "of the needs of less developed countries for a more flexible use of tariff protection to assist their economic development and the special needs of these countries to maintain tariffs for revenue purposes".[16] In other words, developed countries were not supposed to insist on full reciprocity for the concessions they were making.

The Review Session amendments made no major changes in developed-developing country legal relations. Probably their most significant impact was at the level of principle – the fuller and now almost enthusiastic endorsement of the idea that legal freedom "helps" developing countries. Beyond that, the next most significant result was probably the fact of change itself. The Review Session repeated the lesson of the GATT-ITO negotiations that, once a negotiation exists, there has to be something for developing countries to "gain". It also repeated the lesson that the easiest concession to "give" is a little more legal freedom.

LEGAL POLICY AFTER THE REVIEW SESSION

The first steps under the revised Article XVIII did not signal any change in the GATT's "by-the-book" approach. Although Article XVIII was now less restrictive, the developed countries continued to apply it seriously. Indeed, in 1957, when Ceylon tabled a new series of infant-industry measures under Article XVIII, the Contracting Parties responded by appointing a "panel" to investigate and make recommendations.[17] A panel is a group of individual representatives, acting in their personal capacity (that is, not under instruction from their governments) who are charged to make an objective analysis of the facts and legal criteria applicable to a problem. In GATT practice, the appointment of a panel signals a commitment to rigorous and objective application of the rules.[18] The choice of the panel mechanism meant that the Contracting Parties continued to regard Article XVIII as an exception to be controlled very carefully – and, quite possibly, even to be discouraged.

The rigor of the Article XVIII procedure proved to be the dying gasp of a legal policy that was rapidly losing conviction. Only Ceylon ever used the panel procedure, and Ceylon's requests were disposed of by 1960. Developed countries would continue to insist on a certain rigor with respect to formalities, but their interest in actual discipline soon began to wither. The declining interest was not the product of any new *démarche* by developing countries. Nor was it ever formalized in the legal texts of the GATT. It was, rather, the product of a slowly growing sense of hopelessness and frustration, more an attitude than a consciously articulated policy.

One of the major causes of frustration was the lack of progress in solving balance-of-payments problems. By the late 1950s, the GATT's developed countries had pretty well pulled out of the post-war balance-of-payments crisis; for them, GATT legal discipline was becoming increasingly more meaningful as the final push approached.[19] For the developing countries, by contrast, the years 1955–60 produced a growing volume of ever more dramatic studies showing that developing countries were losing ground economically, often in spite of growth that was quite impressive in absolute terms. Instead of becoming fewer, balance-of-payments restrictions were expanding. A GATT report in November 1959 showed that thirteen of the GATT's sixteen developing-country members were now using balance-of-payments restrictions.[20] Peru and Nicaragua, which had not used balance-of-payments restrictions during the first decade of GATT history, had been forced to restrict imports in 1958 and 1959 respectively.[21] It began to look as if emergency restrictions were going to be a permanent feature of developing-country trade regimes, making other GATT obligations irrelevant. It was also becoming clear that the IMF would take the lead in supervising the emergency restrictions, because of its ability to provide on-site consultation and direct financial assistance.

Another discouraging factor was the failure of the tariff negotiating policy. Developed countries were forced to recognize that, despite tough bargaining in the early years, they had not succeeded in binding very many developing-country tariffs in the early GATT negotiations. Thus, for very many products, developing countries could create prohibitive trade barriers, quite legally, by simply raising the tariff.

Given these loopholes, there was not much to be gained from attacking excessive or illegal trade barriers. Some trade would usually be taking place because developing countries tended to spend the foreign exchange they earned. Securing the removal of some illegal measure was unlikely to increase that level of trade because the same protection would probably re-appear, legally, in some other form.

The result of this growing frustration was a subtle change in the way things were done. The review of balance-of-payments restrictions was typical. As required by GATT law, balance-of-payments restrictions remained under periodic legal review. But, by contrast to the reviews of developed countries where there was intensifying pressure to remove trade restrictions as they got closer and closer to balance-of-payments equilibrium, the developing-country reviews became increasingly pro forma as their balance-of-payments problems remained drearily the same.

Nor were any new initiatives taken. The early rush of legal complaints against developing countries did not last. After the four initial complaints in 1948–49, mentioned earlier, there had been eight developed-country complaints against developing countries in the years 1950–56. Then, nothing. No complaint against a developing country was filed between 1957 and 1969.[22]

The declining rigor of GATT legal discipline towards developing countries produced a rather curious legal policy. The substance withered, but the form remained. Developing countries continued to observe the formalities – especially in seeking formal waivers for actions not in conformity with the rules. The overall volume of such formal activities is evident from an examination of almost any GATT agenda over the past 25 years. By volume, developing-country waiver proceedings are actually more frequent than developed-country proceedings. For example, in a GATT Index of all 169 waiver decisions taken by the GATT up to November 1983, developing-country waivers account for 116 of the decisions, as opposed to 51 for the developed countries.[23]

Developing-country delegates would argue that developing countries actually comply with GATT legal formalities more frequently than do developed countries. There is no way to verify such a claim on an overall basis, because there is no way to count the number of non-conforming measures that should have been, but were not, regularized under GATT law. Some quite striking instances can be identified, however, in which it does seem that developing countries have been asked to go through legal formalities that were not required of developed countries for the same measures.

The clearest example is that of "surcharges". The GATT's balance-of-payments exception, Articles XII and VIII(B), allows a country to limit imports when its balance-of-payments position so requires. But the legal text only permits governments to use quantitative import restrictions for this purpose. It does not permit them to use "surcharges" – an across-the-board surtax on all imports.

In the late 1950s, the IMF recommended to several developing countries that surcharges would be a superior instrument to use in limiting imports for balance-of-payments purposes.[24] A number of developing countries followed this advice and sought a GATT waiver to permit surcharges. The waivers were granted, routinely.[25] A few years later, certain developed countries began to experience balance-of-payments difficulties; some of them resorted to surcharges, namely Canada, Denmark, the United Kingdom and eventually even the United States.[26] No developed country ever sought a waiver. The GATT held consultations, but in each case it was agreed to put aside the legal issue and to concentrate on reviewing the key economic issue – whether restraints were being kept at the necessary minimum and whether they were being removed as promptly as possible. Despite these precedents, however, developing countries still had to go through the waiver procedure for their surcharges. Some of the developing-country surcharge waivers are still in force and are still being renewed.[27]

There appear to be two reasons for this curious situation. Part of the pressure for developing-country compliance with formalities is self-induced. Even if no other country really cares, it is nonetheless prudent for a small country to avoid giving larger countries a legal right to use economic pressure – especially once it becomes clear that the formality leads to no real discipline.

The other reason lies in developed-country attitudes. In spite of their general disinterest in enforcing legal discipline, developed countries do find it difficult to accept "pragmatic" stances once a matter of developing-country legal compliance is raised. The explanation for this abnormal interest in formalities seems to lie, paradoxically, in the absence of any other kind of legal relationship. Among developed countries, where a general commitment to a sort of "best-efforts" compliance with GATT legal disciplines is assumed, nothing much is surrendered by waiving compliance with formalities; the objectives of the relationship between the GATT and the country remain clear and the existence of the commitment to those objectives is never in question. With developing countries, though, where there is no common underlying discipline, legal form is all there is to the relationship. Setting aside the formalities would leave the parties in a legal vacuum. They would have nothing else to say to each other.

The situation might be summed up by saying that both sides need to be legalistic because they have agreed not to be legal.

The legal relationship just described did not develop overnight. Nor did it develop in isolation. Many other factors also contributed to the change of attitudes just described. One of the most important was a major shift in the focus of the GATT's relationship with developing countries. From about 1958 onwards, developing countries seized the initiative and persuaded the GATT to concentrate on the behavior of developed countries towards them, rather than on their own behavior. The next chapter deals with this phase in the relationship.

NOTES AND REFERENCES

1. For a list of GATT accessions up to May 1969, see John H. Jackson, *World Trade and the Law of GATT*, op. cit., Appendix E, pp. 898–901.
2. *General Agreement on Tariffs and Trade: Basic Instruments and Selected Documents* (hereafter cited as BISD), 8th Supplement (Geneva: GATT Secretariat, 1960) pp. 99–100.
3. The classification of Portugal and Spain as developing countries in this list is based on their own claims to such treatment at the time. That is the criterion generally used in this study – although it should be noted that nothing very important turns on the precise distinction between developing and developed countries. Note, incidentally, that the line shifts over time, as self-perception changes. Portugal and Spain ceased to be developing countries on the day they became full members of the European Community.
4. *BISD*, 17th Supplement (1970), p. vii.
5. *GATT Focus*, newsletter of the GATT Secretariat, Geneva, No. 47, June 1987.
6. *BISD*, 2nd Supplement (1954), pp. 6 and 40.

7. *BISD*, Vol. II (1952), pp. 20–27. "Volume II" was the title given to the first issue of GATT's annual document series; subsequent issues in the series were titled "Supplement" rather than "Volume". The 1953 issue was called 1st Supplement.
8. *BISD*, 1st Supplement (1953), p. 26.
9. *BISD*, Vol. II (1952), pp. 49–89, and *BISD*, 1st Supplement (1953), pp. 34–43.
10. *GATT Press Release*, GATT Secretariat, Geneva, No. 177, 9 November 1954, quoted in Karin Kock, *International Trade Policy and the GATT 1947–1967*, op. cit., p. 228.
11. See notes 17 and 18 below. In 1983, Indonesia formally notified the Director-General of the GATT of the imposition of new restrictions on imports of food products, stating that they had been imposed in the light of GATT Article XVIII(A) and XVIII(C), GATT Document L/5597, 22 December 1983. Indonesia's notification made no mention of the consultations required under Article XVIII, even though the consultation requirements had actually been reaffirmed in a 1979 decision. See "Safeguard Action for Development Purposes", *BISD*, 26th Supplement (1980), pp. 209–10. The Indonesian notification stated that it was being made "for use as may be deemed fit", suggesting that consultations would probably be a waste of time. To the author's knowledge, no delegation asked for consultations.
12. The four cases may be described as follows:

   (a) *Cuban Consular Taxes*. A complaint by the Netherlands that Cuba's consular tax was being applied in a discriminatory manner in violation of the MFN obligation of Article I. The GATT issued a ruling that the tax was in violation. *BISD*, Vol. II (1948), p. 12. The discrimination was terminated. GATT Document CP.4/4 (1948).

   (a) *Cuban Restrictions on Textile Imports*. A United States complaint charging that various restrictions violated the Article XI prohibition against quantitative import restrictions and also impaired the value of tariff concessions. The practice was eliminated as part of a broader settlement, without a formal legal ruling. GATT Document CP.2/SR. 25 (1948).

   (b) *Brazilian Internal Taxes*. A complaint by France against internal taxes on several products (including cognac) that discriminated against imports in violation of the national treatment obligation of Article III. A working party report, as interpreted, ruled the measure to be in violation. *BISD*, Vol. II (1949), p. 181. The discrimination was eliminated some ten years later, as part of a major tariff overhaul. *BISD*, 7th Supplement (1958), p. 68.

   (c) *Cuban Restrictions on Textile Imports (II)*. A joint submission by the United States and Cuba over the question of whether Cuba was legally entitled to withdraw certain bound tariff bindings. A working party was unable to resolve the disputed factual issues and the case was committed to further negotiation. GATT Document CP. 3/SR.42 (1949).

   The fifth complaint also happened to be against a developing country, but it was brought by another developing country – a complaint by Pakistan against India. See note 23, Chapter 3.
13. On the death of the ITO, see note 25, Chapter 1.
14. The text of the OTC Agreement is published in *BISD*, Vol. I (Revised) (1955), pp. 75–82. Like the ITO Charter, the OTC Agreement meant nothing without

United States participation. The OTC died by the same hand – the refusal of the United States Congress to ratify it.

15. The Review Session Reports appear in *BISD*, 3rd Supplement (1955), pp. 170–252.

16. GATT Article XXVIII(*bis*)(3)(b).

17. *BISD*, 6th Supplement (1958), p. 112. The following year, the Contracting Parties went one step further and drafted a set of permanent procedures for the Article XVIII panels. *BISD*, 7th Supplement (1959), p. 85.

18. For example, the GATT repeatedly refused to use panels to review compliance with the requirements of the balance-of-payments exception, on the ground that such reviews would be more rigorous than countries wanted. The story of the balance-of-payments panels, as well as similar experiences with panels, are reported in Robert E. Hudec, *The GATT Legal System and World Trade Diplomacy*, op. cit., pp. 80–81.

19. For the developed countries, the legal pressure began with an insistence that any restrictions remaining after the balance-of-payments justification ended must be regularized under the very demanding terms of a so-called hard-core waiver. See *BISD*, 3rd Supplement (1955), p. 38. The treatment of succeeding countries became progressively more gentle, but continued to require rather demanding reporting and confrontation procedures into the mid-1960s, including some GATT lawsuits. For a time, the balance-of-payments restrictions remained a separate agenda item, called "residual restrictions". Eventually they lost their distinctive character and became merged with the general problem of non-tariff barriers. For a full description of how the developed-country residual restrictions were treated, see Hudec, *The GATT Legal System and World Trade Diplomacy*, op. cit., pp. 241–60.

20. *BISD*, 8th Supplement (1960), p. 66.

21. *BISD*, 7th Supplement (1959), p. 37, and *BISD*, 8th Supplement (1960), p. 52. Both Peru and Nicaragua resorted to surcharges rather than the quantitative import restrictions permitted by the GATT.

22. The 1950–56 complaints can be described as follows:

   (a) *Greek Increase in Bound Duties*. A 1952 United Kingdom complaint charging simple violation of a bound tariff binding. The violation was admitted and was corrected in 1953 after a devaluation. See *BISD*, 7th Supplement (1959), p. 69.

   (b) *Greek Special Import Taxes*. A 1952 French complaint charging that new taxes violated the national treatment rule of Article III and could not be justified as IMF-sanctioned monetary measures. A panel report clarified the issue. See *BISD*, 1st Supplement (1953), p. 48. The taxes were removed after the 1953 devaluation. See *BISD*, 7th Supplement (1959), p. 69.

   (c) *Brazilian Compensatory Concessions*. A 1953 United States complaint charging failure to implement concessions promised in a previous negotiation. The concessions were implemented in 1954. GATT Document SR.9/27 (1954).

   (d) *Turkish Import Levy*. A 1954 Italian complaint asking for a ruling on whether a new tax could be justified as an IMF-sanctioned monetary measure. The IMF supported Turkey and the complaint was withdrawn. GATT Document SR.9/7 (1954).

(e) *Peruvian Embargo on Exports from Czechoslovakia.* A 1954 Czech. complaint charging that the embargo violated the prohibition of Article XI. The embargo was withdrawn the same year. GATT Document SR.9/27 (1954).

(f) *Greek Luxury Tax.* A 1954 Italian complaint charging that the fax discriminated against foreign goods in violation of the national treatment rule of Article III. The complaint was settled when the tax was removed from some products. GATT Document SR.9/30 (1955).

(g) *Greek Duties on Long-playing Phonograph Records.* A 1956 West German complaint charging that failure to apply a bound tariff rate to a new product within the generic classification violated the tariff binding of the tariff. A ruling in favor of the complaint was made by a panel of customs experts. GATT Document L/580 (1956). The ruling was not approved by the Contracting Parties. GATT Document SR.11/16 (1956). The case was settled with agreement on a compromise rate for the new product. GATT Document L/765 (1957).

(h) *Chilean Auto Taxes.* A 1956 United States complaint that a sharply graduated automobile tax impaired the value of a tariff concession on automobiles. The complaint was withdrawn when Chile enacted new tax legislation satisfactory to the United States. GATT Document IC/SR.31 (1957).

After 1956, no legal complaints were filed against a developing country until a 1969 Danish complaint against Spain concerning restrictions on cod imports. Even that complaint was quite mild and was settled almost immediately. See GATT Document L/3221 (1969). On the pattern of subsequent complaints, see note 15, Chapter 5.

23. The count is taken from the Index to *BISD*, 30th Supplement (1984). Although the number of developing-country waiver proceedings is arguably inflated by the fact that many involve repeated renewals of the same waiver, the repetition is itself a valid measure of relative attention to form.

24. See GATT Document Com.TD/F/W.1 (1965). For a discussion of the background and early history of the issue, see Jackson, *World Trade and the Law of GATT*, op. cit., pp. 711–14.

25. The following is a list of the GATT waivers for developing-country surcharges that were imposed for balance-of-payments reasons, with *BISD* citations to the first and most recent waiver decisions:

Country	First waiver	Latest waiver
1. Peru	7th Supplement 37 (1959)	12th Supplement 54 (1964)
2. Chile	8th Supplement 25 (1960)	13th Supplement 22 (1965)
3. Nicaragua	8th Supplement 52 (1960)	11th Supplement 70 (1963)
4. Ceylon	10th Supplement 35 (1962)	18th Supplement 29 (1972)
5. Uruguay	10th Supplement 51 (1962)	30th Supplement 14 (1984)
6. Turkey	12th Supplement 55 (1964)	30th Supplement 11 (1984)

Not all developing countries have sought waivers for their balance-of-payments surcharges. One documented case was a surcharge by India in the early 1960s. See GATT Document L/2477 (1965) (notice of surcharge removal).

26. *BISD* citations to the relevant reports or (non)decisions are: Canada, 11th Supplement (1963), p. 57; United Kingdom, 15th Supplement (1968), p. 113; United States, 18th Supplement (1972), p. 212; and Denmark, 19th Supplement (1973), p. 120. Also treated outside Article XII and without a waiver were balance-of-payments "import deposits" imposed by Italy, 21st Supplement (1975), p. 121, and by New Zealand, 23rd Supplement (1977), p. 84, and emergency restrictions by France following the "events of May" in 1968, 16th Supplement (1969), p. 57.

27. See the Uruguayan and Turkish waivers cited in note 25. Balance-of-payments surcharges have produced one of the oddest chapters in GATT legal history. The GATT twice attempted to revise its balance-of-payments rules to permit surcharges as an alternative to quantitative import restrictions, in order to bring the rules into conformity with what had become widely accepted practice. The first time was in the Part IV negotiations of 1963–64. The United States supported the amendment, but the European Community opposed and blocked agreement. The author served as one of the United States delegates in these negotiations. As he understood the Community's position, it was that recognition of legal authority to use surcharges that would remove whatever restraining effect the waiver process was exercising on an already very weak commitment to respect existing tariff bindings. Since the balance-of-payments surcharges were, in practical terms, going to be virtually perpetual anyway, saying they were legal would leave nothing to show for the concessions so painfully extracted in years past.

    Then in the 1973–79 Tokyo Round negotiations a second effort was made to change the rules. Again it fell short. But, even though the GATT's rules continued to prohibit surcharges, the Contracting Parties did adopt a "decision" which agreed that all balance-of-payments restrictions, in whatever form (including surcharges), should be submitted to existing procedures of Articles XII and XVIII(B) to determine whether they satisfy the economic criteria required for balance-of-payments quantitative import restrictions. The decision made no mention of any need to obtain a waiver. "Declaration on Trade Measures Taken for Balance-of-Payments Purpose", *BISD*, 26th Supplement (1979), p. 205. In other words, the GATT was prepared to treat surcharges as de facto acceptable, even to the point of regulating them in the same manner as "legal" quantitative import restrictions, but it still was not willing to say that they were legal. That is how the matter now rests. For a further analysis of this situation, see Frieder Roessler, "The GATT Declaration on Trade Measures Taken for Balance-of-payments Purposes: A Commentary", *Case Western Reserve Journal of International Law*, Cleveland, Vol. 12, No. 2, 1980, pp. 383–403.

3

Demands for a New Legal Relationship – 1958–1963

IN THE YEARS following the 1954 Review Session, the question of the GATT's relationship to developing countries continued to grow in importance. According to Karin Kock, the Swedish expert on GATT affairs, the issue became critical once it became clear that a large number of British and French colonies were soon to achieve independence.[1] "Cold War" competition for the loyalty of these emerging countries intensified when the Soviet Union began to press for the creation of a global trade organization, within the United Nations, that would provide an alternative to the Western-dominated GATT. The prospect of a rival United Nations organization grew more substantial each year and finally materialized in the form of the United Nations Conference on Trade and Development (UNCTAD), formally constituted in 1964.[2]

CHANGES IN BARGAINING POWER

By the early 1960s, GATT relations between developed and developing countries had become almost totally centered on competition with UNCTAD in the making. The UNCTAD threat considerably augmented the bargaining power of developing countries. Developed countries believed that a bloc decision not to participate in the GATT would be seriously damaging to Western political interests; they were therefore willing to pay a price to avoid it. Developing countries knew this and asked for a great deal. In the end, however, the UNCTAD threat had its limits. Developing countries knew that the GATT was useful to them and they knew that a United Nations type organization might not be able to replace it. Thus, although it often did not seem so at the time, developing countries actually used the UNCTAD threat with a great deal of caution and patience.

Certain other factors are commonly cited as reasons for the substantial increase in developing-country bargaining power during this period. One is

51

the formation of an effective "bloc" in the early 1960s, the so-called "Group of 77".[3] The presence of effective bloc behavior probably did increase bargaining power and thus consolidated the traditional source of developing-country power – the participation issue – in a most effective way.

It is often assumed that developing countries also increased their bargaining power because of the greater voting power created by their increasing membership in the GATT. In fact, however, most of the main elements of the GATT's new policy were in place by the early 1960s, when the GATT's developing-country membership was still a minority. Besides, the total number of votes rarely matters in GATT affairs, because the GATT almost never votes. The changes that occurred were accomplished by consensus, not by voting majorities.

NEW FOCUS ON EXPORTS

The increase in the bargaining power of developing countries occurred at a time when their trade-policy concerns had begun to change. The conventional description of the change is that developing countries came to see that economic development could not be promoted solely by a policy of import substitution behind trade barriers. Instead they began to take the view that the key to development was very much larger export earnings. As the focus shifted to export earnings, however, evidence began to mount that the export performance of developing countries was actually declining. The message for the GATT was clear. The GATT had promised to create trade conditions that would promote growing exports for everyone; it was failing to achieve this objective for developing countries. If the GATT was to attract and hold developing-country members, therefore, it needed a major new initiative to increase the export earnings of developing countries.

The need for such an initiative was perceived fairly soon after the 1954 Review Session. A meeting of GATT ministers was convened in November 1957 to consider the general state of, and the prospects for, international trade. The ministers' decision cited three major problems:

> . . . the failure of the trade of less developed countries to develop as rapidly as that of developed countries, excessive short-term fluctuations in prices of primary products, and widespread resort to agricultural protection.[4]

The ministers called for a study of these problems by a group of experts. The result was the Haberler Report of October 1958.[5] The report supported the general perception that the export earnings of most developing countries were unsatisfactory in terms of the resources needed for economic development. While the report contained some criticism of developing-country trade restrictions, the main focus was on the need to open the markets of developed countries.

Another meeting of GATT trade ministers was called to consider the Haberler Report. To remedy the problems identified in the report, the ministers adopted an Action Program. One of the three objectives of the Action Program was to expand the export earnings of developing countries. A special working group, called Committee III, was established to work on this objective.[6]

The creation of Committee III marked the beginning of a permanent shift in the emphasis of the GATT's relationship with developing countries. The initiative was now with the developing countries. Their demand for greater market access had become the first issue on the agenda. Because it was a very difficult demand to meet, it tended to absorb almost all the institutional energy allocated to developing-country relations. Moreover, as long as developed countries were unable to meet this first demand, they would find it difficult to muster the kind of moral authority needed to make complaints about the behavior of developing countries. Concern over the trade policies of developing countries would not disappear entirely, but it would be pushed into a distant second place.

CAMPAIGN FOR IMPROVED MARKET ACCESS

Almost from the outset, the Action Program divided its attention between two main fronts. One was traditional trade negotiations, where the effort was to persuade developed countries to use their negotiating authority to the maximum extent, without insisting on very much reciprocity from developing countries. The second was a direct appeal for unilateral trade liberalization by developed countries – without negotiation and without reciprocity.

The first year of the Action Program came to a conclusion in November 1959, at the Fifteenth Session of the Contracting Parties, held in Tokyo. It was decided to hold a new round of tariff negotiations in 1960 to be known as the Dillon Round. In the committee charged with formulating the negotiating rules for the Dillon Round, developing countries asked for various special rules that would take account of their difficulty in providing reciprocity. The committee declined. Noting that Article XXVIII(*bis*) had already made some concession on the reciprocity problem for developing countries, the committee saw no justification for any further negotiating rules on behalf of developing countries. Instead, it re-affirmed the traditional rule that each country makes its own decision as to the adequacy of reciprocity.[7]

The Committee III report to the Fifteenth Session responded to this defeat by proposing a new kind of trade liberalization – a second front. Committee III expressed the view that developing countries could not achieve the necessary degree of trade liberalization by relying on traditional methods of tariff negotiation involving reciprocity. It therefore proposed, and the Contracting Parties approved, a recommendation calling upon developed countries to "examine" barriers to exports from developing countries "with a view to facilitating an early expansion of the export earnings of less-developed countries".[8] This non-binding and gently worded appeal for unilateral trade liberalization by developed countries was the first in what proved to be a long history of such appeals.

The Fifteenth Session had another item of business that warned of the forces opposing the liberalizing objectives of the Action Program. The Contracting Parties agreed to put "market disruption" on the agenda for the following session.[9] This rather harmless looking item was a first step in trying to control the growing number of discriminatory quantitative controls which developed countries were imposing on textile imports – the manufactured product with the greatest export potential for developing countries. Governments of developed countries believed it was impossible for them, politically, to accept the rapid increase in imports in this sector from developing countries. The study of "market disruption" would eventually be used as the basis for the Multi-fiber Arrangement (MFA) – a multilateral agreement authorizing and supervising a virtually permanent regime of quantitative trade controls.[10] The contrasting goals of the Action Program and the trade policy towards textiles were to become a pattern. There would be efforts to increase exports from developing countries, but there would also be new trade restrictions to place limits on that growth.

In November 1960, Committee III reported on the results of its request for unilateral concessions the year before.[11] The results had been few and for the most part consisted of removing balance-of-payments restrictions that were being phased out anyway. Committee III applauded the progress and made another request for more significant unilateral concessions in the coming year.

The Dillon Round negotiations of 1960–61 proved unsatisfactory to most contracting parties. A meeting of ministers in November 1961 agreed to begin work immediately on a new round of negotiations, adopting new procedures. As part of the new procedures, they agreed that "a more flexible attitude should be taken with respect to the degree of reciprocity to be expected from [developing countries]".[12] The statement was an admission that the reciprocity demands of developed countries in the Dillon Round negotiations had been too severe.

On the second front, the same 1961 meeting of ministers adopted a declaration which, for the third year in a row, pressed for unilateral concessions. The 1961 declaration re-stated the needs of developing countries in significantly more urgent terms and it included a great deal more detail about the kind of action that should be taken. For example, governments were asked to "give immediate and special attention to the speedy removal . . ."[13] of whatever. The ministers called for meetings at an early date to establish targets, timetables and deadlines. They singled out duty-free entry, for tropical products as a priority objective. They did not, however, go so far as to make any of this legally binding.

By 1961, the efforts on this second front were beginning to fall into a pattern. There had been few visible results so far and, as experience with this tactic grew, it could be seen that results would continue to be very slow in coming. Governments of developed countries said they supported the objective of unilateral concessions and were willing to participate in the work. But the actual removal of trade barriers would have required these governments to undertake politically difficult actions in their national legislatures, and most governments were not eager to tackle this task. The absence of any real progress led to a continual search for additional forms of activity that would give the appearance of movement. The GATT became very skillful in creating such appearances, primarily by erecting new procedural mountains and then climbing them. The GATT's work evolved into a slow and patient form of bureaucratic slogging – unending meetings, detailed studies of trade flows and trade barriers and repeated declarations in increasingly urgent but never-quite-binding language. The work was tedious, repetitive and often, absurd.

One of the more interesting characteristics of this work was its success, at the level of principle, in securing agreement to the idea of unilateral concessions. In 1962, the United States Congress authorized the elimination of duties on tropical products, without reciprocity.[14] In May 1963, the GATT trade ministers approved another declaration accepting the objective of duty-free access for tropical products, once again with no expectation of reciprocity.[15] Developed-country governments seemed willing to accept the idea that there should be at least some areas of trade policy in which the requirement of reciprocity would not apply.

The developed countries were much less willing, however, to tear up the reciprocity requirement for the new trade negotiations, called the Kennedy Round, that were to start in May 1964. The rules for the Kennedy Round negotiations began by affirming that each participant was free to judge reciprocity for itself – the traditional formula for saying that countries had no obligation to grant non-reciprocal concessions. There was, however, a special rule for developing countries. The first version of the special rule was quite broad:

> ...every effort shall be made to reduce barriers to exports of the less-developed countries, but... the developed countries cannot expect to receive reciprocity from the less-developed countries.[16]

Subsequent refinements, however, added:

> ...the contribution of the less-developed countries to the overall objective of trade liberalization should be considered in the light of the development and trade needs of these countries.[17]

In other words, some "contribution" was expected after all. The issue would be how meaningful the "contribution" had to be.

The operative answer was given in the actual Kennedy Round negotiations. Developing countries were allowed to become formal "participants" in the negotiations on the basis of a declared intention to "contribute". It was then agreed that contributions did not have to be tariff reductions. India claimed to have made a contribution, for example, through the lowering of the United Kingdom's most-favored-nation tariff, which meant that the value of the preferential duties which India enjoyed in the British market were reduced.[18] Many, perhaps most, developed countries did not make a serious effort to extract contributions. The United States did more than most other countries, although the majority of the concessions it received consisted of promises to "bind" existing rates of duties against increase.[19]

The Kennedy Round confrontation over the reciprocity issue can be made to look somewhat ridiculous in retrospect. It was more a matter of principle than practical consequence. Under the GATT's MFN obligation, developing countries were entitled to all concessions made in the negotiations, whether or not they had "participated" in the Kennedy Round negotiations. On, the other hand, mere "participant" status did nothing to induce concessions on products of special interest to developing countries. It was impossible to legislate that non-reciprocity should have as much bargaining leverage as reciprocity.

The issue of principle, however, was an important one. The developed countries were trying to preserve the idea that the GATT should be a bilateral legal relationship. The developing countries seemed equally intent on denying that principle. In terms of formal decisions, the result was a draw, but the actual outcome of the Kennedy Round negotiations constituted an admission that the developing countries had won. By the end of the Kennedy Round negotiations in 1967, the GATT had become pretty much resigned to accepting a one-sided legal relationship with developing countries.

ENFORCING THE LEGAL OBLIGATIONS
OF DEVELOPED COUNTRIES

In late 1961, Uruguay filed a legal complaint under Article XXIII against fifteen developed countries – in effect, against the entire developed-country membership of the GATT. The Uruguayan complaint listed 576 restrictions in the fifteen markets: Uruguay's legal theory was that these restrictions were seriously reducing Uruguayan exports, that Uruguay was thus not receiving the overall level of benefits contemplated by the General Agreement and that this situation constituted a "nullification and impairment of benefits" (in the words of Article XXIII). Uruguay asked the Contracting Parties to remedy the situation.[20]

Article XXIII does in fact contain provisions allowing members to complain about an overall imbalance of benefits and obligations; these provisions were meant to provide a basis for claiming legal adjustments in the case of something like a catastrophic 1930s-type world depression. But, in the approximately 150 complaints filed before and after this one, there has been only one other such broadside – a 1983 complaint by the European Community against Japan charging that its entire trade relationship with Japan had been distorted by the overall orientation of Japanese foreign economic policy.[21] The normal complaint under Article XXIII involves a discrete trade problem, usually a single trade measure that can be remedied by specific action.

The Uruguayan complaint was showpiece litigation – an effort to dramatize a larger problem by framing it as a lawsuit. The complaint was making two points. One was to draw attention to the commercial barriers facing exports from developing countries and the fact that, whether or not these barriers were legal, the GATT was not working if it could not do better than this. Second, although Uruguay carefully avoided any claim of illegality, the fact that many of the restrictions were obviously illegal would, Uruguay hoped, dramatize the GATT's ineffectiveness in protecting the legal rights of developing countries.

Before the Uruguayan case, there had been relatively little litigation involving developing countries, on either side. As noted earlier, the GATT began with a rash of legal claims against developing countries, but these had very quickly dwindled to only the very rare case.[22] Claims by developing countries had accounted for about 15 percent of the GATT's adjudicatory caseload.[23] Of the twenty or so decided cases up to the time of the Uruguayan decision, three had involved successful claims by developing countries: Pakistan against India in 1948,[24] Chile against Australia in 1950[25] and Brazil against the United Kingdom in 1961.[26] Of the approximately thirty-five other legal complaints that had not reached a formal decision, five more had been complaints from developing countries. A complaint in 1952 by India against Pakistan had been settled to India's satisfaction without a decision.[27] Two others became moot when the problem was solved by other means: a complaint in 1952 by Greece and Turkey against the United States[28] and a complaint in 1953 by Turkey against the United States.[29] Two other developing countries had filed complaints without success: Cuba against the United States in 1949 (no violation found)[30] and Greece against the United States in 1953 (no resolution).[31] Taken as a whole, these eight developing-country complaints were pretty typical of the results in developed-country cases.

The relatively small number of legal complaints was interpreted by the developing countries to mean that it was very difficult for them to enforce legal claims against developed countries, primarily because their dependent economic position exposed them to indirect retaliation in so many different ways. In addition, they often argued, developing-country lawsuits had no real force behind them because developing countries simply do not have the market power to injure a developed country by retaliation.

The GATT took the Uruguayan complaint seriously. A panel was appointed and conducted an examination on each listed restriction. Uruguay refused to take any position about the GATT legality of the 576 measures. Neither the panel nor the GATT Secretariat would accept the role of plaintiff in Uruguay's stead. Accordingly, the panel did what a court would have done: it accepted, as uncontested, any claim by defendants that a measure was GATT-conforming. The developed-country defendants did not claim conformity for patently illegal measures and, in these instances, the panel made a finding of nullification and issued a formal recommendation asking that the illegal measure be removed. Follow-up proceedings were held in 1963 and 1964 where each defendant reported some degree of compliance.[32]

Although Uruguay's broader claim of "nullification and impairment" due to an overall imbalance of benefits was clearly cognizable under Article XXIII, Uruguay did not press the claim and the panel chose to ignore it. The panel said it was willing to examine the question of whether individual trade restrictions not in violation of the GATT might be causing an "impairment" of GATT benefits. It ruled, however, that a country claiming such non-violation impairment must show exactly how particular measures impair benefits expected from the General Agreement. This Uruguay refused to do.[33] So nothing came of the narrower "impairment" issue, either.

Uruguay did specifically ask for one legal ruling. It asked the panel to rule on the legality of the variable import levy used by the European Community.

The panel stated that, since the Contracting Parties had previously discussed the issue without reaching agreement, it did not consider it "appropriate" to examine the matter.[34]

At the conclusion of the proceeding, Uruguay noted the removal of certain restrictions, but said that others had been added in the meanwhile and that consequently Uruguay's overall position was no better than before.[35] The lesson to be drawn from the case, according to Uruguay, was that GATT law did not protect developing countries.

Uruguay took this lesson into the 1963–64 negotiations that produced Part IV of the General Agreement, proposing a number of reforms designed to remedy this situation. The law reform proposals added considerable heat to the debate for a while and eventually produced one moderately important reform in 1966.

EMERGENCE OF THE DEMAND FOR TARIFF PREFERENCES

The issue of new tariff preferences was not part of the 1958 Action Program. It seems to have entered the GATT discussions sometime in 1961. By 1963 it had made its way on to the agenda of issues to be studied.[36]

By the time the preferences issue had re-surfaced, GATT legal discipline on the subject of non-discrimination had already begun to slip. The formation of the European Community, itself a legally permitted form of discrimination under Article XXIV, had triggered two important types of legally prohibited discrimination. One was the Community's extension of preferential tariff rates to the former African colonies of certain member states. Before 1957, preferences had existed between individual member states and their respective colonies or ex-colonies; these preferences had been authorized by express exceptions written into Article I of the GATT. The post-1957 preferential arrangements were not covered by this exception in Article I, because they extended the preferences to and from all the other member states of the Community.

The Community argued that these new preferential measures were authorized under Article XXIV, claiming that each was an individual free trade area between the Community and the African state in question. Both legally and practically, the justification did not persuade other GATT contracting parties, for the arrangements had not the least prospect of satisfying the GATT's legal requirement that such unions achieve a prompt and complete removal of substantially all trade barriers between the parties. After a heated debate which led to an *impasse*, however, the GATT agreed to put aside the legal issue and to concentrate on solving, in a "pragmatic" fashion, any actual trade problems that might arise.[37] The European Community had breached the wall. It had successfully granted new preferences.

At about the same time, many developing countries began to view the European Community's rapid economic growth as a lesson that regional integration could stimulate economic development. Developing countries therefore began to form their own customs unions and free trade areas. Whatever their ambitions, none of these efforts came even close to satisfying the legal requirements of Article XXIV concerning prompt and comprehensive liberalization. They were, in effect, nothing more than new preferences between developing countries. Unlike the legal battle that had ensued over the preferential arrangements between the Community and its associated countries and territories, the GATT's review of these developing-country arrangements was gentle and supportive. The agreements were simply passed over with a pragmatic wait-and-see attitude.[38] The developed-country members of the GATT were reluctant to be seen as discouraging this supposedly effective tool of development, even when it was being used illegally.

The crumbling legal discipline against preferences was merely the symptom of a deeper disagreement over the wisdom of the MFN obligation itself. The developed-country position on the GATT's MFN obligation had fragmented. The United States was still opposed to preferences, but, whereas the United States had been able to obtain the support of the entire developed-country bloc in 1948, by 1963 the European Community was on the other side. The Community's chosen instrument for assisting developing countries was preferential tariff treatment along the lines of its African arrangements – selected preferences for selected developing countries.[39] And the Community was not alone. In varying degrees, many other developed countries within the GATT were sympathetic. Preferences began to look like the easiest solution to the increasing pressure from developing countries for trade liberalization. All GATT governments were having difficulty meeting demands for conventional trade liberalization. The greater this difficulty, the greater became the appeal of preferences as an alternative. Preferences required less political sacrifice at home because the main losers were supposed to be third countries. Even if preferences did more harm than good, they were something developed countries could "give".

The United States succeeded in blocking the preferences initiative, both in the GATT and in UNCTAD, during the first half of the 1960s when developed countries were trying to fashion an answer to the demand for a new order. But the preferences issue took its toll nonetheless. The GATT's developed-country bloc was divided. Without unity on this key issue, there was no hope of devising any coherent alternative to the demands of developing countries.

NOTES AND REFERENCES

1. Karin Kock, *International Trade Policy and the GATT 1947–1967*, op. cit., p. 236.
2. As its name implies, UNCTAD began life as a mere international conference. The conference, held in Geneva in 1964, voted to transform itself into an organization. See UNCTAD, Final Act, United Nations Document E/CONF.46/141 (1964). The institution was established by a subsequent resolution of the General Assembly. United Nations Document, General Assembly Resolution 1995 (1965). See generally, *The History of UNCTAD 1964–1984*, United Nations Document UNCTAD/OSG/286 (New York: United Nations, 1985).
3. The term "Group of 77" refers to a 77-member voting bloc organized by developing countries for the 1964 UNCTAD Conference. Its membership is now well in excess of 100. Not all Group of 77 members participate in GATT affairs. See Karl P. Sauvant, *The Group of 77: Evolution, Structure, Organization* (New York: Oceana Publications, 1981).
4. *BISD*, 6th Supplement (1958), p. 18.
5. Gottfried Haberler et al., *Trends in International Trade*, Report by a Panel of Experts (Geneva: GATT Secretariat, 1958), hereafter cited as the Haberler Report.
6. *BISD*, 7th Supplement (1959), pp. 27–29.
7. *BISD*, 8th Supplement (1960), pp. 108–10.
8. Ibid., p. 23. See also pp. 135–41 (report of Committee III).
9. Ibid., pp. 22–23.
10. The process began with a simple report defining the phenomenon of "market disruption", for the purpose of giving it standing as a special problem that would justify special measures. *BISD*, 9th Supplement (1961), p. 26. Subsequent textile arrangements then provided for discriminatory quantitative import restrictions, under multilateral supervision, as a means of dealing with market disruption. The current agreement is known as the Multi-fiber Arrangement (MFA). The agreement is formally called the Arrangement Regarding International Trade in Textiles. The most recent full text appears at *BISD*, 21st Supplement (1975), p. 3. The MFA was most recently extended in 1986 for five more years.
11. *BISD*, 9th Supplement (1961), p. 144.
12. *BISD*, 10th Supplement (1962), p. 26.
13. Ibid., p. 29.
14. Trade Expansion Act of 1962, Section 213, 76 Statutes at Large 874. The Act did require, however, that other developed countries do likewise, a condition that was not met because the European Community refused to remove its duties on tropical products, in order to protect preferences in these products granted to certain African countries.
15. *BISD*, 12th Supplement (1964), pp. 36–40. The European Community's ministers dissented, but for other reasons. Their statement indicated that they, too, agreed with the non-reciprocity principle itself.
16. Ibid., p. 48.
17. *BISD*, 13th Supplement (1965), p. 111.
18. John W. Evans, *The Kennedy Round in American Trade Policy: the Twilight of the GATT?* (Cambridge, Massachusetts: Harvard University Press, 1971) p. 249.
19. Ibid., p. 253.

20. GATT Document L/1647 (1961).
21. GATT Document L/5479 (1983).
22. See notes 12 and 22 in Chapter 2.
23. For a comprehensive list of GATT legal complaints, and the settlement reached, up to 1975, see Robert E. Hudec, *The GATT Legal System and World Trade Diplomacy*, op. cit., pp. 275–96. For an extension of the list to July 1985, see *Review of the Effectiveness of Trade Dispute Settlement under the GATT and the Tokyo Round Agreements*, Publication No. 1793 (Washington: United States International Trade Commission, 1985). The GATT also published such a list in 1986: *Analytical Index – Notes on the Drafting, Interpretation and Applications of the Articles of the General Agreement on Tariffs and Trade* (Geneva: GATT Secretariat, 1986) pp. XXIII-87 to XXIII-128.
24. Pakistan claimed that denial of a tax rebate on exports to Pakistan, but not on exports to other countries, violated the MFN obligation of GATT Article I. GATT Document CP.2/SR.11 (1948). The Contracting Parties ruled in favor of Pakistan and, although India continued to disagree on the merits, the two countries agreed to eliminate the discrimination as part of a broader settlement. GATT Document CP.3/SR.19 (1949).
25. Chile complained that a change in an Australian consumption subsidy, although legal under the GATT, had nullified the benefits of a tariff concession to Chile. The Contracting Parties ruled in favor of Chile. *BISD*, Vol. II (1950), p. 188. Although Australia continued to disagree on the merits, the parties reached a settlement satisfactory to Chile. GATT Document CP.5/SR.6 (1950).
26. Brazil charged that the United Kingdom was proposing to increase the margin of preference in its tariff on bananas, in violation of the terms of a waiver permitting such increases, GATT Document SR.19/12 (1961). A panel ruled in favor of Brazil, GATT Document L/1749 (1962). The proposed increase was abandoned, GATT Document SR.20/2 (1962).
27. GATT Document L/82/Add.1 (1953). The complaint had involved discriminatory export fees on jute.
28. The complaint charged that a United States escape-clause action on dried figs did not conform to Article XIX. GATT Documents L/40, L/44 (1952). Turkey took the compensation it was entitled to by means of retaliation. *BISD*, 1st Supplement (1952), p. 28. The United States then withdrew the tariff concession permanently under Article XXVIII, thereby removing the legal issue. GATT Document L/284 (1954).
29. The complaint charged that quotas on filbert nuts impaired GATT concessions. GATT Document G/46/Add.3 (1953). The United States withdrew the quotas one month later.
30. The complaint charged that a reduction in an MFN tariff rate impaired a previous concession binding the level of a preferential rate on the same item. See GATT Document CP./SR.34 (1949) and *BISD*, Vol. II (1949), p. 11.
31. Greece charged that an export subsidy on sultana grapes ought to be removed because of trade damage caused to Greece. GATT Document L/39 (1952). There was no legal basis for the complaint and eventually the United States refused to discuss the issue further. GATT Document SR.8/12 (1953).

32. For the text of the three panel reports, see *BISD*, 11th Supplement (1963), p. 95, and *BISD*, 13th Supplement (1965), pp. 35 and 45.
33. *BISD*, 11th Supplement (1963), p. 100.
34. Ibid.
35. GATT Document L/1662 Rev.1 (1964).
36. See *BISD*, 12th Supplement (1964), p. 44 (GATT ministerial declaration of May 1963 agreeing to establish a working group to study the preferences proposal).
37. *BISD*, 7th Supplement (1959), p. 70.
38. For a detailed survey of GATT's attitude to the developing-country arrangements during these years, see Kenneth W. Dam, "Regional Economic Arrangements and the GATT: the Legacy of a Misconception", *University of Chicago Law Review*, Vol. 30, No. 4, 1963, pp. 615–65.
39. For a statement of the European Community's policy at the GATT Ministerial meeting in May 1963, see GATT, *BISD*, 12th Supplement (1964), pp. 39–40.

4

Defining the New Relationship – 1964–1971

THE SCHEDULING of the UNCTAD conference for the spring of 1964 precipitated an effort within the GATT to demonstrate more forcefully its commitment to the interests of developing countries. The first step was a decision to draft amendments to the legal text of the General Agreement that would consolidate the various strands of the GATT's emerging policy towards developing countries. Initially, it was contemplated that the new legal text would be placed in Article XVIII. The new text grew so long, however, that at the last moment it was re-packaged as a new Part IV of the General Agreement.[1]

PART IV OF THE GATT

The importance of Part IV is not easy to describe. From a technical point of view, Part IV added nothing to the existing legal relationship between developed and developing countries. Part IV was only a slightly more impressive statement of the urgent but non-binding texts that the Action Program had been issuing over the preceding five years, giving them a permanent form in the text of the General Agreement. The language of Part IV was a bit more legalistic, giving the illusion of greater commitment. Indeed, the title of the new Article XXXVII, "Commitments", actually said so. In fact, however, the text of Part IV contained no definable legal obligations.

The drafting reached new heights in suggesting commitment where there was none. Instead of "should", the text now said "shall" several times. But the "shall" never went anywhere:

Article XXXVII(1)
The developed contracting parties shall to the fullest extent possible – that is, except when compelling reasons, which may include legal reasons, make it impossible – give effect to the following provisions.

Article XXXVII(3)
The developed contracting parties shall:

(a) make every effort . . .
(b) give active consideration . . .
(c) have special regard to . . .

The text contained a special procedure for enforcing these "commitments", but it provided only for consultations, not for specific legal rulings. Wisely so.

Interestingly, the "commitments" of developing countries towards each other were equally empty of obligation. The seldom-noticed text of Article XXXVII(4) says that developing countries (then called "less-developed countries")

> . . . *agree* to take appropriate action in implementation of Part IV for the benefit of the trade of other less-developed contracting parties, *insofar as such action is consistent with* their individual present *and future* development, financial and trade needs, *taking into account* past trade developments as well as the trade interests of less-developed contracting parties as a whole. (emphasis added)

The developing countries made a serious effort to put more substance into the developed-country commitments in Part IV, but there was never much chance of making them legally binding. Most developed-country delegations simply did not have instructions allowing them to consider new legal obligations. Delegates from developing countries knew this. In some ways, the legal emptiness of Part IV is a measure of how little developed countries were willing to spend to save the GATT from UNCTAD – or, perhaps, a measure of how little it took to persuade developing countries that abandoning the GATT was not in their own best interest.

Developing countries also tried to improve Part IV in two other respects. First, they sought to win new kinds of legal freedom. Serious efforts were made to include an authorization for preferences and to settle the reciprocity question by making it clear that no reciprocity of any kind should be requested. Both these efforts were rejected. Part IV did not mention preferences. And the Part IV text on reciprocity was merely a repetition of the vague Kennedy Round negotiating rule.

Second, led by Uruguay and Brazil, the developing countries asked for a major reform of GATT adjudication procedures to cure the problems that had been demonstrated, in their view, by the Uruguayan Article XXIII case. They asked that the GATT adopt new sanctions for legal violations, including both money compensation and retaliation by the Contracting Parties as a whole.

They also asked that the GATT Secretariat assume a prosecutorial role in GATT lawsuits to relieve small countries of the political onus that befalls a plaintiff.[2] The developed countries refused to include any of these proposals in Part IV. As a compromise, the proposals were referred to the GATT's soon-to-be-created Trade and Development Committee.[3]

The major significance of Part IV was its force as an agreed statement of principle. At the time, developed-country delegates tended to scoff: "Why not agree? It doesn't mean anything." The GATT, they pointed out, was a place where governments dealt in concrete, meaningful trade actions. In such a setting there was simply no value to the sort of pious declarations so common in other international organizations.

The tough-minded delegates of the 1960s under-estimated the effect of agreeing to these principles. Developing countries returned to these principles again and again in the years that followed. When they did, developed-country delegations always searched for ways to do things that could be seen as satisfying the moral commitments expressed in them. Much, perhaps even most, of the activity has been meaningless and even cynical. But no observer of the GATT for the past twenty years can deny that developed countries have spent an increasing amount of time every year dancing to the whip of these agreed principles. They are not law, but they do control the GATT's agenda.

The other important consequence of Part IV came on the procedural front. The Contracting Parties agreed to create a permanent Trade and Development Committee which would have as its mandate all the objectives of Part IV. There was now a permanent bureaucracy attending to developing-country concerns and preparing the agenda called for by their agreed principles.

LEGAL DISCIPLINE IN THE 1960S

In addition to Part IV, the GATT's effort to prove its value vis-à-vis UNCTAD also produced a very interesting statement summing up GATT policy on the subject of legal discipline. In March 1964, the GATT Secretariat published a pamphlet entitled *The Role of GATT in Relation to Trade and Development*.[4] The pamphlet was primarily addressed to the governments of developing countries. In addition to reviewing the various Action Program efforts, the pamphlet gave a full description of the rights and obligations of GATT members, giving special attention to the legal discipline expected of developing-country members. In so doing, it emphasized the considerable legal freedom that developing countries enjoyed, while at the same time having the right to benefit from MFN application of developed-country obligations. The 1963 non-reciprocity rule adopted in the Kennedy Round negotiations was quoted.[5] The rule was then repeated with emphasis when describing the tariff negotiations required when countries accede to the General Agreement:

> While less-developed countries have made some tariff concessions on their accession, relatively little reciprocity is expected from them and it is accepted that they must, in general, retain freedom to use their tariff flexibility in the light of their development needs.[6]

The pamphlet then went on to explain that developing countries who make tariff concessions will find it relatively easy to withdraw them later, because Article XVIII recognizes the legitimacy of industrial development reasons. And then, as though the very mention of tariff concessions might be frightening, it hastened to remind readers that Article XVIII was needed *only* where a tariff was bound and that where the tariff was unbound " – which is the case over by far the major part of the tariffs of most [developing-country members] – they are free to set their tariffs at any level".[7]

The granting of waivers for balance-of-payments surcharges was mentioned, showing the GATT's willingness to waive legal rules when prohibited trade measures are found to be appropriate to the circumstances. The Article XVIII(C) rules allowing quantitative restrictions were described with similar emphasis on the ease of application. And, with regard to Article XXIV on regional integration, the pamphlet mentioned the several developing-country unions and pointed out that GATT practice had been to set aside legal questions for the time being and to direct attention to specific and practical problems.[8]

On the whole, the pamphlet gave a quite accurate description of the GATT's legal discipline for developing countries. What was interesting was its effort to portray the absence of legal obligations as a virtue. This is perhaps the clearest demonstration there is of the link, during this time, between the GATT's legal policy towards developing countries and its very strong desire to attract and hold developing-country members.

KENNEDY ROUND NEGOTIATIONS

Part IV produced no dramatic changes. Nor did the decision, at the 1964 UNC-TAD conference, to make UNCTAD a permanent organization. If anything, the reality of UNCTAD was probably less threatening to the GATT than the various pre-UNCTAD visions of what it might be like. Developing countries remained very active in the GATT. They continued to press for improved market access and the GATT continued to encounter obstacles in its effort to get something done.

With the opening of the Kennedy Round negotiations in 1964, most of the efforts towards trade liberalization shifted to this forum. Trade negotiations were the forum where the developed countries had legal authority to do something. This was also where they wanted to do something. The United States, in particular, wanted to persuade developing countries that liberalization could be achieved only through business-like negotiations on specifics, rather than by voting for sweeping statements of principle.

Twenty-five developing countries declared themselves "participants" in the negotiations. Special procedures were established to give attention to the concerns of developing countries. The Kennedy Round rules provided for a "linear" tariff reduction by the major developed countries – an across-the-board cut of 50 percent, with a rule that all exceptions had to be listed and justified. Developing countries were invited to table their demands for tariff reductions on products of interest to them, and developed countries were required to consider these demands when formulating their offers. Then, after all this preparation, developed countries tabled their initial offers. After developed countries had "confronted" each other's exceptions from the 50 percent linear cut, participants from developing countries were given an opportunity to confront the developed countries on the exceptions which excluded products of interest to them. After this first round of confrontations, developed countries then revised their lists of exceptions, a process that required a good deal of cliff-hanging negotiation among developed countries. The developing-country demands, meanwhile, were dealt with in pretty much a unilateral fashion.[9]

At the end of the day, developing countries found that they had not really "participated" in the negotiations. Except for some not-very-effective efforts by the United States, developed countries made no effort to extract more than token concessions from them. Consequently, with no economic benefits on the table, the developed countries had felt free to treat developing-country requests for liberalization as simply yes-or-no issues that needed no negotiation.

The results of the Kennedy Round negotiations were the proverbial glass of water – both half full and half empty. Unquestionably, many products of considerable importance to developing countries, such as cotton textiles, were essentially excluded from the linear tariff reductions. Developed countries had decided that they were not willing to make major political sacrifices where weak domestic industries were already being threatened. The tariff reductions on tropical products – the priority area established by the Action Program – were also disappointing. No reduction at all was made on approximately half the volume of dutiable imports.[10] According to UNCTAD calculations, the average tariff reduction on products of interest to developing countries was less than the average on products figuring in developed-country trade – 26 percent and 36 percent respectively.[11]

Developing countries declared the results a failure, as did UNCTAD. The GATT and its supporters argued the contrary, pointing out the many important cuts that were made, asserting that an average reduction of 26 percent was a very large cut by historical standards and pointing out, also, that the cuts on many other products not currently identified as developing-country products would create long-term opportunities. The defense of the Kennedy Round achievements was necessary to maintain perspective, but there was never any chance it would prevail. It was clear that a massive liberalization had not occurred and that no extraordinary sacrifices had been made. Given these facts, no one could have expected that developing countries would stop pressing for more. That being so, the rest of the debate was merely jockeying for rhetorical advantage.

The Kennedy Round negotiations had been advertised as the long-awaited answer to demands by developing countries for improved access to developed-country markets. Its equivocal results strengthened the hand of those urging more radical solutions. The conventional approach had been given its chance and it had not proved capable of doing enough. Even if one believed that the technique of multilateral trade negotiations should be tried again, the world would not be ready for another such effort for at least a decade. Governments would have to have something else to "give" in the interim. Enter preferences.

GENERALIZED SYSTEM OF PREFERENCES

In the second UNCTAD conference of 1968, one year after the close of the Kennedy Round negotiations, the United States formally reversed its position and voted to support a "generalized system of preferences" (GSP) under which developed countries would grant tariff preferences to all (or almost all) developing countries, without reciprocity, on all (or almost all) products.[12] Actual implementation was delayed for several years while certain subsidiary issues were worked out.[13] The United States had accepted the GSP with the hope that it could use its own participation in the GSP as leverage to force the European Community to abandon its policy of special preferences to certain Mediterranean and African countries and, in particular, the "reverse preferences" that recipient countries were required to give to the Community. The United States achieved the abolition of the reverse preferences, but eventually it had to abandon its opposition to the special preferences given by the Community. Consequently, while the United States and others limited themselves to one worldwide preference scheme, the Community went on to institute both a GSP scheme applicable to all developing countries and an elaborate system of additional preferences for selected developing countries with whom it had special ties.[14]

Reflecting the gradual shift in attitudes, the GATT had begun to accept ad hoc preference agreements as early as 1966.[15] It was not until 1970, however, that the main implementing details of the GSP itself were settled, not in the GATT but in UNCTAD. Then, in 1971, the GATT adopted two waivers permitting two types of preference schemes.[16] One was a ten-year waiver setting aside the MFN obligation in Article I to the extent necessary to permit the institution of the GSP. The other was a waiver, subject to review in ten years, permitting developing countries to exchange tariff preferences among themselves, under the terms of a Protocol requiring that participation be open to all GATT developing countries. After twenty-three years in the wilderness, Article 15 of the ITO Charter had finally been welcomed into the GATT. (Nine years later, in 1979, both waivers would be made permanent in the so-called Enabling Clause decision.)[17]

It should be noted that the legal status of the GSP program was permissive and not mandatory. In UNCTAD, governments of developed countries had agreed in principle to grant preferences, but that agreement was never reduced to a contractual obligation, either in UNCTAD or in the GATT. The only GATT legal instrument on the GSP was the waiver allowing governments to introduce preferences if they chose.

The terms of the GSP waiver require that preferences be made generally available to all developing countries, but the details are not controlled. Consequently, it is up to the government of each developed country to decide what products will be covered, what the margin of preference will be and what quantitative or other limits will be imposed on preference benefits. Each developed-country government has done something different. The United States legislation had a number of conditions that could be used to disqualify unworthy recipient countries, as well as other quantitative limits to make sure that preferences will be applied only when "needed".[18] The European Community's scheme contained its own elaborate set of limitations designed to prevent its GSP scheme from interfering with the commercial advantage of its special preferences for Mediterranean and African countries.[19]

The two waivers of Article I in 1971 can be viewed as the end of the period of upheaval that began with the 1957 ministers resolution which called forth the Haberler Report. By 1971, the GATT's new relationship with developing countries had been defined.

MORE ON LEGAL DISCIPLINE: THE RISE OF PRAGMATISM

While the campaign for market access was slowly grinding forward through Part IV, the Kennedy Round negotiations and the 1971 waivers to permit preferences, the campaign on the legal front went into reverse. The late 1960s saw a sharp decline of legal discipline among all Contracting Parties, developed and developing. Between 1963 and 1970, there were only a few initiatives that could be called legal complaints, none really being pressed towards a legal ruling.[20] A theology of "pragmatism" grew up to replace the GATT's earlier interest in effective legal procedures. It was probably the lowest point in the GATT's history in terms of respect for the legal character of GATT engagements.

The pragmatist era was primarily a developed-country reflex – a doctrine to justify a decline in the legal discipline of developed countries. Non-compliance was expanding. While most developed countries had liberalized balance-of-payments restrictions with reasonable promptness after reaching equilibrium, a fair number of "residual restrictions" remained in force, primarily in agriculture. An increasing number of new quantitative import restrictions, many of them discriminatory, were being imposed on competition from Japan and other newly emerging exporters – first in textiles, then in other manufactures. Japan, in turn, held on to a particularly large number of restrictions into the late 1960s and beyond. And finally, the formation of the European Community had involved a number of aspects that were quite debatable from a legal point of view, especially its side agreements with Africa and the Mediterranean countries and its highly protectionist common agricultural policy. The GATT very much needed a period of relaxed discipline in order to work out the new legal relationship that the Community's arrival required.

Notwithstanding this adverse legal climate (or perhaps because of it), the developing-country attack on the legal front continued after the earlier Part IV reform initiative had been defeated. Brazil and Uruguay submitted proposals in the Trade and Development Committee, in 1965, repeating the request that the GATT Secretariat initiate and prosecute legal complaints and repeating, too, the various proposals for increased sanctions – financial compensation and multilateral retaliation.[21]

These developing-country reform proposals once again met with relatively little success. Indeed, they probably made things worse rather than better. The mid-1960s were a time of radical change – UNCTAD, the Group of 77, preferences and so forth. The reform proposals calling for money compensation and joint retaliation looked like part of the same movement. Developed-country officials envisaged wave after wave of lawsuits against themselves, launched by countries which did not regard themselves as bound by the rules and which, therefore, would have no lawsuits to fear in return. The developed countries reacted by adopting an even more intense commitment to pragmatism, lecturing developing countries (and each other) on the unwisdom of seeking legal solutions to trade problems and threatening to treat any resort to law as a hostile act. Whatever the origins of this pragmatist movement, it was clearly made worse by fear of developing-country claims.

While the more extreme proposals for reform were once again rejected, the new initiative did result in a decision in 1966 creating a new GATT adjudication procedure for developing-country legal complaints under Article XXIII.[22] The most significant element in the 1966 procedure was the agreement that developing-country complaints would automatically be referred to a panel if mediation failed and that time limits would be imposed to prevent the use of delaying tactics by the defendant (typically a developed country). This was a significant change from the usual practice of seeking the agreement of each party to each successive step in the procedure. The special rule was adopted in order to meet the complaint that large developed countries had the political and economic power to refuse to proceed, arbitrarily, when the plaintiff was a developing country.

The new procedure, however, still required a developing country to initiate the proceedings. Efforts to assign this role to the GATT Secretariat were once again rebuffed. For this reason the new procedure was not viewed by developing countries as a very significant victory. The reluctance to initiate complaints was undoubtedly a serious problem. No developing country invoked the 1966 procedure until 1972 and, after that, not again until 1977.[23] Given the hostile attitude towards legal claims in the late 1960s, the reluctance is not hard to understand.

Developing countries could, of course, find one gain in these legal developments. The pragmatist climate during this period more or less guaranteed that nothing much would be done to re-assert legal discipline over their own conduct. True, developing countries were still attending to the formalities of balance-of-payments reviews and waivers on surcharges, but these were mere formalities and had been so for some time. The pragmatist mood of the late 1960s ensured that they would remain that way.

NOTES AND REFERENCES

1. *BISD*, 13th Supplement (1965), p. 2 (protocol introducing Part IV).
2. GATT Document L/2195/Rev.1, Annex 4 (1964).
3. The Trade and Development Committee inherited the unfinished work of the Legal and Institutional Committee that had drafted Part IV. See *BISD*,

13th Supplement (1965), p. 76. The 1965–66 Trade and Development Committee negotiations on the Brazil-Uruguay proposals are discussed in the documents cited in notes 21 and 22.

4.   *The Role of GATT in Relation to Trade and Development* (Geneva: GATT Secretariat, 1964). The pamphlet is not identified by Sales Number or other document number.

5.   Ibid., p. 7.

6.   Ibid., p. 8.

7.   Ibid., p. 9.

8.   Ibid., pp. 16–17

9.   John W. Evans, *The Kennedy Round in American Trade Policy*, op. cit., pp. 245–53.

10. *BISD*, 15th Supplement (1968), p. 150.

11. *The Kennedy Round Estimated Effects on Tariff Barriers*, Report by the Secretary-General, United Nations Document TD/6/Rev.1 (Geneva: UNCTAD Secretariat, 1968). For another detailed quantitative analysis of the Kennedy Round results, see Ernest H. Preeg, *Traders and Diplomats: An Analysis of the Kennedy Round of Negotiations under the General Agreement on Tariffs and Trade* (Washington: Brookings Institution, 1970).

12. United Nations Document UNCTAD, Resolution 21 (II) (26 March 1968). For a description of change in the United States' position, see Rachel McCulloch, "United States Preferences: the Proposed System", *Journal of World Trade Law*, Geneva, Vol. 8, No. 2, 1974, pp. 217–18.

13. See the United Nations Document TD/B/332, Supplement I (1971) (the "agreed conclusions"). Most observers believe that the issues were not finally settled until an informal United States–European Community agreement, known as the Casey-Soames Understanding, was reached in meetings in March and August, 1973. According to the story, the European Community agreed to give up reverse preferences in exchange for a United States undertaking not to challenge the GATT legality of the (manifestly GATT-illegal) Lomé preferences.

14. The European Community's current GSP scheme is contained in Regulations 3601/81, 3602/81 and 3603/81 *Official Journal of the European Community*, No L 365, 7.12, 1981. The special preferences are currently provided for in the Second Lomé Convention of 1 January 1981, described in *BISD*, 29th Supplement (1983), p. 119 (working party report). The Community's legal justification for Lomé preferences is as a free trade area under Article XXIV, a justification which other countries tolerate without conceding. See ibid., p. 125.

15. The GATT's first step towards the GSP was a waiver permitting Australia to give preferences to developing countries. *BISD*, 14th Supplement (1966), p. 23. The first explicit experiment with preferences on trade between developing countries was a 1968 "decision" (not a waiver) permitting a preferences agreement between India, the United Arab Republic and Yugoslavia, open to participation by all other developing countries. *BISD*, 16th Supplement (1969), p. 17.

16. *BISD*, 18th Supplement (1972), pp. 24 and 26.

17. See note 29, Chapter 5. The subsequent history of the waiver for preferences on trade between developing countries is discussed in Chapter 6.

18. Trade Act of 1974, Title V, Sections 501–505, 19 United States Code 2461–2465. The 1974 legislation has been replaced with 1984 legislation extending the United States'

GSP program; the special conditions of both laws are discussed in Chapter 6. For a comparative description of the GSP schemes of the United States and the European Community and a summary of their own and other research on the trade effects of these programs, see Rolf J. Langhammer and André Sapir, *Economic Impact of Generalized Tariff Preferences*, Thames Essay No. 49 (Aldershot, Brookfield and Sydney: Gower, for the Trade Policy Research Centre, 1987). See also Barry H. Nemmers and Ted Rowland, "The US Generalized System of Preferences: Too Much System, Too Little Preference", *Law and Policy in International Business*, Washington, Vol. 9, 1977, pp. 855–911.

19. See legal sources cited in note 14. See also Langhammer and Sapir, *Economic Impact of Generalized Tariff Preferences*, op. cit.; Axel Borrmann et al., *The European Communities' General System of Preferences* (The Hague: Martinus Nijhoff, 1981).

20. See Robert E. Hudec, *The GATT Legal System and World Trade Diplomacy*, op. cit., pp. 223–28 and pp. 292–93.

21. GATT Documents Com.TD/F/W.1, and Com.TD/F/W.4 (1965).

22. *BISD*, 14th Supplement (1966), p. 18.

23. Israel invoked the special procedure in 1972 in a complaint involving United Kingdom textile restrictions. A panel was appointed, but the case was settled before any legal ruling was made. See *BISD*, 20th Supplement (1974), p. 237 (panel report of settlement). The next instance was Chile's invocation in a 1977 complaint concerning export subsidies of the European Community on malted barley. The complaint was later withdrawn, before a panel was appointed. See GATT Document C/M/123 (1977) (referral to consultations). The only other two invocations known to the author were an Indian complaint against Japanese restrictions on leather in 1980 and a Mexican complaint against various import charges on petroleum and petroleum products in 1987. The former complaint was settled, at least temporarily, with some undertakings worked out in connection with a United States complaint proceeding concerning the same restrictions. See GATT Document L/5623 (1984). The latter was referred to a panel, together with complaints by Canada and the European Community on the same subject.

5

Testing the New Relationship – 1972–1979

IN THE EARLY 1970s, GATT governments began to plan the Tokyo Round of multilateral trade negotiations, known formally as the Multilateral Trade Negotiations, or MTN. Discussions began in 1972, and GATT trade ministers formally convened the negotiations and established the negotiating rules in Tokyo in September 1973.[1] The negotiations started very slowly and did not end until the summer of 1979. Implementation of the Tokyo Round agreements took several more years.

LEGAL POLICY OF THE UNITED STATES

The decade in which the Tokyo Round negotiations took place witnessed a sharp turn – or at least an attempted sharp turn – in GATT legal policy. A serious effort was made to revive legal discipline among developed countries. In the very simplest terms, the effort can be seen as a change in the United States' policy towards GATT law. In the 1960s that policy had been dominated by two factors:

(a) The United States had a strong and growing economy.
(b) The political interests of the United States called for effective European integration and the growth of a strong and stable Japan.

During the 1960s both the European Community and Japan had employed a number of market-distorting measures in pursuit of their own economic and political development. It is not clear that such measures were actually beneficial, but the governments seemed to think they were and so the United States had tolerated them. The economy of the United States had been strong enough to absorb the effects of whatever market disadvantage was involved.

Towards the end of the 1960s, an increasing number of producers in the United States began to encounter strong competition from imports, leading many political leaders in the United States to conclude that their economy no longer enjoyed what had once seemed a comfortable margin of competitive superiority. Meanwhile, Japan and Western Europe were experiencing rapid economic growth and were beginning to look like economic superpowers equal to the United States. The collapse of the dollar in August 1971 dramatized the rather sudden end of the economic dominance of the United States. These events persuaded many political leaders in the United States that their country no longer had either the capacity, or the need, to tolerate deviant trade policies of the European Community or Japan. A new understanding was needed: Everyone had to return to playing by the same rules.

There were many contradictions in this new policy of the United States. In the first place, it was a bit more self-righteous than was appropriate, for the United States itself was by no means innocent of major GATT rule violations. It was also somewhat disingenuous, for many of those who complained about European Community and Japanese behavior were protectionists who wanted to emulate the Community and Japan, not reform them. And finally, it tended to set unrealistic goals because the government of the United States, in its desire to silence protectionists in its own country, was promising legal reforms that ignored quite basic schisms in GATT policy. With all its contradictions, however, it clearly was a new legal policy and it was pursued vigorously.

The new policy involved two kinds of legal reform. First, there had to be some clearer and more demanding rules in key areas; these would be negotiated in the Tokyo Round deliberations in the form of new "codes" on certain problem areas. Second, both the new rules and the old rules would need more vigorous enforcement. The GATT's dust-covered machinery for adjudicating legal disputes had to be made to work again. The best way to achieve this was to give the machinery something to do and, if it did not work any more, then improvements would also have to be devised in the Tokyo Round negotiations. The two kinds of legal reform were often lumped together and described as an assault on "non-tariff trade barriers".

The new legal policy of the United States had a special component for developing countries, called "graduation". The volume of exports from the more advanced developing countries was beginning to cause discomfort to producers in the United States. Those producers had begun to complain about the one-sided nature of the GATT legal relationship with developing countries, using their complaints as a justification for new trade restrictions against them. The United States Administration proposed to silence these complaints by compelling the more advanced of the developing countries to accept greater legal discipline as their export trade grew. Brazil, the Republic of Korea and Taiwan were examples of countries targeted.

LEGAL POLICY OF DEVELOPING COUNTRIES

The new legal policy of the United States appeared at a time when the developing countries were themselves mounting a major campaign to change the law of the international economic order. The objective of the developing countries was the same as it had been – to enlarge the area of preferential treatment for their products. The campaign peaked in 1974 with two historic Resolutions of the United Nations, the Declaration of a New International Economic Order (NIEO) and the Charter of Economic Rights and Duties of States.[2]

When the Tokyo Round rules were being put together in 1973, GATT developing countries were ready with a law reform agenda of their own. They asked that the Tokyo Round rules contain a general negotiating rule recognizing that developed countries were entitled to "differential and more favorable treatment" in all areas of the negotiations.[3] The term applied both to improved access and to further relaxation of GATT legal discipline. With regard to access, developing countries were asking for new trade liberalization, MFN or discriminatory. With regard to legal discipline, they wanted still wider, and more permanent, exemptions from the GATT's rules.

The United States chose not to bring the conflict in legal positions to a head at the outset of the Tokyo Round negotiations. Relying on the considerable ambiguity in the developing-country position, the United States and other developed countries accepted the differential-and-more-favorable-treatment formula as the basis of developing-country participation in the Tokyo Round negotiations. Moreover, they acceded to the inclusion of these principles in the two United Nations resolutions the following year, again without indicating any reservations.[4] By contrast to their very sharp opposition to some of the other proposals being debated in these NIEO resolutions, the developed-country position on preferential trade-policy treatment had all the qualities of a warm endorsement. Once again, the developed countries were under-estimating the significance of a "non-binding" principle.

The conflict between the position of the United States and the objectives of the developing countries did not fully emerge until the closing phases of the Tokyo Round negotiations and beyond. To recount the story properly, it is necessary to begin with an overview of the trade liberalization achieved during the 1970s and then to examine, in some detail, the steps taken by the United States in pursuit of its new legal policy.

TRADE LIBERALIZATION IN THE 1970S

There were two kinds of tariff reduction on developing-country exports during the 1970s. One was the Generalized System of Preferences (GSP) and the other was the Tokyo Round negotiations on tariffs.

The GSP tariff reductions were, and will no doubt continue to be, criticized for their failure to go further than they did. Many important products were excluded or were limited in quantity. Other rather arbitrary limitations abounded.[5] Nonetheless, GSP schemes did reduce or eliminate tariffs on a substantial proportion of developing-country exports. After a decade or more of pious declarations about the need for unilateral concessions, developed countries had actually done something. No reciprocity was asked. Although the GSP tariff reductions were not legally binding, they were in fact made effective (which does not always happen with GATT legal obligations).

Despite growing attention to "graduation" and other ways of limiting GSP benefits, national GSP schemes have generally maintained or expanded the level of overall trade benefits being granted. And even though grumbling seems to increase every year, developed-country governments still keep signing declarations that they owe developing countries some form of GSP and that it should be made even "better" over time.[6]

Although somewhat overshadowed by the law-reform business of the Tokyo Round negotiations, the tariff reductions made in those negotiations were also significant. Governments followed the same special procedures for developing-country interests as in the Kennedy Round negotiations. The developed countries pressed a little harder for some reciprocity from the larger developing countries, but not very much. This time, the average tariff cut on all industrial products in the ten major developed countries was about 33 percent. The average tariff reduction on industrial products of immediate interest to developing countries was once again smaller – about 26 percent.[7] These tariff reductions began from lower tariff rates to start with and therefore had less commercial impact than the Kennedy Round cuts, but they were far from meaningless. Developing countries once again had received substantial tariff reductions without making any very substantial trade concessions in return.

To put these tariff results into perspective, however, it must be noted that quantitative restrictions on "sensitive" (or "disruptive") exports from developing countries were increasing during the 1970s. Many were in the form of so-called "voluntary export restraints", where the threat of quantitative restrictions on imports would induce developing countries to agree to limit exports at the source. In other words, while it was true that the general level of protection in developed-country markets was being reduced, the resulting growth in exports was being capped in certain important industries. Since these restraints would typically affect products where developing-country producers had the greatest comparative advantage, they were curtailing the most valuable gains from trade.

The proliferation of such quantitative restraints was a main item on the agenda of the Tokyo Round negotiations, in the form of a proposal to rewrite the increasingly ineffective rules of Article XIX governing such measures. The new rules were to be incorporated in a separate side agreement on emergency protection to be called a safeguards code. In spite of agreement on several parts of the safeguards code, however, governments were unable to reach agreement on how to deal with discriminatory trade restrictions, voluntary export restraints and a few other key issues. Thus the negotiators at that time were not able to realize a safeguards code.[8]

In sum, developing countries did manage to achieve two rather substantial tariff liberalizations during the 1970s, both on essentially unilateral terms. These gains were curtailed, though, by a growing network of quantitative restraints, so that the net growth in exports was less than it could have been. The lesson seemed to be that the legal policy being pursued by developing countries was capable of generating positive action by developed countries, but was having difficulty in securing the full realization of those gains.

It was against this background of growing, albeit insecure, developing-country achievements that the United States launched its Tokyo Round law-reform campaign.

REVIVING THE ADJUDICATION MACHINERY

The effort of the United States to revive the GATT adjudication machinery has been described in detail elsewhere.[9] The United States filed an initial spate of legal complaints in 1970–72 in order to get the old machinery working again. It then secured agreement that strengthening the machinery would be an item on the agenda of the Tokyo Round negotiations. Soon other governments began to file legal complaints. Even before the Tokyo Round negotiations had ended, the GATT was having difficulty processing the high volume of litigation that had already been generated by all this attention. The Tokyo Round negotiations eventually produced some new procedural rules that strengthened the adjudication machinery further.[10] The development of stronger procedures continued in the years following the Tokyo Round negotiations, including a lengthy and important declaration by GATT ministers in 1982.[11]

It is still too early to tell whether these dispute-settlement reforms, as this area is called, have been successful. Some of the elements seem to be working quite well. Governments now appear able to bring complaints without generating political hostility. The procedure usually moves forward with reasonable promptness, and the quality of the legal decisions, although spotty, has been getting much better. The main issue that remains is the critical one – acceptance and compliance. A discouraging number of deadlocks have occurred during the 1980s.[12]

Developing countries have generally supported the position of the United States on GATT dispute settlement insofar as it seeks to establish a prompt and automatic right to legal rulings. Small countries usually place a rather high value on "law" as something that can help to neutralize the power of larger countries.

Legal complaints filed by developing countries, although still not very numerous, have been increasing since 1977. According to the author's count, the GATT received sixty-one formal legal complaints between 1977 and 1985. Of these, twelve were complaints by developing countries against developed countries.[13] That was about double the pre-1960 rate. More important, seven of the twelve complaints were pressed to formal proceedings before a GATT panel – almost double the number in the preceding thirty years.[14] Developed-country defendants have generally behaved very "correctly" in these cases, and the GATT has gone out of its way to see that the cases were handled promptly and with respect. Although developing countries still experience considerable trepidation about bringing a developed country into court, each new case adds to the precedent and to the momentum that will make the next case somewhat easier.

While it is difficult to point to any stunning results that developing-country complaints have achieved, developing-country complainants who have won a clear legal ruling usually report some improvement in the practices about which they complained. This has not been the case, however, with complaints involving political embargoes – the European Community's embargo against Argentina during the war in the Falklands, or recent United States actions against Poland and Nicaragua.

The revival of the GATT's adjudication machinery since 1970 also produced a modest number of complaints in the other direction, complaints against violations by developing countries. Of the approximately eighty complaints filed between 1970 and 1985, eight were complaints by developed countries (usually the United States) directed against developing-country practices or against illegal discrimination favoring developing-country trade.[15] Four of these were pressed to a formal decision by a GATT panel.[16]

Far from improving legal discipline in this area, the lawsuits against developing countries have tended to produce results confirming its demise. Each of the four cases pressed to decision has triggered an unusual reaction protecting the developing country from GATT rules. In a 1971 decision against Jamaica, for example, a panel was compelled to agree with a highly technical United States' claim of legal violation, but in the same report it recommended an immediate waiver.[17] Even though the panel's instinct was sound (it was a silly complaint), panels would not normally rush to help in this way. The waiver recommendation showed an extreme sensitivity to potential developing-country objections about uncalled-for discipline.

The three other cases involved a more serious kind of pressure on the substantive rules themselves. One was a case involving a legal claim against Spain where a panel made some quite unsound legal rulings in what appeared to be an effort to give a poor country some extra leeway with the rules.[18] More serious were two cases in which the United States attacked another developed country for illegally discriminating in favor of developing countries. One was a 1972 complaint involving British discrimination in favor of certain Caribbean countries;[19] the other was a 1982 complaint involving discrimination by the European Community in favor of certain Mediterranean countries.[20]

In both instances, the United States had to fight through a swarm of protests by developing-country beneficiaries (and their allies) just to get the case heard. The panel in the British case went to extraordinary lengths to settle the issue informally; it all but refused to decide the complaint and eventually did succeed in persuading the United States to settle. Although the case of the European Community was complicated by other unusual difficulties, the intense opposition of developing countries delayed the process substantially. The panel did eventually issue a ruling, finding that the European Community had "nullified" benefits owing to the United States, for which the United States was entitled to compensation. The Community indicated it would not accept that decision, but the parties eventually reached a settlement.

The developing-country position in these cases tends to be based on the legal position that Part IV of the GATT excuses governments from GATT legal obligations whenever the effect of the government's action is to further the economic development objectives of Part IV. The words of Part IV, of course, do not contain any specific exemption from GATT rules. The position is based on the principles of Part IV which recognize the need to accelerate the process of economic development. The idea is that any market distortion favoring a developing country furthers Part IV objectives.

Developing countries felt the need to assert this legal position recently in a case entirely between two developed countries. The case involved a 1982 complaint by the United States against certain trade-distorting elements of Canada's Foreign Investment Review Act (FIRA). The legal principle of the complaint by the United States would have applied to similar laws in dozens of developing countries. Developing countries entered into the first rounds of the discussion in the GATT Council with some vigor, at times seeming to argue that the GATT should sustain their own legal view (that such laws were not covered by the GATT or, in any event, were excused by Part IV) by refusing even to hear the United States complaint against Canada. They also sought to exercise some control over the panel's terms of reference, for the same purpose.[21] Once again the decision of the GATT panel responded to the developing-country protests. The panel found some parts of the Canadian law to be in violation of the GATT, but the panel's decision took special care to say that nothing in its decision was meant to cover the situation of a developing country.[22] Most observers doubted that developing countries would have voted to approve the report without its special disclaimer.

These cases represented a potentially important development in the GATT's legal relationship with developing countries – but clearly not the development for which the United States was looking. The cases seem to be providing developing countries with a tactical opportunity to establish their concept of Part IV legal immunity. When the United States sues, the claim of Part IV legal immunity comes up in a defensive posture, where it can "win" merely by blocking a decision, as in the 1972 complaint against the United Kingdom, or by forcing a decision in which the "road block" is circumvented, as in the 1982 FIRA complaint. So far, the defensive use of this legal position has proved fairly effective. Although these precedents do not establish the developing-country position definitively, each has added a little more authority to it.

If there was a lesson to be learned from these lawsuits, it was that something more was needed to restore legal discipline in this area. Part of the answer, it was hoped, would be found in the new "codes" that were being drafted in the Tokyo Round negotiations.

TOKYO ROUND CODES AND FRAMEWORK AGREEMENTS

Writing new GATT rules is not an easy thing to do. Changing the legal text of the General Agreement requires approval by at least two-thirds of all GATT members. Even then, members who do not sign the new rules are not bound by them, but instead continue their legal relationships with other GATT members under the rights and obligations of the original text. Where unanimous agreement is unlikely, therefore, an amendment would leave both the old and the new texts operative for most member countries. It is undesirable to divide up the master legal instrument in this way, especially when reform may require a long process involving many separate amendments.

Before the Tokyo Round negotiations, the GATT had experimented in a few cases with making changes in rules by means of separate side agreements. The 1954–55 Review Session agreed to an amendment prohibiting export subsidies for non-primary products (Article XVI[4]), but the amendment was arranged in such a way that, while the language became part of the General Agreement, the operative obligation required a separate declaration to which only the major developed countries subscribed.[23] In the early 1960s, governments agreed to a program of discriminatory quantitative import restrictions for textiles, which would otherwise have been in violation of the GATT, by means of a judicially separate agreement that amounted to a de facto relaxation of the relevant GATT disciplines – the agreement currently known as the Multi-fiber Arrangement (MFA).

In the Kennedy Round negotiations, governments wanting to tighten and refine the discipline on the use of anti-dumping duties once again resorted, in 1967, to a separate agreement. They placed the new rules in a separate code which any interested country could sign.[24] Although only the major developed countries and a few others signed, the signatories were pleased with the way the code approach had worked. Governments had been able to make the code effective among themselves, without a two-thirds vote of all GATT members. The signatories were also able to administer the rules among themselves and by themselves. Because it was limited to those willing to accept the new obligations, the committee of signatories was a much more cohesive group and, therefore, it was more easily capable of reaching consensus.

The attraction of the code approach grew in proportion to developed-country irritation with developing-country interventions in everyday GATT business. By the late 1960s, such irritation was much in evidence. It had become difficult to consider any subject in GATT meetings without finding developing countries insisting forcefully on some special measure for their own benefit. Developing countries viewed this continual nagging as a tactic fully justified by their urgent economic needs. They were prepared to block action, anywhere, until attention was given to those needs. Unfortunately, the nagging often seemed more ceremony than substance because developed countries were usually unwilling or unable to do anything meaningful. In those cases, the developing countries would often consume a great deal of time to obtain nothing more than few additional words in a document pledging, for the hundredth time, that developing-country needs would be "taken into account".

The code approach had very important implications for the legal relations between developed and developing countries. It proposed a new legal community, limited to those members who were willing to subscribe to the rules. If developing countries wished to participate in the new community, they would have to accept equal obligations. If, on the other hand, they continued to insist on a one-sided relationship, they would find themselves excluded from the really serious work and left with only a GATT membership increasingly empty of any substance.

The developing countries had quickly appreciated the potential of the 1967 Anti-dumping Code and moved to counter it. The key to maintaining the existing one-sided legal relationship in the GATT was the unconditional MFN obligation stated in Article I of the General Agreement, requiring each GATT contracting party to extend measures of trade liberalization to all GATT members, whether or not the other member had "paid" for that treatment with reciprocal obligations. In 1967, and again in 1968, the Indian delegation asked the GATT Secretariat for a legal ruling on whether the GATT's MFN obligation required code signatories to apply the Anti-dumping Code's more favorable anti-dumping rules to the trade of non-signatories. The answer was yes; non-signatories were entitled to the same favorable treatment as signatories.[25] This established a formal legal brake on the code approach, but it remained to be seen whether impatient developed countries would respect it.

In its planning for the Tokyo Round negotiations, the United States pressed for more extensive use of the code approach. The main objective of the United States was a code providing for greater discipline on the use of subsidies. The United States wanted this new subsidies discipline as a quid pro quo for agreeing to restrict the scope of its own countervailing-duty law. Another major goal was a code on government procurement in which each signatory would eliminate "buy-national" preferences so that foreign producers could compete on equal terms for procurement contracts. New disciplines in the area of customs valuation and product standards were also high on the United States' agenda.

It is probably fair to say that the main reason for the code approach was simply the desire to escape from the cumbersome ratification procedures of the formal GATT amendment process. A close second, however, was the desire to protect the enterprise from a developing-country veto. The new rules would go into effect with, or without, the blessing of the developing-country bloc. This naturally raised the question of where developing countries would stand if they did not sign. The United States announced an intention to pursue a conditional MFN approach for the Subsidies Code and the Government Procurement Code (the two codes involving the most tangible trade benefits). The United States said it would apply the more favorable code rules only to the trade of other signatories.

The aggressiveness of the United States approach was tempered by a little caution. The caution lay in the selective approach. The subject of government procurement lay outside the GATT's MFN obligation.[26] The Subsidies Code does lie within the GATT's MFN domain, but the United States persuaded itself that it could make a credible legal defense for discrimination in this case as well.[27] Publicly, therefore, the United States was not asserting an intent to flout GATT law. Although private statements promised that the United States would not be bound by the MFN rule if reciprocity was not forthcoming, the restraint that the United States Administration exercised in public showed that it was of two minds on this matter.

The conflict between the substantive objectives of the United States and the developing countries carne to the fore only in the closing months of the Tokyo Round negotiations when smaller governments were finally brought into the process. When the time for decision came, the developing countries managed to force a considerable softening of the United States' position.

First, the United States did not oppose a long list of demands from developing countries for new exceptions from the existing GATT rules, nor several demands for stronger legal affirmations of exceptions granted previously. Developed countries agreed to all of these demands in a series of legal texts known as the "Framework Agreements".[28] The Framework texts included a decision of the GATT Contracting Parties, called the Enabling Clause, which was meant to be a de facto amendment of the MFN obligation in Article I. The Enabling Clause gave permanent legal authorization for:

(a) GSP preferences.
(b) Preferences in trade between developing countries.
(c) "More favorable" treatment for developing countries in other GATT rules dealing with non-tariff trade barriers.
(d) Specially favorable treatment for the least-developed developing countries.[29]

Another Framework text half-legalized the use of surcharges by developing-countries for balance-of-payments reasons; it also relaxed some of the other requirements for reviews of developing-country balance-of-payments restrictions.[30] A third Framework text broadened the exception for "infant-industry" protection in Article XVIII. Although little noticed at the time, the changes in

Article XVIII succeeded in undermining the key elements of the legal discipline that had been fought over so vigorously in 1947 and in 1954–55, removing the requirement of advance approval (a major concession) and broadening the right to protect existing non-infant industry.[31] Finally, the Framework text also re-stated the "non-reciprocity" principle in terms which, although still short of total non-reciprocity, inched slightly closer to that position.[32] (As in 1964, a GATT Secretariat report at the end of the negotiations celebrated these relaxations of legal discipline as positive GATT contributions to developing countries.[33])

In exchange for all these Framework texts, the United States did manage to achieve recognition of its own central "graduation" objective. After considerable resistance, developing countries agreed to say that:

> Less-developed contracting parties expect that their capacity to make contributions or negotiated concessions or [to] take other mutually agreed action . . . would improve with the progressive development of their economies and improvement in their trade-situation and they would accordingly expect to participate more fully in the framework of rights and obligations under the General Agreement.[34]

While the United States did not press for any generalized application of this principle, it did make what it thought were appropriate demands for reciprocity from selected developing countries. If reports to the Congress by the negotiators can be believed, the United States managed to obtain a more-than-symbolic amount of reciprocity from these countries.[35]

The contending viewpoints collided over the form of the new codes. Codes were drafted in the exclusionary form proposed by the United States. Obligations applied only to other signatories and only signatories had any say in administering the codes. At the outset, the codes were negotiated between developed countries alone, with the result that the rules contained no exceptions for developing countries. In the final phase of the negotiations, however, the new codes were presented to developing countries for acceptance. The United States, with some support from other developed countries, brought considerable pressure on more advanced developing countries to sign. The developing-country bloc refused to yield without special provisions carrying out the principle of "differential and more favorable treatment" agreed to in the 1973 negotiating rules. Developed countries then agreed to add a separate provision to most of the codes, usually entitled "Special and Differential Treatment for Developing Countries", and known to negotiators as "S and D provisions".[36]

The content of the S and D provisions varied. Some were merely non-binding assurances of technical assistance to help developing countries learn how to comply with the new rules. Others were status exemptions from the new obligations. Some of these status exemptions were quite limited and non-controversial. In codes dealing with technical matters, such as customs valuation and import licensing, developing countries were in agreement that such devices should not be used in a protective manner by anyone; the S and D provisions in these codes were limited to exemptions thought to be necessary because of the limitations of developing-country administrative capacity.[37] On the other hand, in codes that dealt with the level of trade distortions *per se*, developing countries insisted that they should be entitled to protect, or subsidize, more than other countries. Here, after considerable controversy and threats not to participate, the developing countries generally won some recognition of their position.

The developing countries felt most strongly about the issue of subsidies, arguing that such measures were a proper and necessary tool of development. Their bargaining position was strengthened by the fact that the developed-country consensus about subsidies was quite weak to begin with. The S and D provision of the Subsidies Code reflected this situation, for it excused developing countries from virtually all the new discipline contained in the code.[38] This was clearly a defeat for the United States.

In two other codes of this kind, the Government Procurement Code and the Standards Code, developing countries also obtained recognition of the right to weaker discipline, but the provisions were vague and, in essence, left the exact measure of discipline to future decision.[39] The only code to emerge with no S and D provision at all was the Aircraft Code, an agreement to remove all trade barriers to trade in civil aircraft.[40]

Judged by the texts alone, the Tokyo Round codes represented a stand-off between the contending points of view. The events following the drafting had much the same mixed quality, but, as had been the case for the GATT itself, the trend seemed to point to a continuing line of small concessions to the developing-country point of view.

IMPLEMENTING THE TOKYO ROUND CODES

Of the sixty-five or so developing countries in the GATT, only a handful signed the Tokyo Round codes. As of June 1986, the number of developing-country signatories was: Standards, fourteen; Subsidies, thirteen; Import Licensing, ten; Customs Valuation, nine; Anti-dumping, nine; Procurement, three.[41] On the other hand, the signatories invariably included a majority of the ten or so most advanced developing countries – the prime "graduation" candidates. The only code that was not signed by a majority of the advanced developing countries was the Government Procurement Code, an understandable result in view of the limited capacity of most developing countries to compete for procurement contracts of the size covered by the code – 150,000 special drawing rights (SDRs) on the IMF.

The United States did carry out, to some degree, its threat of denying benefits to non-signatories. The one clear case was the Government Procurement Code, where the law of the United States expressly denied non-signatories the right to compete. The denial may have been more symbolic than real, however, for, as just noted, it is unlikely that very many developing countries would be able to compete for contracts valued at over 150,000 SDRs anyway. Moreover, as noted earlier,[42] the United States was not violating the GATT in this case, because procurement matters are expressly exempted from GATT legal obligations, including the MFN obligation.

The United States also initiated a policy of denying benefits to "non-signatories" of the Subsidies Code. (In fact, the S and D exceptions in the Subsidies Code were so broad that the United States refused to grant benefits to any developing country, even code signatories, unless they agreed to make some more rigorous bilateral commitments about subsidy policy.) Developing countries affected by this policy fought back. Pakistan used the political leverage of the Afghanistan crisis to obtain code benefits on the basis of a very weak bilateral commitment that contained little or no added discipline on subsidies. India then brought a complaint in the GATT charging that the United States' denial of code benefits to it was a violation of Article I. Rather than carry out its threat to violate the GATT, the United States backed away and settled by granting Subsidy Code benefits to India on the same easy terms offered to Pakistan.[43]

It is difficult to be certain about how other developed countries are treating non-signatories. It appears that, with the exception of the Government Procurement Code, most have applied the new code rules on an MFN basis to all GATT Contracting Parties. A GATT decision in 1979 reaffirmed that the GATT's basic MFN obligations are not affected by the codes, meaning that, even though non-signatories have no rights under the codes themselves, their existing GATT rights – specifically their MFN rights under Article I – entitle them to equally favorable treatment.[44]

Administration of the codes has preserved some of their exclusionary aspects, but once again the original design has been compromised. Signatories have established their right to meet in private and often do so. Non-signatories, however, have made a point of insisting on the right to observer status,[45] and the various code committees have recognized that right as a general principle. The result is that code committees meet sometimes in private and sometimes in public. They also argue a lot about which is proper. Although the developed countries have defended the separatist position for some time now, a certain fatigue over the constant confrontations on these procedural issues is becoming evident. Such fatigue is usually a prelude to retreat.

In 1982 the Contracting Parties agreed to conduct an enquiry into the reasons why developing countries were not adhering to the Tokyo Round codes and what could be done about it.[46] The reasons, of course, were perfectly clear. The only issue was whether the developed-country signatories would be willing to meet them by offering still greater exemptions from code disciplines. The agreement to study the issue may have been mere stalling, but it could also have been the first step in an even larger retreat from the code design.

TOKYO ROUND IN RETROSPECT

As time goes on, it begins to look more and more as if the momentum of the Tokyo Round proposals for greater legal discipline over developing countries has become spent and that the legal demands of developing countries have regained the initiative. At the present time, it is difficult to foresee any real movement in the direction of greater legal discipline.

The reasons for this outcome turn out to be the same basic reasons that have existed since 1947. First, the developed countries themselves have been of two minds about legal discipline. Even for the United States, there is a real question as to the depth of the commitment to legal change. So far, the "get tough" message seems to have been aimed primarily at domestic audiences, carried out only to the extent necessary to satisfy those audiences. It is by no means clear how much unpleasant discipline the United States itself is prepared to accept. Until now, it has primarily occupied the position of unsatisfied *demandeur*; thus it has had little occasion to confront the question.[47]

The major problem on the developed-country side, however, has been the unwillingness of other GATT developed countries to go even as far as the United States. The European Community is unwilling to abide by many of the policy norms being asserted by the United States. Because of this resistance, the United States has not even been able to achieve a greater legalization of its relationship with the Community. So long as this basic policy schism exists, the Community will certainly not support the efforts of the United States to increase legal discipline in any other sector. In addition, it is likely that the Community has little enthusiasm for the substantive content of the United States' legal policy towards developing countries. The Community's developing-country policy is built around its regional agreements with Mediterranean countries and with African and other selected developing countries. These are the developing countries of interest to the Community and it obtains the legal relationship it wants with these countries through non-GATT agreements. For these relationships, strengthening the GATT would, at best, be a wasted effort; at worst, it would introduce additional norms (for example, non-discrimination) that would undermine them.

The second reason why the law-reform proposals have become bogged down is the ever-present "membership" issue. However much they care about legal discipline, GATT developed countries always seem ready to retreat if it means jeopardizing developing-country membership in the GATT. Perhaps the best indication of the current influence of that phenomenon in the GATT's legal relationship with developing countries was the report on the Tokyo Round negotiations written by the GATT Secretariat immediately after the negotiations ended.[48] The report was written primarily for developing-country consumption. It was written quickly (but very thoroughly) in order to pre-empt the kind of negative evaluation that UNCTAD had made after the Kennedy Round negotiations. Because it was written for a developing-country audience, it naturally celebrated all the "victories" achieved by the Group of 77. And once again, a central element of the "victories" was all the new legal freedoms developing countries had won, especially those which involved discriminatory special and differential treatment.

The year was 1979. Here was the GATT, still thoroughly preoccupied with holding the allegiance of developing countries and still making a virtue of the fact that GATT rules do not apply to developing countries. The link between the two was as strong as ever.

NOTES AND REFERENCES

1. *BISD*, 20th Supplement (1974), p. 19.
2. There were two United Nations resolutions on the New International Economic Order: (i) a Declaration and (ii) an Action Program. See General Assembly Resolutions 3201, 3202 (S-IV), 1 May 1974 (adopted without vote). The Charter was also in the form of a resolution, General Assembly Resolution 3281 (XXIX), 12 December 1974 (vote of 120–6, 10 abstentions).
3. The original formulation of the term in the Tokyo Round declaration was "differential measures . . . which will provide.. special and more favorable treatment . . . ", *BISD*, 20th Supplement (1974), p. 21. GATT usage never settled on a uniform shorthand expression. Some Tokyo Round documents used the shorthand "special and differential treatment" (in GATT parlance often reduced to S and D), while others used the formulation quoted in the text.

4. Both the New International Economic Order documents and the Charter of Economic Rights and Duties of States covered the entire spectrum of international economic relations. The trade provisions repeated all the demands that had ever been made in GATT-ITO negotiations and included specific endorsement of bigger and better GSPs in the future. While developed countries by no means agreed with everything in either set of documents, they made virtually no protest about the idea of special and differential treatment in general, or about GSP in particular. For the NIEO "reservations" of the major developed countries (expressed after the resolutions were adopted by "consensus"), see United Nations Documents A/PV.2229–2231, 1–2 May 1974, reprinted in *International Legal Materials*, Vol. 13, 1974, pp. 744–66. For a discussion of similar positions regarding the Charter, see *1974 United Nations Yearbook*, p. 399; see also Robert F. Meagher, *An International Redistribution of Wealth and Power: a Study of the Charter of Economic Rights and Duties of States* (New York: Pergamon Press, 1979) pp. 57–59. Such developed-country opposition as there was to the S and D principle was addressed, not to the trade area, but to provisions urging that it be extended into other, ill-defined areas of economic relations.

5. See sources cited in notes 18 and 19, Chapter 4.

6. See, for example, the GATT ministerial declaration of 1982, *BISD*, 29th Supplement (1983), pp. 13 and 22.

7. See *The Tokyo Round of Multilateral Trade Negotiations*, Report by the Director-General of the GATT (Geneva: GATT Secretariat, 1979) pp. 118–22. For UNCTAD's assessment, see *Assessment of the Results of the Multilateral Trade Negotiations*, United Nations Document TD/B/778/Rev.1 (Geneva: UNCTAD Secretariat, 1982).

8. The Contracting Parties, however, decided to continue the Safeguard Code negotiations. *BISD*, 26th Supplement (1980), p. 202. No agreement was reached and the item was placed on the agenda for the Uruguay Round negotiations.

9. See Robert E. Hudec, *Adjudication of International Trade Disputes*, Thames Essay No. 16 (London: Trade Policy Research Centre, 1978), and "GATT Dispute Settlement after the Tokyo Round: An Unfinished Business", *Cornell International Law Journal*, Ithaca, Vol. 13, No. 2, 1980, pp. 145–202.

10. See "Understanding Regarding Notification, Conciliation, Dispute Settlement and Surveillance", *BISD*, 26th Supplement (1980), p. 210.

11. *BISD*, 29th Supplement (1983), pp. 13–16.

12. The main source of problems has been a series of complaints by the United States against agricultural trade measures of the European Community, namely export subsidies on wheat flour and pasta, production subsidies on canned fruits and raisins and tariff discrimination on citrus products. Both sides have found it difficult to abide by adverse rulings, and the GATT's legal machinery has found it difficult to produce persuasive decisions in support of those rulings. In large part, the reason is that there never has been a solid substantive consensus underlying the rules applicable to the problems in this area, not even the new 1979 rules of the Subsidies Code.

The United States must take some responsibility for the deadlocks which have occurred. The most celebrated instance was a 1973 complaint by the European

Community charging that the United States legislation establishing a tax-reducing device called DISC (Domestic International Sales Corporation) constituted an export subsidy in violation of GATT Article XVI(4). The United States responded to the complaint in a rather arrogant manner, refusing to submit to adjudication until several major conditions were met. Eventually a panel was constituted and in 1976 it ruled that the DISC law was in violation of Article XVI(4); it also ruled, in three companion cases brought by the United States, that three European tax laws were in violation for essentially the same reason. See *BISD*, 23rd Supplement (1977), p. 98 (DISC report); and pp. 114, 127 and 137 (reports on French, Belgian and Dutch tax laws). Most GATT countries agreed that the three European decisions were in error, but for five years the United States refused to agree to set them aside unless its own violation was treated similarly. Finally, in 1981, the United States agreed to a GATT decision that effectively separated the two legal issues and set aside the European rulings. See *BISD*, 28th Supplement (1982), p. 114.

In 1984, the United States passed legislation repealing DISC and substituting FSC (Foreign Sales Corporation), a new tax remission scheme somewhat closer to what GATT permits. See Title VIII, Deficit Reduction Act of 1984, Public Law No. 98–361, 98 Statutes at Large 494 and 985. While observers could take some comfort in the amount of effort the United States Administration expended in order to pass this legislation, the overall story – including the fact that so much effort was required – presented a pretty discouraging picture of United States responsiveness to GATT legal norms.

13. The count of 61 complaints in the period 1977–85 is based on the author's own, as yet unpublished, research. (For published sources listing the cases, see the sources cited in note 23, Chapter 3, and note 9 of this chapter.)

Here, the category of formal legal complaint includes either a formal invocation of Article XXIII procedures or a formal request for an equivalent legal ruling/legal action by the Contracting Parties under some other provision (or, sometimes, without actually citing any provision at all). The twelve developing-country complaints are:

(a) Chile: *European Economic Community Export Refunds on Malted Barley*. Referred to conciliation, then withdrawn. See GATT Documents L/4588 and C/M/123 (1977).

(b) Republic of Korea: *European Economic Community Article XIX Restrictions on Televisions*. Settled. See GATT Documents C/M/124 (1978) and C/M/134 (1979).

(c) Hong Kong: *Norwegian Restrictions on Textiles*. Panel ruling of GATT violation. See *BISD*, 27th Supplement (1981), p. 119.

(d) Brazil: *European Economic Community Export Refunds on Sugar*. Panel report, unable to make definite ruling. See *BISD*, 27th Supplement (1981), p. 69.

(e) Chile: *European Economic Community Restrictions on Imports of Apples*. Panel ruling of GATT violation. See *BISD*, 27th Supplement (1981), p. 98.

(f) India: *Japanese Import Restrictions on Leather*. Invoked special Article XXIII procedure for developing countries (see text at notes 22 and 23, Chapter 4): Case settled in 1981. See GATT Document L/5653 (1984).

(g) India: *United States Countervailing Duty Without Injury Finding*. Panel appointed, settled after first hearing. See *BISD*, 28th Supplement (1982), p. 113.

(h) Hong Kong: *European Economic Community (French) Quantitative Restrictions*. Panel ruling of violation. See *BISD*, 30th Supplement (1984), p. 129.

(i) Argentina, Brazil, Colombia, Cuba, Dominican Republic, India, Nicaragua, Peru and Philippines (with Australia): *European Economic Community Sugar Regime (Export Subsidies)*. Further proceedings deferred pending commodity agreement negotiations. See GATT Documents L/5309 (1982) and C/M/166 (1983).

(j) Argentina: *European Economic Community Falklands War Embargo*. Claim of violation not resolved. Decision concerning Article XXI procedures adopted. See GATT Document L/5317 (1982) and *BISD*, 29th Supplement (1983), p. 23.

(k) Nicaragua: *United States' Discriminatory Quotas on Sugar*. Panel ruling of GATT violation. See *BISD*, 31st Supplement (1985), p. 67 (panel report).

(l) Nicaragua: *United States' Trade Measures Affecting Nicaragua*. Panel ruling of non-justiciability. See *GATT Focus*, No. 42, November-December 1986, p. 4.

The above list does not include a Brazilian complaint against Spanish tariffs on coffee. *BISD*, 28th Supplement (1982), p. 102 (panel report). Nor does it include a Polish complaint against American tariff treatment: GATT Document L/5390 (1982).

14. The seven cases are items (c), (d), (e), (g), (h), (i) and (j) in the previous note. Item (g), the Indian complaint about United States countervailing duty laws, was pressed forward to the first panel meeting and then settled on the basis of a United States offer that met India's demand – a victory for India.

15. The eight complaints are:

(a) United States: *Greek Tariff Preferences*. Settled without panel proceedings. See GATT Documents L/3384, C/M/62, and C/M/65 (1970).

(b) United States: *Jamaican Margins of Tariff Preference*. Panel ruling of GATT violation and recommendation of waiver. See *BISD*, 18th Supplement (1972), p. 183.

(c) United States: *United Kingdom Dollar Area Quotas on Citrus*. Panel adjudication, settled after several hearings. See *BISD*, 20th Supplement (1974), pp. 230 and 236.

(d) United States: *Spanish Restrictions Affecting Soybeans*. Panel ruling of no GATT violation, but possibility of non-violation nullification; ruling not approved. See GATT Documents C/M/152 (1981). The panel report was never de-restricted.

(e) United States: *European Economic Community Tariff Discrimination on Citrus*. Panel ruling of non-violation nullification; settled, but decision neither adopted nor rejected. See GATT Documents C/M/160–162 (1982) and C/M/167–168 (1983). The report has not been de-restricted.

(f) United States: *Brazilian Export Subsidies on Poultry*. Subsidies Code complaint, still pending at the end of 1986.

(g) European Economic Community: *Spanish Homologation Requirements*. Standard Codes complaint resolved by decision of Standards Committee recommending compliance. See *BISD*, 31st Supplement (1985), p. 239.

(h) European Economic Community: *Chilean Measures Affecting Imports of Dairy Products*. Still pending at the end of 1986.

16. The four cases are items (b), (c), (d) and (e) in the previous note.

17. Item (b) in note 15. The issue was whether Jamaica, which had acceded to the GATT in 1963 under the provisions of Article XXVI(5)(c) allowing newly independent countries to succeed to the rights and obligations of their parent countries, was bound by the United Kingdom's obligations as they stood in 1947 when the United Kingdom acceded to the GATT, or as they stood in 1962 when the United Kingdom first undertook to apply the GATT to Jamaican trade. Jamaica (and everyone else) had proceeded for about ten years on the assumption that 1962 was the applicable date. To everyone's surprise, a literal reading of GATT Article XXVI required application of the United Kingdom's 1947 obligations. The 1947 obligations would have required Jamaica to reduce some 1962 margins of tariff preference to their 1947 levels. The waiver allowed Jamaica to continue applying the 1962 margins.

18. Item (d) in note 15. The decision of the GATT Council merely to "take note" of the report was a polite way of rejecting its conclusions.

19. Item (c) in note 15.

20. Item (e) in note 15.

21. See, for example, GATT Documents G/M/156 and C/M/160 (1982).

22. *BISD*, 30th Supplement (1984), p. 158, para. 5.2.

23. The complex technical status of GATT Article XVI (4) is explained in detail in John H. Jackson, *World Trade and the Law of GATT*, op. cit., pp. 373–76.

24. "Agreement on Implementation of Article VI of the General Agreement on Tariffs and Trade" (1967 Anti-dumping Code). *BISD*, 15th Supplement (1968), p. 24.

25. GATT Document L/3149 (1968).

26. The MFN obligation of GATT Article I applies to tariffs and other border charges and also "to all matters referred to in paragraphs 2 and 4 of Article III". Paragraph 4 of Article III applies to "all laws; regulations and requirements affecting . . . [an imported product's] internal sale". By itself, the language in paragraph 4 would clearly cover a buy-national rule or regulation governing purchases by the government. But paragraph 8(a) of Article III states that the provisions of Article III shall not apply to non-commercial government procurement. Although it could be argued that the text of paragraph 8(a) does not literally excuse procurement from Article I obligations, but only from Article III obligations, GATT practice has been to read the 8(a) exemption as applicable to Article I as well.

27. The defense centered on two ideas: (i) It was clear that under the reservation for existing legislation in the Protocol of Provisional Application, the United States was permitted to apply countervailing duties without an injury finding. The United States was prepared to argue that it was entitled to surrender that privilege under the Protocol of Provisional Application in pieces, country-by-country, without violating the MFN obligation of Article I. (ii) The United States would argue that countervailing duties cannot be deemed to be subject to the MFN obligation because, even when imposed under uniform criteria, they necessarily involve the imposition of discriminatory duties (that is, only against the subsidizing country).

See Senate Report No. 96–249, 96th Congress, 1st Session (1979) p. 45. The author finds neither defense persuasive.

28. *BISD*, 26th Supplement (1980), pp. 203–18, reprinted separately as an unnumbered GATT pamphlet entitled *Agreements Relating to the Framework for the Conduct of International Trade* (1979).

29. *BISD*, 26th Supplement (1980), pp. 203–04, paragraphs 1–4.

30. Ibid., pp. 205–09. The content of the amendments and the meaning of the term "half-legalized" are explained in note 27 of Chapter 2.

31. Ibid., pp. 209–10. The effect of these changes is discussed in Chapter 9.

32. Ibid., p. 204, paragraphs 5–6.

33. *The Tokyo Round of Multilateral Trade Negotiations*, op. cit., pp. 148–53. Although the report covers every aspect of the Tokyo Round negotiations, it was addressed primarily to a developing-country audience. The GATT had been "burned" after the Kennedy Round negotiations when, having prepared no such detailed evaluation, its silence had permitted a quite negative UNCTAD evaluation to hold center stage long enough to become the accepted wisdom among developing-country governments. To avoid a repetition of this public relations disaster, the GATT Secretariat completed and published its Tokyo Round report the moment the negotiations were over. UNCTAD's evaluation (see note 7 of this chapter) came three years later.

34. *BISD*, 26th Supplement (1980), p. 205, para. 7. The graduation text was expressly presented to the United States Congress as the *quid pro quo* that justified accepting the other, pro–developing-country Framework texts. See House Report No. 96–317, 96th Congress, 1st Session, (1979), pp. 198–99.

In its Arusha Program of February 1979, the Group of 77 had adopted the following text:

> "The Group of 77 rejects the concept of 'graduation' sought to be introduced by developed countries in the trading system, which would, *inter alia*, allow developed countries to discriminate among developing countries in a unilateral and arbitrary manner."

Arusha Program for Collective Self-Reliance and Framework for Negotiations, United Nations Document TD/236 (1979) p. 35, reprinted in *Proceedings of the United Nations Conference on Trade and Development, Fifth Session* (Manila), United Nations Document TD/269, Vol. 1, 1981, p. 145.

35. The United States Administration reported concessions from 22 developing countries on some $3 billion worth of trade. House Report 96–317, 96th Congress, 1st Session (1979), p. 12. According to Oswaldo de Rivero, the European Community's demands for reciprocity were also greater than expected during the Tokyo Round and also caused considerable consternation among developing countries. Oswaldo de Rivero, *New Economic Order and International Development Law* (New York: Pergamon Press, 1980) p. 40. According to the GATT Secretariat's report, twenty-six developing countries recorded concessions in the Tokyo Round negotiations. *The Tokyo Round of Multilateral Trade Negotiations*, Supplementary Report by the Director-General of the GATT (Geneva: GATT Secretariat, 1980) pp. 3–4.

36. The only exception was the Import Licensing Code, where developing-country exemptions appeared in the text of the relevant rule or in a footnote thereto. See "Agreement on Import Licensing Procedures", *BISD*, 26th Supplement (1980), p. 154.

37. The Import Licensing Code, cited in the previous note, established new obligations concerning the procedures used in implementing quantitative import restrictions. Its purpose was to ensure that the administration of quantitative import restrictions did not lead to additional restrictive effects. The main S and D reservation was a statement in Article 1(2) qualifying the Code's statement of general purpose with a vague acknowledgement of the need to take account of development needs. The specific exceptions all have to do with excusing developing countries from the more burdensome tasks required – for example, the exemption in footnote 2 of the Code relieves developing countries from the requirement of meeting certain time limits.

     The Customs Valuation Code, cited as "Agreement on Implementation of Article VII of the General Agreement on Tariffs and Trade", ibid., p. 116, had as its objective to revise and strengthen GATT obligations on customs valuation, by requiring governments to use transaction value in most cases, by limiting and defining the cases where other valuation methods could be used and by establishing a hierarchy of alternative methods. A first special-and-differential-treatment provision, Article 21, merely granted a five- to eight-year grace period for developing countries. When this proved unacceptable to a significant number of developing countries, more S and D treatment was provided for in the protocol of acceptance, ibid., pp. 151–53. The protocol provided for deletion of one obligation entirely, a promise of favorable consideration for extensions of the grace period, advance acceptance of reservations from certain specified obligations and quasi-acceptance of a reservation that would set aside virtually the entire Code "on a ... transitional basis" for developing countries wishing to preserve a system of fixed customs values. Although extensive, these derogations all rested on problems of administrative capacity and not on a policy of allowing developing countries to use trade-distorting valuation standards for development purposes.

38. The Subsidies Code is cited in "Agreement on Interpretation and Application of Articles VI, XVI, and XXIII of the General Agreement on Tariffs and Trade", ibid., p. 56. The Code refines GATT Article VI rules limiting the use of countervailing duties and expands the obligations of GATT Articles XVI and XXIII prohibiting or limiting the use of export subsidies and other trade-affecting subsidies. Article 14 of the Code is the separate provision for developing countries. It begins by excusing developing countries from the central obligation of subsidies discipline – the flat prohibition of export subsidies on non-primary products in Code Article 9. (Although the GATT has contained such a prohibition since the late 1950s, in GATT Article XVI[4], developing countries had never accepted XVI[4].) Code Article 14 also excuses developing countries from the one new nullification and impairment remedy created by the Code, for subsidies affecting third-market sales. When the other Article 14 provisions declaring subsidies to be a legitimate tool of development policy are considered, it is fair to say that the Subsidies Code certainly did not tighten the GATT's existing legal discipline applicable to developing-country subsidies and may even have weakened it.

Despite their very vigorous claim of entitlement to use subsidies, the developing countries were not able to roll back the existing law that permits countries to levy countervailing duties against any subsidy that causes material injury to a domestic industry. The Subsidies Code contains no provisions calling for S and D treatment under countervailing duty laws.

The Subsidies Code had a companion code – the Anti-dumping Code of 1979, cited as "Agreement on Implementation of Article VI of the General Agreement on Tariffs and Trade", ibid., p. 171. The Anti-dumping Code dealt only with the remedial measure of anti-dumping duties, the analogue to countervailing duties. Its only S and D provision was a one-paragraph exhortation, in Article 13, asking developed countries to consider more "constructive" remedies (presumably some sort of minimum price agreement) as an alternative to anti-dumping duties.

39. The Government Procurement Code, "Agreement on Government Procurement", ibid., p. 33, requires "national treatment" for large-scale procurements by whatever government agencies ("entities") a government lists in its schedule to the agreement. Each government's list of entities is established by negotiation, based on reciprocity. The Code also contains further obligations concerning procurement procedures, designed to remove hidden barriers. Article III of the Government Procurement Code contains the S and D provisions. It establishes no legally effective status exemptions as such and so it might be considered among the most strict on developing-country discipline. But it does contain a number of non-binding exhortations promising special consideration for developing-country requests for exemption – exemption from having to give full reciprocity on the initial list of covered entities, permission to make ad hoc withdrawals of entities already on the list and ad hoc exemptions from other Code obligations. (Two final "notes" to the agreement establish two further exemptions, neither of which reduces obligations significantly below the level for developed countries.) The Standards Code, "Agreement on Technical Barriers to Trade", ibid., p. 8, contains necessarily vague obligations requiring that technical standards not be formulated, or applied, in ways that create unnecessary obstacles to trade. The Code contains some specific obligations concerning procedures for formulating standards and for testing products. Article 12 of the Code contains several non-binding exhortations to take account of development needs. It also contains, however, one legally effective exemption that could be used to excuse wholesale non-compliance. The exemption states that developing countries "shall not be expected" to use trade-neutral standards or procedures that are "not appropriate to their development, financial and trade needs", p. 20. The same text indicates that developing countries will be justified in using standards "aimed at preserving indigenous technology and production methods and processes compatible with their development needs". The effect of this exemption will depend on how the Code is administered.

40. "Agreement on Trade in Civil Aircraft", ibid., p. 162. Although there were some developing-country producers of aircraft, such as Brazil, and others who would have some interest in developing such capacity, the Aircraft Code seems to have been looked upon as a private deal between the major producers. Actually, since the Code signatories liberalized trade barriers on an unconditional MFN basis, developing countries such as Brazil obtained the benefits without even participating.

41. *GATT Activities in 1985* (Geneva: GATT Secretariat, 1986) pp. 74–75. The numbers have been somewhat depleted by the fact that Spain and Portugal ceased being "developing countries" on joining the European Community.

42. See note 26.

43. See GATT Documents L/5028 (1980) (complaint) and *BISD*, 28th Supplement (1982), p. 113 (panel report announcing settlement). The decision to accept these not-very-demanding commitments in satisfaction of United States reciprocity demands eventually brought forth Congressional objections and demands that the negotiation of any further agreements be halted pending a Congressional review of the entire policy. *International Trade Reporter*, Bureau of National Affairs, Washington, Vol. 2, 1984, p. 704.

44. *BISD*, 26th Supplement (1980), p. 201. The decision was part of the Tokyo Round package and was understood to be part of the price for developing-country acquiescence in the code approach. The decision was in the form of a formal decision of the GATT Contracting Parties – the full membership of the GATT. It also contained an additional paragraph exhorting everyone to maintain the "unity" of the GATT system and two other paragraphs stating (i) that the GATT Contracting Parties (that is, the full membership of the GATT) would receive "adequate information" about the workings of the various codes and (ii) that non-signatories would be able to follow the proceedings of code signatories as observers. In the best GATT tradition, the last two paragraphs were drafted in the passive in order to slide around the awkward fact that codes were juridically separate agreements, over which the Contracting Parties had no power to "decide" anything (except, of course, to deny the use of GATT facilities).

45. For a discussion of the first four year's efforts to deal with the problem, see GATT Document L/5582 (1983) (GATT Council report to Thirty-ninth Session) pp. 9–12.

46. *BISD*, 29th Supplement (1983), p. 18.

47. The occasions when the issue has been confronted have not been too encouraging. See the cases discussed in note 12.

48. *The Tokyo Round of Multilateral Trade Negotiations*, op. cit.

6

Developments in the 1980s – Form without Substance

THE FIRST half of the 1980s has produced no important change of direction in developing-country policy. The events of this period could generally be described as a further elaboration of the main themes laid down in the previous twenty years. At the level of formal recognition, the commitment of governments to current developing-country policy has continued to escalate. Practical elaboration of these general principles has also moved ahead slightly, but not with the same sense of progress. Indeed, there is a growing sense that the practical benefits of this policy may be very small, perhaps even non-existent.

The current situation, then, presents a rather odd picture of things moving in different directions. Even though there is an increasing awareness of problems at the implementing level, the formal commitment to the current policy continues to get stronger every year. As criticism of the policies of developing countries increases, so do the rhetorical and institutional barriers to reconsideration.

The present chapter describes recent developments in three areas which illustrate the current situation.

EMERGING INTERNATIONAL LAW OF DEVELOPMENT

In 1974, the United Nations adopted two major resolutions, one calling for the New International Economic Order and the other declaring a Charter of Economic Rights and Duties of States. Shortly after, legal experts in various parts of the world began working in earnest on the question of whether the principles affirmed in these documents deserved to be recognized as rights and obligations of international law proper. For some, this project was a matter of relatively objective scientific enquiry into current national and international practice, while for others it was more a question of advocacy seeking to provide developing countries with a new legal tool to support their claims.

Certain NIEO principles, such as those applicable to expropriation, had been the object of a long-standing legal debate going back many years. Others, such as the principle of preferential and non-reciprocal treatment in trade affairs, represented a more or less new topic. In all cases the question was the same – whether the principles in question had become sufficiently well recognized in international agreements, and in the practice of governments, that they could now be acknowledged as obligations binding in customary international law.

In 1978, the International Law Commission of the United Nations issued a report containing a draft text of a model MFN clause, consisting of some thirty articles designed to clarify and elaborate the MFN concept. Among the provisions of the draft text were two articles providing that preferences given to developing countries should be exempt from the standard MFN obligation.[1] The Commission justified the provisions by arguing that the agreement of both the GATT and UNCTAD to this principle had established its general observance. Although the model MFN clause itself has never been adopted by the United Nations, the Commission's recognition of the exception for preferences was regarded as a major step forward.

In 1979, the General Assembly of the United Nations adopted a resolution directing the Secretary-General to study the "consolidation and progressive development of the principles and norms of international economic law relating in particular to the legal aspects of the New International Economic Order".[2] The study, which was to encompass all aspects of international economic relations, was subsequently assigned to the United Nations Institute for Training and Research (UNITAR). The UNITAR study began with scholarly compilations of legally relevant activities under the various major principles of the NIEO. Among these was an extremely thorough monograph on the principle of preferential and non-reciprocal treatment, written in 1982 by Professor Wil D. Verwey, of the University of Grainger, demonstrating the very extensive volume of legal activity, particularly in the trade field, in which that principle has been applied by governments and international organizations.[3]

The final UNITAR report was published in October 1984.[4] It was a fairly conservative document. The report stressed the slow and incremental nature of the "progressive development" process and made relatively few claims of new legal obligations. With regard to principles calling for positive action by developed-country governments, the report took a particularly cautious position. It expressed the view that such principles:

> ... can only define their aim or objective in general, but not the extent to which this objective is to be realized nor the ways and means of achieving

it, which have to be worked out in particular cooperative schemes tailored to the specificities of each situation. Thus, the normative prescription can at most, in addition to defining the objective in general, create a duty or an obligation to negotiate with a view to defining more precisely the targets to be reached and the ways and means of reaching them.[5]

With respect to the principle of preferential and non-reciprocal treatment in particular, the final report presented a surprisingly brief statement that focused entirely on the precedent of the GSP, calling attention to its incomplete execution by developed countries as evidence that the principle was not yet wholly accepted.[6]

The United Nations study has encouraged a large and growing number of other scholarly writings, conferences and research projects on the same issue.[7] Perhaps the most ambitious, apart from the United Nations' study itself, has been the work of the International Law Association, which has created a Committee on Legal Aspects of a New International Economic Order.[8] These various collateral projects promise that the somewhat conservative conclusions of the UNITAR study will not be the last word. On the contrary, legal scholars appear to be making a greater effort than ever to make sure that the "progressive development" of NIEO principles continues to move towards the creation of new legal norms.

The case in favor of greater legal recognition for the principle of non-reciprocal and preferential treatment usually centers on three main points.

First, at the most abstract level there appears to be fairly broad agreement that some kind of preferential treatment is an appropriate response to economic inequality – that "affirmative action" or "reverse discrimination" is called for in order to correct the economic inequalities of the world. Governments have expressed the idea in a variety of ways. One form of expression that has won a large following among scholars and commentators is to describe the duty of preferential treatment as a refinement of the principle of equality. For example:

> From a legal point of view the first step on which a consensus should be easy to reach is the statement that the equality principle (or non-discrimination principle) means that equal cases should be treated equally and unequal cases unequally.[9]

Second, with some exceptions, there is an almost axiomatic assumption that trade-policy rules which call for preferential treatment will make a positive contribution to curing the economic inequality of developing countries, in much the same way as preferential tax treatment would better the conditions of poor people. This was the premise of all the NIEO drafting, of the GSP and, of course, of everything the GATT itself has said on the subject. When the economic assumption is merged with the idea of "equality", it comes out looking like this:

> The principle of economic equality of States demands a new approach, correcting it to include preferential treatment for developing countries. The most favored-nation [sic] clause cannot be applied in the relations between the industrially developed and developing countries.[10]

Third, scholars have managed to pull together a fairly impressive array of precedents showing that the principle of preferential and non-reciprocal treatment has been given a great deal of legal and quasi-legal recognition in actual practice. The main source of legal recognition has been the contractual provisions of the General Agreement itself. Many GATT obligations can be so characterized. Every development-based exception allowing developing countries to escape a general GATT obligation – from Article XVIII to the Enabling Clause to the Tokyo Round codes – creates a fully effective legal right based on this principle. Although it might be argued that such rights involve no positive duties on the part of developed countries, they do in fact require developed countries to continue observing GATT obligations in cases where, but for the preferential legal excuse, a developing country's failure to observe the same obligation would normally justify non-observance by the developed country in return.[11]

At the present time, it is difficult to predict how much legal recognition these NIEO legal studies will eventually accomplish. Many commentators have already felt comfortable saying that the principle of preferential and non-reciprocal treatment has some kind of legal standing in international law.[12] On the other hand, the studies are also bringing forth a growing number of critics who dispute these claims – not only on the technical question of whether present practice constitutes recognition of this or that duty as law, but also on the broader question of whether it is even possible to create an effective international obligation requiring one group of governments to grant preferential treatment to another.[13] The rather conservative conclusions of the UNITAR study tend to reinforce this criticism.

What does seem clear, however, is that the sheer volume of activity by serious and sober scholars has lent a certain *prima facie* credibility to the legal claims being made at least as a political matter. This itself promises to be a factor of some importance in the future of GATT policy. Even if developed countries are not much moved by all these legal arguments, developing countries probably will be. What greater validation of current GATT policies could there be than an assurance from legal scholars that such policies rest on fundamental obligations of international law?

GLOBAL SYSTEM OF TRADE PREFERENCES

The 1979 Enabling Clause was meant to create a firmer legal footing for preferential trade measures. Further elaboration and implementation of the preferences principle was expected to follow during the 1980s. One of the areas in which further development was expected was preferences between developing countries. Two initiatives were involved, one in the GATT, the other in UNCTAD.

The GATT initiative began with the 1971 Protocol Relating to Trade Negotiations among Developing Countries.[14] The Protocol is a mini-GATT between developing countries, containing both a schedule of negotiated "concessions" (discriminatory tariff preferences) and a collection of GATT-like rules, some twenty-two in all, that provide a legal framework for the concessions. Interestingly, the rules of the Protocol pay considerable attention to the phenomenon of reciprocity. Developing-country governments must "negotiate" to join the Protocol and be entitled to its benefits; the process of negotiation is designed to require entrants to contribute whatever reciprocity is appropriate to their economic status. Moreover, the rules of the Protocol contain numerous provisions spelling out adjustments that may be needed to maintain the balance of concessions in certain situations – withdrawal, emergency restrictions and the like. Even where the Protocol creates exceptions for the very poorest countries, which are not required to contribute anything, it goes on to make clear that such countries do not have the same rights to "compensation" for withdrawals made by others.[15] The 1971 GATT Protocol did not receive any further impetus from the Enabling Clause decision in 1979. The Protocol began with sixteen signatories in 1971 and, by the end of 1984, it had had a net gain of only two members. Signatories continue to meet annually under the aegis of the GATT's Trade and Development Committee, and they have occasionally discussed the possibility of holding another round of negotiations. So far, however, no such negotiation has occurred.

Instead, UNCTAD seems to have captured the initiative. The UNCTAD Secretariat launched its own study of the subject in 1976 with a paper presented to the fourth UNCTAD session in Nairobi.[16] The paper called for a "global system of trade preferences" (GSTP) – a worldwide system that would supplement the various regional preference systems then in place and would cover all trade measures rather than just tariffs. The proposal was developed in a series of further UNCTAD Secretariat papers, ending with a 1981 paper entitled

"Outline of Possible Elements for the Initial Phase of the GSTP Nego-tiations".[17] Then, in a 1982 ministerial declaration, the Group of 77 declared that it was formally opening negotiations to conclude the GSTP. (The UNC-TAD itself was not called upon to sponsor the negotiations, although its Secre-tariat always assists in such matters.) In May 1986, another ministerial declara-tion pronounced the negotiations open and prepared a draft on a GATT-like agreement in which the results of the GSTP negotiations could be embodied.[18] The negotiations were to begin in Geneva in early 1987.

The most interesting document in this second GSTP initiative was the UNCTAD Secretariat's blueprint for the program of trade preferences. The blueprint was a detailed plan for structuring preferential border measures, with numerous refinements to ensure that actual trade outcomes would involve "an equitable distribution of benefits to all participating parties". Although the more extreme refinements of the blueprint appear not to have been incor-porated into the 1986 negotiating mandate, the blueprint remains a dramatic illustration of what trade policy might look like if structured in rigorous com-pliance with NIEO principles.

The blueprint proposes that the first step be a linear tariff reduction of 10 percent, with least developed countries permitted to limit their own cut to 5 percent.[19] The tariff reduction would be preferential, of course, applying only to products from other developing countries. Next, before any reductions are made, the likely trade effects of such preferential access would have to be studied in order to measure the likely distribution of benefits. The blueprint acknowledges that the actual trade effects would probably be quite disparate, owing to the diverse nature of protection in different developing countries. Much of the protection in developing countries is very high and often two and three layers deep. Before going ahead, therefore, adjustments would have to be made to correct for such disparity of benefits.

Several kinds of adjustment are proposed. First, the linear tariff reduction itself might be adjusted. For countries with extremely high tariffs, where a 10 percent cut might have no impact, a maximum rate (for developing-country products) might be established. To help very poor developing countries, more advanced countries might also undertake a two-tier reduction, giving such poor countries even lower tariffs, a preference within the preference.[20] In the other direction, it is recognized that some very poor developing countries might find that any cut in protection would harm local industry; such countries might be permitted to satisfy their preference obligation by raising their MFN tariff (with appropriate GATT waivers, of course).

The UNCTAD blueprint also proposes adjustments with respect to non-tariff measures. The general design for GSTP contemplates that the preferential system will be extended to non-tariff measures and to quantitative import restrictions in particular. Preferential treatment would be given by providing developing countries with some kind of preferred access to quota licenses; either a specific share of the import quota would be set aside for developing countries, or some other kind of preferential status would be given when licenses are awarded. The UNCTAD Secretariat's proposals contemplate that the duty to provide preferential access under quantitative restrictions might be adjusted according to the effects achieved by tariff preferences. Countries receiving greater benefits from the tariff preferences would be required to give greater access under quantitative restrictions than countries benefiting less.[21]

The final adjustment device would be a "solidarity fund" that could make payments to countries which, after all other adjustments, are still receiving fewer benefits than required by the reverse discrimination norms of the equality principle. The fund could be financed either by general subscription or by a tax levied in proportion to the volume of benefits that each country receives from GSTP.

Now comes the complex part. The intricate relationship just described would produce an acceptable distribution of benefits in a two-dimensional world – that is, a world in which there were no other preferential relationships that had to be worried about. Unfortunately, the world does contain other preferential relationships to which UNCTAD and the Group of 77 are also committed. These are the many regional and sub-regional preference systems among developing countries, usually in the form of customs unions or free trade areas. From the beginning, the UNCTAD blueprint for GSTP took it as given that these other preferential trade relationships are economically beneficial and must be preserved. (It was the coexistence of such regional groupings that required adding the word "global" to the title of GSTP.)

The preferences required under GSTP would impair the economic benefits of these regional groupings if they reduced the preferential advantage that members of the regional group now enjoy vis-à-vis other developing countries. To preserve the present level of advantage, further refinements were made in the overall design of the GSTP. In effect, each element of preference would need to have two tiers – or even three tiers if the special advantages for least developed countries were to be preserved.

The UNCTAD blueprint suggested that preferential tariff advantages within regional systems could be preserved simply by reducing the intra-regional tariff rate to the same extent that the outside rate is reduced for GSTP countries. If the intra-regional rate is already too low to permit such additional reductions, the blueprint suggested the obvious solution – the regional grouping must grant its GSTP preferences to non-member developing countries, not by reducing the tariff rate that they must pay, but by raising the MFN tariff rate applicable to developed countries.[22] As for non-tariff measures, such as quantitative import restrictions, a parallel set of internal preferences would also have to be designed. The UNCTAD blueprint speaks of setting aside a special share of quotas, within the special share for developing countries, that would be open only to members of the regional grouping.[23]

The UNCTAD blueprint is, if nothing else, a rigorous application of NIEG principles and assumptions. There will, indeed, be a lot of work to do if the benefits of international trade are to be redistributed according to need.[24]

UNITED STATES' GSP LAW OF 1984

One of the dangers inherent in GSP-type schemes is that developed countries will use their power to discriminate selectively, either to bargain for commercial advantage in return or to punish those developing countries whose behavior is somehow found wanting. The early debates on the GSP and the concern about discriminatory practices were described in Chapter 4. In those early debates the United States seemed to be the developed country most concerned to prevent such discriminatory use of the GSP. The United States delegates asked for a fairly strict non-discrimination requirement on the granting of preferences – a sort of internal MFN policy requiring that preferences be generalized to all developing countries. They also asked for a non-reciprocity requirement, preventing developed countries from asking for anything in return. The non-reciprocity element was finally accepted, with the European Community agreeing to abandon the reverse trade preferences it had enjoyed under special preference agreements with certain Mediterranean and African developing countries. The United States, however, was unable to obtain a complete ban against discriminatory preferences; the European Community insisted on the right to grant additional, selective preferences to developing-country members of its existing agreements.

Notwithstanding the efforts made in these early debates, the actual implementation by the United States of its GSP schemes has exhibited a persistent drift towards the very dangers of which warning was given. The United States' position began to change as soon as it began to implement the GSP. The 1974 legislation creating the GSP scheme contained a number of provisions denying benefits to individual developing countries. Some of these exclusions were based on criteria indicating that discriminatory assistance was no longer necessary and thus the exclusions were consistent, at least in principle, with the idea that GSP was supposed to help those who needed help.[25] Other exclusions, however, were based on judgments of moral desert, including the country's behavior towards the economic interests of the United States. This latter category included provisions requiring or authorizing the President to deny GSP benefits to:

(a) Countries dominated or controlled by international communism.
(b) Members of the Organization of Petroleum Exporting Countries (OPEC) or similar commodity cartels which engage in actions that, *inter alia*, raise prices to "an unreasonable level."
(c) Countries that expropriate United States property without paying prompt, adequate and effective compensation.
(d) Countries that fail to cooperate with United States narcotics law enforcement.
(e) Countries that fail to act in good faith in recognizing or enforcing arbitral awards.[26]

In addition, among the conditions the President was required to consider before designating any developing country as a beneficiary was the following:

. . . the extent to which such country has assured the United States it will provide equitable and reasonable access to the markets and basic commodity resources of such country.[27]

During the 1980s, the United States has taken several additional steps towards a more discriminatory use of preferences. After opposing European Community–type special preference agreements for many years, the United States enacted its own version in 1983, the so-called Caribbean Basin Initiative, which provides extra preferences to selected developing countries in that region.[28] Likewise, after repeatedly questioning the economic validity of the European Community's many free trade areas with individual developing countries, the United States concluded what is clearly a "special relationship" free trade area with Israel.[29]

The most important developments, though, occurred in the 1984 legislation extending the GSP arrangements. The legislation encountered considerable opposition. To secure its passage a number of other conditions had to be attached to GSP in order to make it appear more clearly an instrument of United States' self-interest.

The list of disqualifying conditions was expanded.[30] The exclusion for countries that expropriate without adequate compensation was expanded to include appropriation of intellectual property rights. An earlier amendment excluding countries that harbor international terrorists was reaffirmed. And another new ground of exclusion was added – failing to afford "internationally recognized workers' rights". Likewise, the list of criteria to be considered before giving benefits to any country was expanded by adding:

(a) The extent to which the country has assured the United States it will refrain from unreasonable export practices, especially copper exports.
(b) The extent to which the country protects the intellectual property rights of businesses in the United States, especially against counterfeiting.
(c) The extent to which the country has acted to (i) liberalize foreign investment and (ii) liberalize trade in services.
(d) The extent to which the country has acted to recognize workers' rights.[31]

Far more important, the 1984 law created an elaborate new mechanism which made GSP benefits into a bargaining chip to induce developing-country governments to accept reciprocal obligations. The main targets were advanced developing countries which were to be "graduated" by being persuaded to accept greater obligations. The new mechanism involved two steps. First, the President was given authority to limit GSP benefits under the "competitive need" standard. Then the President was given authority to waive these limitations whenever he finds that such action will serve in the national economic interest. The key considerations of national interest are to include:

(a) Whether the country in question is providing reasonable access to its markets and to its commodities.
(b) Whether the country is providing adequate and effective protection of intellectual property rights.[32]

The Report of the Ways and Means Committee in the House of Representatives, in explaining this mechanism, is quite open about its purpose:

> The purpose of granting the President this waiver authority is to provide him with additional tools to achieve United States trade interests with BDCs [Beneficiary Developing Countries], such as greater market access for United States exports . . . [33]

So far, the United States has not made much use of these several kinds of exclusionary authority. Decisions under the various exclusion authorities were in most cases deferred for two years. Punitive discrimination may not be as strict as the words of the law might suggest, for there does appear to have been a certain amount of Congressional posturing in the enactment of some of these conditions. On the other hand, when Congress began to consider trade legislation in 1987, the Administration did produce some demonstration punishment.[34]

Even though the exact degree of enforcement remains to be seen, the overall significance of the 1984 legislation is already clear. The idea of unilateral, non-reciprocal trade benefits has been put to a severe political test and it has failed. GSP has survived, but only when treated as a form of largesse similar to foreign aid – a tool to be used to win friends and punish enemies. Indeed, the House Report expressly cites the foreign aid practice of the United States as a precedent for some of the conditions attached to GSP benefits.[35]

As a preview of the future that will be created by the principle of non-reciprocal and preferential treatment, the 1984 GSP legislation has to be viewed as a most disquieting event. Like GSTP, it looks like an·idea that has somehow got out of hand.

NOTES AND REFERENCES

1. *Report of the International Law Commission to the General Assembly on the Work of its Thirtieth Session*, United Nations Document A/33/10 (1978), reprinted in *1978 Yearbook of the International Law Commission* (New York: United Nations, 1979) p. 8. Articles 23 and 24 are the provisions on developing country preferences.

2. United Nations Document, General Assembly Resolution 34/150 (17 December 1979), adopted by vote of 112–6–25. The 1974 United Nations resolutions declaring the NIEO are cited and discussed in notes 2 and 4, Chapter 5.

3. Wil D. Verwey, "The Principle of Preferential Treatment for Developing Countries", printed in *Progressive Development of the Principles and Norms of International Law Relating to the New International Economic Order: Analytical Papers and Analysis of Texts of Relevant Documents*, United Nations Document UNITAR/DS/5 (New York: United Nations Institute for Training and Research, 1982) pp. 6–218.

   Other studies in the series are: Wolfgang Benedek, "Stabilisation of Export Earnings of Developing Countries", ibid.; pp. 219–90; "Permanent Sovereignty over Natural Resources", ibid., pp. 291–465 (UNITAR staff paper); Augusto-Caesar Espiritu, "The Principle of the Right of Every State to Benefit from Science and Technology", printed in *Progressive Development of the Principles and Norms of International Law Relating to the New International Economic Order: Analytical Papers and Analysis of Texts of Relevant Documents*, second volume, United Nations Document, UNITAR/DS/6 (New York: United Nations Institute for Training and Research, 1983) pp. 1–153; A. Peter Mutharika, "The Principle of Entitlement of Developing Countries to Development Assistance", ibid., pp. 154–351; Harry Wunsche, "The Principle of the Common Heritage of Mankind", ibid., pp. 437–564; "The Principle of Participatory Equality of Developing Countries, in International Economic Relations: Analysis of Texts", ibid., pp. 353–436 (UNITAR Staff Paper); Milan Sahovic, *The Principle of Participatory Equality of Developing Countries in International Economic Relations: "Analytical Paper"*, United Nations Document UNITAR/DS/6/Add.1 (New York: United Nations Institute for Training and Research, 1984) pp. 1–54.

UNITAR has also published the key NIEO documents up to 1978. See Alfred George Moss and Harry N.M. Winter (eds), *A New International Economic Order: Selected Documents 1945–1975*, two volumes, United Nations Document UNITAR/DS/1 (New York: United Nations Institute for Training and Research, no date); Hideko Makiyama (ed.), *A New International Economic Order: Selected Documents 1976*, United Nations Document UNITAR/DS/2 (New York: United Nations Institute for Training and Research, 1980); Hideko Makiyama (ed.), *A New International Economic Order: Selected Documents 1977*, United Nations Document UNITAR/DS/3 (New York: United Nations Institute for Training and Research, 1982).

For an overview of the issues raised by the UNITAR study, see Thomas M. Franck and Mark M. Munansangu, *The New International Economic Order: International Law in the Making*, Policy and Efficacy Studies No. 6 (New York: United Nations Institute for Training and Research, 1982).

4. *Progressive Development of the Principles and Norms of International Law relating to the New International Economic Order: Report by the Secretary-General*, hereafter cited as the UNITAR Report, United Nations Document A/39/504/Add.1 (New York: United Nations, 1984). The study was discussed at length in the Sixth Committee during the 39th session of the General Assembly, but the question of what follow-up action to take was deferred pending the submission of further comments and proposals by governments in 1985. See United Nations Document A/C.6/39/SR.63, 5 December 1984.

5. United Nations Document A/39/504/Add.1, paragraph 134, p. 73.

6. Ibid., paragraphs 136–47, pp. 74–78. In the author's view, the UNITAR conclusions correctly direct attention to what is probably the most important factor in assessing the current legal status of the preferential/non-reciprocal principle, namely the fact that, in the most important application of that principle, actual practice is falling far short of the rhetorical endorsement. Somewhat surprisingly, however, the conclusions do not try to make very much out of the large quantity of rhetorical and precedental material described so carefully in the study by Verway, "The Principle of Preferential Treatment for Developing Countries", op. cit., and thus presents a much less optimistic picture of the "dynamics" than most legal scholars from developing countries would give.

7. A list of the recent books in English would include: Mohammed Bedjaoui, *Towards a New International Economic Order* (New York: Holmes & Meier, for the United Nations Educational, Scientific and Cultural Organization, 1979); Rene Jean Dupuy (ed.), *The New International Economic Order: Commercial, Technological and Cultural Aspects* (The Hague: Martinus Nijhoff, 1981); Marthinus Gerhardus Erasmus, *The New International Economic Order and International Organizations* (Frankfurt-Main: Haag und Herchen, 1979); Kamal Hossain (ed.), *Legal Aspects of the New International Economic Order* (London: Frances Pinter, 1980); Oswaldo de Rivero, *New International Order and International Development Law*, op. cit.; Pieter Verloren van Themaat, *The Changing Structure of International Economic Law* (The Hague: Martinus Nijhoff, 1981); and Abdulqawi Yusuf, *Legal Aspects of Trade Preferences for Developing States* (The Hague: Martinus Nijhoff, 1982).

8. The International Law Association actually initiated its own study in 1978, before the 1979 United Nations resolution. For a report on the Association's work, as

well as a comprehensive description of activities in other form, see "Third Report of the International Committee on Legal Aspects of a New International Economic Order", in *Report of the Sixty-first Conference* (London: International Law Association, 1965) pp. 107–53.

9. Recommendation of the Rapporteur of Sub-committee I, Committee on Legal Aspects of the New International Economic Order, quoted in ibid., pp. 131–32.

10. Milan Bulajic, "Legal Aspects of a New International Order", in Hossain (ed.), *Legal Aspects of the New International Economic Order*, op. cit., pp. 45–67 and p. 61. One of the most common ways the economic assumption appears is through characterizing the pre-NIEO legal order as harmful to developing countries. For example:

> "The international economic order essentially based on the GATT principles was actually very favorable for developed countries and very unfavorable for developing countries. Hence the need to have a New International Economic Order appearing as a guiding force."

Dupuy (ed.), *The New International Economic Order*, op. cit., pp. 209–10 (remarks of Professor Virally): A few authors recognize that the economic assumptions of this position are not self-evident and so they explain why they hold them. See, for example, de Rivero, *New International Order and International Development Law*, op. cit., pp. 2–5. Even rarer is the legal analysis of NIEO principles that actually challenges the economic assumptions. The only such work known to the author is Ernst-Ulrich Petersmann, "International Trade and International Trade Law", Discussion Paper for the International Law Association's International Committee on Legal Aspects of the New International Economic Order (1986).

11. The non-reciprocity statement in Part IV of the GATT, Article XXXVI(8), is also relevant in this regard. The provision does not create any obligations to grant concessions. See Verwey, "The Principle of Preferential Treatment for Developing Countries", op. cit., p. 44. Article XXXVI(8) does come very close to having legal effects, however, when it applies to Article XXVIII withdrawals of concessions by developing countries. In that context, Article XXXVI(8) is supposed to permit developing countries to satisfy the obligation to compensate by offering partial compensation and thus to bar developed countries from withdrawing substantially equivalent concessions if appropriate partial compensation is offered. Unfortunately, the standards of appropriateness – what degree and kind of protection is or is not necessary for economic development reasons – does not appear to be a standard that can actually be applied to any specific dispute.

12. See, for example, the International Law Association Report, op. cit., pp. 129–30; Subrata Roy Chowdbury, "Legal Status of the Charter of Economic Rights and Duties of States", in Hossain (ed.), *Legal Aspects of the New International Economic Order*, op. cit., p. 93 n.33; Yusuf, *Legal Aspects of Trade Preferences for Developing States*, op. cit., p. 168 (". . . at an incipient stage, but is acquiring a gradual concretization in international law".)

13. See, for example, Darnien Hubbard, "The International Law Commission and the New International Economic Order", *1979 German Yearbook of International Law*, Vol. 22 (Berlin: Duneker and Humblot) pp. 80–99. See also Petersmann,

"International Trade and International Trade Law", op. cit. The issue is discussed further in Part II at notes 10–13 of Chapter 10.

14. *BISD*, 18th Supplement (1972), p. 11. The complete text of the 1971 agreement, including schedules, was reprinted in 1981 in an unnumbered GATT publication, *Protocol Relating to Trade Negotiations among Developing Countries*. A cursory examination of the schedules shows that several participants gave relatively few concessions (Uruguay with six, Brazil with twelve including "polo sticks"). The preferential rates established by most participants were still fairly high. Most of Brazil's were over 30 percent *ad valorem*; all of Chile's were over 40 percent. Among the countries with more numerous concessions, Greece's preferential rate on almost all concessions was 80 percent of the MFN rate; the Indian preferential rate was 50 percent of the MFN rate, but the MFN rates in question were all 30 percent or more, several being at 60 percent and 100 percent. At the end of 1979, however, participants reported that trade under the preferential rates had grown to $329 million from about $15 million in 1972. Annual reports of the activities of Protocol signatories are published in the BISD series, beginning with the 21st Supplement, under the heading "Trade Negotiations among Developing Countries".

15. See, for example, paragraph 2 of the identical protocols for the subsequent concession-free accession of Paraguay (1975) and Bangladesh (1976). *BISD*, 23rd Supplement (1977), pp. 154 and 156.

16. United Nations Documents TD/ 192 and TD/192/Supplement 2 (1976).

17. United Nations Document TD/B/C.7/47 (1981). Earlier papers included TD/B/C. 7135 and 35/Add. l (1979) (S and D treatment of LDDCs), and TD/B/C.7/42 (1980) (survey of issues). Also important was a statement of principles and objectives contained in the Group of 77's Arusha Program cited in note 34 of Chapter 5. For a general account of the development of the GSTP up to 1982, see B.G. Ramcharan, "Equality and Discrimination in International Economic Law (XII): the Proposed Global System of Trade Preferences Among Developing Countries", in *The Yearbook of World Affairs 1984* (London: Stevens, for the London Institute of World Affairs, 1984) pp. 191–215.

18. The declaration, issued on 23 May 1986, was entitled "Brasilia Declaration on the Launching of the First Round of Negotiations within the Global System of Trade Preferences Among Developing Countries". In addition to the declaration, the ministers also produced a brief document entitled "Guidelines for Techniques and Modalities for the First Round of GSTP Negotiations" and a rather lengthy draft agreement entitled "Agreement on the Global System of Trade Preferences Among Developing Countries". The draft agreement contains thirty-three articles plus annexes; the legal text involves an extremely interesting mixture of GATT and UNCTAD/NIEO bloodlines, well worth a study of its own.

    In general, the Brasilia documents eschewed the more refined elements of the UNCTAD Secretariat's blueprint discussed here; at least for the moment, the attainment of equal benefits was left to reciprocity-type negotiations between the parties.

19. As the author understands the proposal, the reduction would be 10 percent of the existing rate, rather than 10 percent *ad valorem*. Thus, if the current rate were 20 percent *ad valorem*, it would be reduced to 18 not 10 percent.

20. United Nations Document TD/B/C.7/24 (1980), para. 54.

21. "... countries whose markets are most open to penetration from tariff-preference receiving countries relative to their own ability to take advantage of such preferences should be least obliged to extend quota preferences, and, conversely, those countries with the greatest propensity to take advantage of tariff preferences relative to the operation of their own markets should accept the greatest obligation to extend quota preferences." United Nations Document TD/B/C.7/47 (1981), para. 13.

22. Ibid., para. 27. The UNCTAD Secretariat's paper goes on to say, however, that tariff increases should be viewed only as a short-term solution, with the long-term solution being the eventual merging of regional groups into a global free trade area for all developing countries.

23. Ibid., para. 31.

24. It is interesting to note that, in a study of developed-country protection published the year following the GSTP proposals, the UNCTAD Secretariat, having made a rather pessimistic forecast about access to developed-country markets for developing-country goods, recommended as a long-term strategy a greater effort to increase trade between developing countries. *Protectionism and Structural Adjustment in the World Economy*, United Nations Document TD/B/888/Rev.l (Geneva: UNCTAD Secretariat, 1982) pp. 25–27.

25. The primary limitation of this kind was the so-called "competitive need" limitation, which provided that a certain volume of imports from one developing country ($25 million [1974] or 50 percent of total imports) was proof that the exporting country was sufficiently competitive to render GSP unnecessary, and so justified removing GSP treatment for that country, on that product. Trade Act of 1974, Section 504, 88 Statutes at Large 2070, as amended, 19 United States Code 2464.

    Frequently, United States officials also explain the limitations as the sort of reverse discrimination that developing countries themselves use in their own GSTP preference schemes; that is, exclusion of "competitive" developing countries is meant to redirect GSF benefits to the poorer countries who need them more. Unfortunately restoration of the MFN rate does not necessarily have that effect, for it is impossible to know whether there are any other, poorer developing countries able to take advantage of the situation and, besides, the United States' law does not even ask that anyone should look.

26. Ibid., Section 502(b), 88 Statutes at Large 2067, as amended, 19 United States Code 2462(b).

27. Ibid., Section 502(c)(4), 88 Statutes at Large 2068, as amended, 19 United States Code 2462(c)(4).

28. Caribbean Basin Economic Recovery Act, 97 Statutes at Large, 384, 19 USC 2701. The United States obtained a GATT waiver for the tariff preferences and plans to seek another GATT waiver to permit the extension of the Caribbean Basin Initiative (CBI) discrimination to non-tariff matters – specifically, preferential treatment in government procurement matters. See *International Trade Reporter*, Vol. 2, 1985, p. 1488. Canada now proposes to add a nice refinement to all this by offering special preferences to the Commonwealth countries in the Caribbean. See *GATT Focus*, No. 38, March 1985, p. 2.

29. Legislative authority for the free trade area was given in Title IV of the Trade and Tariff Act of 1984, 98 Statutes at Large 3013. The agreement was concluded in 1985.

30. Ibid., Section 503(b), 98 Statutes at Large 3019, amending 19 United States Code 2462(b). For an overall description of the 1984 GSP law, see Gregory C. Dorris, "The Very Specialized United States Generalized System of Preferences", *Georgia Journal of International and Comparative Law*, Vol. 15, No. 1, 1985, pp. 39–81.

31. Ibid., Section 503(c), 98 Statutes at Large 3019, amending 19 United States Code 2462(c). In explaining these additions, the House Ways and Means Committee said:

> "The Committee strongly believes that countries wishing to reap the benefits of preferential duty-free access to the US market must fulfill international responsibilities in these . . . important areas."

Generalized System of Preferences Renewal Act of 1984. Report of the Committee on Ways and Means, House of Representatives, House Report No. 98–1090, 98th Congress, 2nd Session, p. 12 (1984).

32. Trade and Tariff Act of 1984, Section 505(b), 98 Statutes at Large 3020, amending 19 United States Code 2464(c) and (d). The same section of the 1984 Act also provided for totally removing GSP benefits from any country with a per capita gross national product of $8,500, a figure that is to be adjusted for inflation. At the time the law was passed, the developing country with the highest per capita GNP was Singapore with approximately $5,900.

33. House Report No. 98–1090, op. cit., p. 19.

34. On 1 April 1987, Mexico was denied GSP treatment for thirty-four products reportedly on the ground that it had failed to make sufficient progress towards protecting intellectual property rights.

35. House Report No. 98–1090, op. cit., p. 12.

PART II

A LEGAL CRITIQUE OF THE GATT'S
CURRENT POLICY

INTRODUCTION

THE HISTORY of the GATT's legal relationship with developing countries points to one major question throughout. Is the current GATT legal policy in the best interest of the developing countries themselves, or would developing countries achieve better results if they were to agree to a legal policy based on the GATT's two main principles of reciprocity and non-discrimination?

This question has been debated ever since 1947. It is still being debated today. Despite the GATT's repeated formal endorsement of the principle of non-reciprocal and preferential treatment, opposition to that principle is probably greater today than at any other time. The governments of developed countries sign the declarations, but they do not believe in what they are doing. A growing number of governments in developing countries have doubts. And commentators, especially those from developed countries, become more critical every year.[1]

The disagreement has a paralyzing effect on GATT reform. All participants agree that the GATT system has been losing ground since the mid-1970s and that it needs to move forward in order to regain its effectiveness. On matters of policy towards developing countries, however, the GATT membership finds itself pulling in opposite directions, with one group of countries calling for extension of the current policy while another group asks that it be discarded as a failure.

The criticism of the GATT's current policy towards developing countries falls into two broad categories – economic and legal. The main target of criticism over the years has been the economic assumptions of the policy, primarily the belief that the economies of developing countries will benefit from trade protection. A substantial body of opinion challenges this assumption and argues that trade protection actually reduces economic welfare. While the author agrees with this line of criticism, it is not the purpose of this study to examine it in any depth. The economic criticism has already been developed rather extensively and, although not everyone agrees with it, most professionals understand it quite clearly, and they are able to discuss points of agreement and disagreement with some precision.

This study will concentrate on the legal assumptions of the current policy. The policy assumes that trade policies of developed countries can be influenced most effectively by demands based on the obligation of the rich to assist the poor. The main criticism of this legal policy has been that one-sided legal systems do not work. Critics argue that reciprocity is necessary to induce meaningful and legally secure improvements in market access and that the doctrine of non-reciprocity is really an impediment, rather than an aid, to achieving such market access. In addition, they argue, the dynamics of policies based on discrimination make it likely that preferential legal structures will eventually cause governments to do more harm than good to the supposed beneficiaries of such discrimination.

Unlike the economic criticism, this legal criticism does not rest on any well-developed body of theory. The arguments on both sides rest mainly on experience, intuition and random analogies to national law. The absence of any larger framework makes it difficult to evaluate conflicting arguments or even to identify the basis of disagreement between them.

This part of the study attempts a more systematic analysis. As a theoretical framework for that analysis, the study will try to state a coherent view of the ways in which international legal institutions affect decision-making in national governments, based on an examination of the practical realities of such decision-making. The main focus of attention will be decisions made in the area of trade policy because the configuration of political forces in this area has a tendency to be unique.

The analysis will concentrate on two major kinds of impact that international legal obligations can have on government decision-making. One is their impact on the decision-making processes of the governments that are considering accepting them – in this case, their impact on the trade-policy decisions of developing-country governments. Although often ignored, the role of international legal obligations as a form of self-imposed restraint is perhaps their most important function in the trade-policy area. The second type of impact that is analyzed is the effect of international obligations on the decision-making processes of the governments that the potential member country is hoping to influence – in this case, the trade-policy decisions of the governments of developed countries.

Part II is divided into six chapters. Chapter 7 opens the analysis with a brief summary of the current legal criticism, seeking to make certain at the outset that the major legal objections to the GATT's current policy are understood. Chapter 8 then tries to clarify the distinction between these legal issues and the economic issues that usually are raised at the same time. Chapter 9 begins the legal analysis proper by taking up the issue of internal impact – the ways in which GATT obligations can affect the decision-making processes within developing countries. Chapters 10 and 11 then take up the issue of external impact – the ways in which GATT obligations affect the decisions of developed-country governments. Chapter 10 examines the impact of the doctrine of non-reciprocity and the likely impact of an alternative legal policy based on reciprocity. Chapter 11 then examines the impact of the policy of preferential treatment, as compared with the likely impact of a policy based on the MFN obligation. Chapter 12 summarizes the conclusions and recommendations of the preceding analysis.

NOTES AND REFERENCES

1. For a lucid exposition of both economic and legal criticisms and one that presents the ideas of many other prominent critics as well, see Martin Wolf, "Two-Edged Sword: Demands of Developing Countries and the Trading System", in Jagdish N. Bhagwati and John Gerald Ruggie (eds), *Power, Passions and Purpose: Prospects for North-South Negotiations* (Cambridge, Massachusetts: MIT Press, 1984) pp. 201–30.

   A 1985 report to the GATT prepared by a group of seven distinguished experts has brought this kind of criticism right to the GATT's doorstep. The group, containing three distinguished experts from developing countries, was chaired by Dr Fritz Leutwiler, then President of the Swiss Central Bank and the Bank for International Settlements. The group's report expressed the view that:

   > "Developing countries receive special treatment in the GATT rules. But such special treatment is of limited value. Far greater emphasis should be placed on permitting and encouraging developing countries to take advantage of their competitive strengths and on integrating them more fully into the trading system, with all the appropriate rights and responsibilities that this entails."

   Fritz Leutwiler et al., *Trade Policies for a Better Future: Proposals for Action*, the Leutwiler Report (Geneva: GATT Secretariat, 1985) p. 44.

7

Basic Elements of the Legal Criticism

THE LEGAL debate does not involve any open disagreement about ultimate objectives. Both critics and supporters of the current policy speak of the same ultimate goal – the maximum possible improvement in the economic welfare of developing countries. Critics of the current policy never say that it gives developing countries too many economic benefits. On the contrary, they argue that the present policy does not give developing countries as much economic benefit as would some alternative policy. The central issue is not whether, but how to provide greater economic benefits.

AGREEMENT ON A COMMON GOAL

One line of argument that sometimes puts this common goal into question is the "graduation" doctrine of the United States – the concept which argues that advanced developing countries should grant reciprocity as their economic development improves. Taken at face value, the mercantilist rationale for this doctrine seems to be saying that advanced developing countries who do not grant reciprocity are keeping for themselves economic benefits that properly belong to developed countries and that these benefits should be paid over. But, while domestic advocates of the graduation concept sometimes sound like this, the concept is simply never presented this way in government-to-government discourse in the GATT. No developed country would ever ask a developing country to decrease its own level of economic welfare and especially not for the purpose of improving developed-country welfare. When pressed, United States officials invariably explain that the "payment" they are seeking is merely trade liberalization and that liberalization will actually be beneficial to developing countries. In other words, the graduation doctrine is merely a kind of coercive paternalism.

If there is any exception to this agreement on a common goal, it comes from the developing-country side. Overall economic welfare is not the only value that governments try to maximize. Governments sometimes decide that other values, such as social justice or national independence, require policies that interfere with optimal economic performance. Statements about GATT legal policy made by developing countries sometimes suggest the influence of such competing values. For example, delegates from developing countries express concern that GATT legal discipline may provide excuses for economic coercion against smaller countries, indicating that the non-discipline of current GATT policy might well be preferred for reasons of national independence, even if it were acknowledged to be detrimental to economic welfare.

In this study, both critics and supporters of the present legal policy will be taken at their word; the debate will be treated as one in which both sides share the common goal of maximizing the economic welfare of developing countries. Other values may well be relevant to the final decision, but it is the author's belief that the issue of economic welfare at least comes first. It is impossible to weigh other policy values without some idea of their economic welfare cost.

TARGET OF THE LEGAL CRITICISM

A recapitulation of the essentials of the present GATT policy towards developing countries might be useful. Developing countries have effectively been excused from legal obligations regarding their own trade-policy measures; developed countries have accepted several formal texts obliging them, in principle, to grant concessions without reciprocity. In addition, all countries in the GATT are excused from MFN obligations to the extent necessary to give preferential advantages to developing countries and, once again, the GATT texts imply an obligation in principle to grant such advantages.

The typical economic criticism of this policy would declare the policy in error from top to bottom. It would assert that the greatest economic benefits flow from a policy of more or less free trade and would urge that all the market-distorting measures currently permitted should be abandoned. The legal criticism has a narrower target. Most legal critics merely ask developing countries to adopt the same GATT obligations as everyone else. The legal obligations of the GATT do not require anything even close to a free trade policy. They impose only three major requirements:

(a) The government must use only approved instruments of trade protection.

(b) The government must employ those instruments in a generally non-discriminatory manner.

(c) The government must be prepared to subject all existing protection to a long-term process of binding obligations and reduction through negotiation.

This is all that has ever been asked of any government in the GATT system.

It is important to stress the limited nature of this legal criticism. The target is not the fact that the current policy towards developing countries tolerates market-distorting measures as such, but rather that it abandons any meaningful effort to limit, or to control, the use of such measures by developing countries. The legal debate is not about free trade versus protection. It is about some restraints on the use of measures which restrict trade versus no restraints at all. The central issue is whether this extra margin of legal freedom is really needed – whether it is beneficial or harmful.

HARMFUL EFFECTS IDENTIFIED BY CRITICS

Critics of the current policy argue that it harms developing countries in two different ways.

First, and most often, it is argued that the absence of reciprocal legal discipline makes it more difficult for governments of developed countries to reduce trade barriers to exports from developing countries. Lack of reciprocity also makes it more difficult to resist claims for additional protection when developing-country exports cause competitive discomfort to industries in developed countries. In the same way, the argument runs, developing-country exemption from the MFN obligation has weakened the MFN obligations of developed countries, with the result that the latter now find it more difficult to avoid discriminating against developing-country trade when import relief measures are being considered. In both cases, the premise is that developed countries would be able to treat developing-country exports better if developing countries accepted the same rules.[1]

Second, some critics have begun to argue that the current legal policy can also have deleterious effects on the decision-making process within developing countries. External legal restraints, it is argued, can make it easier for governments of developing countries to resist claims for protectionist measures they know to be unwise. The current legal policy not only fails to provide such assistance to developing-country governments in this situation, but it actually makes things worse by giving greater legitimacy to claims for trade protection.[2]

ASSUMPTIONS ABOUT THE BEHAVIOR OF DEVELOPED COUNTRIES

Officials in developed countries are among the most frequent critics of the current GATT policy towards developing countries. The tenor of the criticism from this quarter usually includes the implication that governments of developed countries are doing a much better job of observing GATT obligations.

While it is true that the developed countries in the GATT do accept a more demanding legal discipline on paper and that they have, in fact, achieved a quite substantial degree of trade liberalization on the industrial side, their actual policies fall considerably short of their GATT obligations. It should not be assumed, therefore, that any developed country would be willing, or able, to live up to all the requirements implied in the typical criticism of the GATT's legal policy towards developing countries. Indeed, it may well be that much of the criticism from developed countries is a sham – that many developed countries are really quite happy with the absence of legal discipline over developing countries because it gives them an excuse for the illegal trade barriers they themselves are imposing.

The present study is limited to the GATT's legal policy towards developing countries because that policy is in fact a discrete issue worth separate analysis. There is no intention to imply a judgment that developing-country behavior is somehow worse than that of developed countries. Most independent critics of developing-country legal policy would make the same disclaimer.

NOTES AND REFERENCES

1. Many observers have seen a connection between the increasing acceptance of the policy of non-reciprocity and preferential treatment and the increasing incidence of protectionism and discrimination against developing countries during the same period. Also influential have been the calculations of the developing countries themselves purporting to show how badly they did in the Kennedy Round and Tokyo Round negotiations; see note 11, Chapter 4 and note 7, Chapter 5. For three recent expressions of this view, see, (i) Fritz Leutwiler et al., *Trade Policies for a Better Future*, op. cit., pp. 20–21; (ii) G. Michael Aho and Jonathan D. Aronson, *Trade Talks: America Better Listen!* (New York: Council on Foreign Relations, 1985), pp. 96 and 98; (iii) Anne O. Krueger and Constantine Michalopoulos, "Developing Country Trade Policies and the International Economic System", in Ernest H. Preeg (ed.), *Hard Bargaining Ahead: US Trade Policy and Developing Countries* (New Brunswick, New Jersey: Transaction Books, for the Overseas Development Council, 1985), pp. 51–53.

   The author himself has contributed to this school of thought:

   "By the latter part of the 1960s, most developed-country members of the GATT had come to view the developing countries as non-paying participants who had lost their standing to enforce legal claims."

Robert E. Hudec, *The GATT Legal System and World Trade Diplomacy*, op. cit., p. 211.

2. Attention to the GATT's internal impact has been less widespread and more recent. The author's first attempt in this direction was Hudec, "GATT or GABB? The Future Design of the General Agreement on Tariffs and Trade", *Yale Law Journal*, Vol. 80, No. 7, 1971, pp. 1315–28. Other authors who have examined the issue include: Frieder Roessler, "The Scope, Limits and Function of the GATT Legal System", *The World Economy*, London, Vol. 8, September 1985, pp. 287–98; Jan Tumlir, *Protectionism: Trade Policies in Democratic Societies* (Washington, DC: American Enterprise Institute, 1985); Tumlir, *Economic Policy as a Constitutional Problem*, Fifteenth Wincott Memorial Lecture, Occasional Paper No. 70 (London: Institute of Economic Affairs, 1985); Kenneth W. Abbott, "The Trading Nation's Dilemma: the Functions of the Law of International Trade", *Harvard International Law Journal*, Vol. 26, No. 2, 1985, pp. 521–25; Stephanie Lenway, *The Politics of US International Trade* (Boston: Pitman Publishing, 1985).

The only work systematically addressing the GATT's impact on decision-making in developing countries in particular is Ernst-Ulrich Petersmann, "International Trade Order and International Trade Law". The subject is, however, a frequent topic of discussion among trade policy officials.

Although most of the above writings, as well as this study, have been influenced by the "public choice" writings that go back to Mancur Olson, *The Logic of Collective Action* (Cambridge, Massachusetts: Harvard University Press, 1965), Stephanie Lenway's book represents, to the author's knowledge, the first explicit effort to examine the GATT's influence in light of these works, and *vice versa*.

The "public choice" scholarship currently being undertaken in the area of trade policy will clearly have a bearing on the further development of the ideas about GATT influence presented in this study and in the others cited above. The directions of enquiry laid out by the works of Robert E. Baldwin and J. Michael Finger, in particular, seem very worthwhile. See, for example, Robert E. Baldwin, *The Political Economy of US Import Policy* (Cambridge, Massachusetts, MIT Press, 1985) and J. Michael Finger, H. Keith Hall and Douglas R. Nelson, "The Political Economy of Administered Protection", *American Economic Review*, Vol. 72, June 1982, pp. 452–66.

8

Separating Legal and Economic Issues

SEPARATING legal and economic issues is difficult because the two sets of issues tend to occupy the same ground. In the GATT, legal measures are never taken for their own sake. They are taken to encourage a particular kind of conduct because that conduct is thought to be economically beneficial. For a legal measure to be "effective", it must have two consequences. It must induce the kind of conduct desired (legal effectiveness) and the desired conduct must in turn achieve the economic benefit desired (economic effectiveness). Debates over "effectiveness" have a tendency to slide from one issue to the other, usually without warning.

Neither issue is necessarily controlling when it comes to selecting the optimal government policy. Even if the government of a developing country is persuaded that certain market distortions are economically harmful and ought not to be employed, considerations of legal policy might still militate against undertaking GATT legal obligations prohibiting such distortions. For example, the government might believe (i) that it was perfectly capable of adopting liberal trade policies by itself without the aid of GATT obligations and (ii) that GATT obligations may cause political hardships for developing countries by legitimizing the use of economic coercion by developed countries. Alternatively, even if a government believed that certain market distortions were economically beneficial, it could still logically oppose adopting them on the grounds of legal policy. For example, the government of a developing country might believe that GSP preferences would be economically beneficial by themselves and yet still oppose the current GSP policy on the ground that it is likely to trigger a chain reaction of other, and more harmful, discrimination that will outweigh whatever economic benefits the GSP preferences might have.

In short, the GATT's current policy towards developing countries could be supported or attacked either on legal or on economic grounds – or on both.

It is essential, however, for critics to be clear which ground is being argued. Failure to be clear can lead to several problems. On the legal side, it can lead authors to use arguments that appear to rest on legal analysis when in fact the reasoning depends on assumptions about economics that have never been identified (and may not even have been perceived). Legal conclusions reached in this manner are not only misleading but tend to reinforce unstated (and unproved) economic assumptions by building them into the legal structure. The following section presents a leading example of this problem.

A SAMPLE PROBLEM: THE EQUALITY ANALYSIS

As noted at the end of Part I, some legal scholars have argued that the current one-sided legal relationship in the GATT represents an important new development in the concept of equality under international law. This new concept is one that rejects the traditional definition of equality in terms of identical legal obligations for all countries. Such formalistic equality, it is argued, is no more just than the law in Anatole France's celebrated epigram – the law which, in all its majesty, prohibited both rich and poor from sleeping under bridges. True equality, the argument runs, requires legal rules that differentiate according to the needs and abilities of each individual subject. To repeat the usual formulation:

> . . . the equality principle (or non-discrimination principle) means that equal cases should be treated equally and unequal cases unequally.[1]

This concept of equality is often illustrated by reference to national tax legislation which taxes the rich more heavily than the poor.

Legal scholars have found GATT law to be an important precedent in the international recognition of this principle. They view it as a law which also taxes the rich more than the poor. The GATT's "taxes", of course, are its legal obligations that require governments not to employ certain trade restrictions. Developing countries are taxed less in that they are required to observe fewer obligations. The unstated assumption is that freedom to use trade distortions is, like freedom from taxes, an extra benefit for the poor.

The citation of GATT law as a source of authority for this new equality principle is a form of legal analysis commonly used to establish a normative legal conclusion. Scholars examine patterns of government behavior in order to demonstrate widespread implementation, and thereby recognition, of a certain normative principle. Sufficient recognition, coupled with the inherent normative validity of the principle itself, can support a conclusion that the principle deserves to be called law, thus raising the principle to an even higher level of obligation. The analysis will usually yield two related conclusions: (i) that the principle itself deserves to be called law; and (ii) that behavior of governments used as a precedent for the new principle – in our example here, governments' acceptance of the GATT's one-sided legal relationship – is an act required by that legal obligation.

The second of these two conclusions, however, does not always follow. Governmental action may reinforce a principle by claiming to rest on it, even when that action turns out to be an ineffective means of achieving the principle's objective. The legal principle is one thing; the adequacy of means, another. To make this clear, a careful statement of the equality principle would say something like this: "It is simply not legally relevant to know whether any of the GATT's "favorable" treatment actually benefits developing countries. All that is needed for the legal conclusion is the finding that governments have recognized a duty to give extra benefits to the poorer country and have acted with the intent of doing so. The fact that the parties chose a wrong means or, indeed, the fact that it may not even be possible to give extra benefits in this area is not relevant to the legal conclusion. The legal principle merely describes the duty, not the economic means to achieve it."

For the most part, the legal analysis of GATT law as an expression of the new equality principle simply ignores the underlying economic issue.[2] It leaves untouched the initial assumption that fewer GATT obligations will increase the economic welfare of poorer countries. Indeed, it reinforces that assumption by implying that the GATT's current legal policy is required by basic principles of equality in international law.

Raising the economic issue would add an important dimension to the legal analysis, for it would at least expose the possibility that the GATT's legal policy is quite the opposite of what it seems. That is, if the legal freedom to use trade distortions might actually be harmful to developing countries, then GATT legal policy may actually be a gross perversion of the equality principle being cited to sustain it. It would be something like a law proclaiming that concern for the poor requires giving them greater legal freedom to use narcotic substances. The narcotics metaphor should not be dismissed as mere hyperbole. If the GATT's history is viewed through the lens of the contrary economic assumption, there are some rather striking parallels between GATT's developing-country policy and penny gin.

The first step in avoiding the problem of unstated economic assumptions is to try to identify underlying economic issues at the outset and for views, if any, about these issues to be made clear. The rest of this chapter is devoted to doing so. It examines three main sets of economic assumptions that appear to underlie the main tenets of the GATT's current policy towards developing countries.

The first is the rather simple and intuitively appealing set of ideas usually called "mercantilism" – basically, the idea that exports are economically beneficial while imports are economically harmful. The second is the considerably more sophisticated justification of trade protection that is loosely called the "infant-industry" rationale – the idea that comparative advantage can be changed by learning and that government assistance is often necessary to overcome various market imperfections that impede socially profitable investment in the learning process. The third is the somewhat separate set of economic assumptions that underlie demands for preferential treatment of developing countries such as the Generalized System of Preferences.

ECONOMIC ASSUMPTIONS: MERCANTILIST DOCTRINE

Mercantilism is a quite familiar concept. It posits that nations gain by expanding exports because exports create larger markets for a country's own producers, thereby creating more profit for those producers and more employment for their workers. It likewise assumes that nations suffer a loss when they increase imports for the same reasons in reverse – a smaller market share for a country's own producers, leading to smaller profits and less employment.

Mercantilist doctrine as such is now thoroughly discredited among professional economists. No serious economist today would accept the mercantilist ideas of economic gain and loss as a starting point for any analysis. The starting point of any serious analysis today is the theory of comparative advantage, which postulates that trade distortions of any kind cause economic loss to all countries affected by them, because resources are directed into less efficient uses. Although the economics profession still produces plenty of arguments for using market-distorting measures in particular circumstances, all begin by accepting the teachings of the theory of comparative advantage and only then go on to explain why the theory does not apply to the case at hand.[3]

The most difficult thing to understand about mercantilism is its durability. Notwithstanding its professional disrepute, mercantilism remains, in political and business circles, the most widely accepted explanation of how international trade works. How can a doctrine so discredited among professional economists have such a firm grip on the views about trade policy of everyone else?

Part of mercantilism's popular appeal is due no doubt to its congruence with intuitive economic perceptions that selling (earning) is economically beneficial, while buying (spending) is something that ought to be done less. These thrifty precepts can be seen most prominently, perhaps, in the widely held view that a balance-of-payments surplus is the optimal result in foreign trade.

Mercantilism's durability in political life turns out to be a quite logical phenomenon. The precepts of mercantilism happen to be a wholly effective formula for maximizing short-term political approval: Increasing exports usually makes exporters happy without displeasing anyone, and decreasing imports usually gives considerable pleasure to import-competing industries while causing generally less noticeable pain among those who lose by it.

The strength of mercantilism's appeal at the intuitive and political levels has been reinforced by the way that governments have responded to that widespread appeal. Instead of combatting mercantilist ideas directly, governments have chosen to justify the GATT's policy of reducing trade barriers in mercantilist terms. Thus, for example, GATT doctrine places very strong emphasis on reciprocity, showing that reduction of trade barriers at home (increased imports) will be matched by a similar reduction abroad (increased exports). Indeed, governments often go even further and try to demonstrate that, by skillful bargaining, they have "won" a particular trade negotiation by securing more trade opportunities than they gave up.

One result of such officially sponsored mercantilist explanations is a somewhat surrealistic situation of the world's leading organization in the field of international trade explaining its policies to the world in terms of voodoo economics, rejected by virtually every professional economist in the field.[4] A more serious consequence, however, is that official adoption of mercantilist ideas has given them even greater currency and legitimacy than they had before. For example, except for economists, virtually all authors who write about the GATT – including most legal scholars, it seems – simply repeat the very plausible mercantilist economics they have been taught by the GATT's own doctrine. This has been one of the costs of trying to use bad economics to justify good economic policy.

The bottom line with respect to mercantilism itself is that, although not worth arguing about as an intellectual matter, it remains a vital force in public discourse. Thus, although this study will ignore mercantilism as a relevant policy argument, it will treat these ideas with great respect as a political fact.

ECONOMIC ASSUMPTIONS: INFANT-INDUSTRY DOCTRINE

Although there has been fairly broad agreement within the economics profession on the desirability of a policy of free trade for developed countries, the same cannot be said for the profession's views on trade policy for developing countries. The more difficult circumstances faced by developing countries have led a substantial number of economists over the years to recommend more interventionist solutions.[5] To be sure, there has also been a strong body of contrary opinion favoring free market policies, and support for this view has strengthened considerably in the past decade or so.[6]

The debate over intervention in trade matters has involved two different kinds of intervention that need to be treated separately. Most of the attention has been focussed on intervention by the developing country itself, in its own market, usually by means of import protection. More recently, the debate has expanded to include the issue of preferences, interventions that other governments are asked to make, in their own markets, by giving preferential treatment to developing-country trade. The present section examines the economic debate over import protection; the next section examines the debate over preferences.

At the practical level, the post-war experience offers a variety of lessons on the wisdom of import protection. Developed countries have practiced a great deal of such protection since World War II. Comparative advantage theory would teach that the cost of that intervention was probably quite high and that greater economic gains would have occurred without it. Nonetheless, it cannot be said that such protection as there was caused the economies of developed countries to fall below politically satisfactory levels of economic growth during most of the period.

The United States, which practices protection less, seems to be better off today than Western Europe, which practices it more, but the relative levels of protection are surely not the only relevant variable. Then, of course, there is the Japanese experience. Japan appears to have practiced more protection than either the United States or the European Community (at least in the early post-war years), and yet Japan was certainly able to grow vigorously and efficiently under those conditions. Although Japan might have gained even more from a more liberal trade policy, few governments would turn down the Japanese growth rate as it was.

The experience of developing countries is likewise less than fully illuminating. Hong Kong and Singapore are cited as examples of buoyant economic growth based on free trade policies, but the relative success of Brazil, Mexico and Korea appear to show that substantial government intervention does not preclude periods of very strong growth. More recent studies have shown, however, that among developing-country governments practicing intervention, those which had a relatively more liberal trade policy grew more rapidly during the 1960s and 1970s than those which were more closed and inward-looking.[7] On the other hand, other studies carried out concurrently with the present study describe the experience of many developing countries which, having adopted liberal trade policies at one time or another in the post-1945 era, have encountered economic difficulties that led them to retreat to more protectionist measures after a fairly short time.[8] The cause of the economic difficulties usually seems to have been destabilizing pressures elsewhere in the society, but the end result, nevertheless, has been that liberal trade policies have had a difficult time in the social and political conditions that exist.

At the level of theory, the main outlines of the debate look like this: Those who favor free market policies begin with the textbook prescription – like everyone else, developing countries should set an appropriate exchange rate, lower trade barriers and let the market identify the export industries in which the country has a comparative advantage. The theory allows for cases in which market distortions or other competing objectives might call for government intervention, but it states that governments should always use the least-distorting form of intervention in order to minimize unwanted side effects; protection of trade is rarely, if ever, optimal for this purpose.[9] In addition, proponents of this view usually express considerable scepticism about whether governments have the ability to intervene effectively to correct market distortions.

The theoretical case on the other side is based on the assertion that the market forces facing developing countries contain an especially large number of imperfections and distortions, that market-directed investment is therefore often not optimal, that the situation can be improved by properly managed intervention by the government and that developing-country governments must intervene by means of trade protection because they do not have the sophistication to use more refined policy instruments. The primary case for such intervention is the "infant-industry" situation where potentially efficient new industries can be identified, but where market forces will not make the needed (and socially profitable) investment – either because the capital market itself is imperfect or because additional investments are needed to overcome other distortions that will impair the functioning of the infant industry.[10] The same arguments can also be applied to existing industries in difficulty.

The theoretical case for infant-industry intervention is certainly a respectable one. There are, indeed, many imperfections in developing-country markets, and where these imperfections exist, market forces will not necessarily direct investment to its optimal uses. Intervention by any government can increase national economic welfare if it redirects investment to a more efficient use, provided that the efficiency gain exceeds the cost of the intervention.[11] And, even though trade protection is not the optimal instrument, it may well be the only instrument suited to the regulatory capacity of many governments in developing countries.[12]

In the author's view, however, the theoretical case for intervention becomes less persuasive when the capacity of governments to operate such a policy is examined. When governments intervene in their home markets, their

decision-making process is prey to several forces that tend to misdirect it, causing them to make wrong choices that channel investment towards even less
efficient uses. All investors, of course, make mistakes. The issue is whether the
forces working on government intervention policies will misdirect intervention
often enough so that the resources wasted in bad investments will exceed the
gains from whatever beneficial interventions are made.[13] Three major forces
of misdirection need to be considered.

1. The first misdirecting force is the average government's own ineptitude
as an investor. Three separate sources of government ineptitude have to be
worried about. The first is simply the difficulty of the task governments assign
themselves. It is not difficult to identify industries that are doing badly, but it
is extremely difficult to identify those industries where government assistance
will accomplish something beneficial for the economy. Industries that require
perpetual assistance are never a good investment. Governments must be able,
therefore, to identify industries where assistance will enable the enterprises to
overcome, or otherwise adjust to, the handicap in question, so that they can
stand on their own feet. It is very difficult to know what effects intervention
will have in this regard. Some market imperfections, such as barriers to foreign
markets, cannot be changed by the action of a developing country; in these
cases, intervention would make sense only if the barrier is temporary or if intervention could somehow enable the infant industry to develop the capacity to
overcome it. Other market imperfections, such as gaps in local infra-structure,
may even be made worse by government intervention; for example, if government intervention pre-empts the growth of market-based institutions that
might in due course meet the need and remove the problem.

A second source of ineptitude lies in the relatively slow reaction of governments to change. As the mobility of capital and technology throughout
the world continues to increase, so does the pace of change in world markets. Rational investment behavior requires constant attention to new developments, the ability to move quickly when opportunity presents itself and a
constant readiness to adjust to new information. Governments tend to be slow
to move initially. They tend to be even slower to change direction once begun,
remaining committed to protection of an industry long after it becomes clear
that the industry will never be able to stand on its own feet. This tendency to
hang on to bad investments deprives governments of what may be the market's
most important asset: its reaction time to error.

The final source of government ineptitude is the way decisions are made.
Can the reward structure for government officials who make investment decisions be made sufficiently attractive, and sufficiently responsive, to yield an
acceptable percentage of sound decisions over time? Large bureaucracies tend

to develop internal standards of performance that have little or nothing to do with their original objectives. This is also true of large private corporations, but they, at least, must eventually confront market forces. The only outside control on the quality of government investment performance is the political process which, unfortunately, can often be appeased by promising to do worse rather than better.

2. The second misdirecting influence on government intervention policies is a tendency of "misbehavior" on the part of enterprises being assisted. Even where government intervention happens to select worthwhile investments, private enterprises, and even public managers, do not always respond by using the assistance to realize their potential efficiency. Enterprises that come to life, or remain alive, by means of government protection often relax their pursuit of greater efficiency thereafter. Instead, it becomes more "efficient" to pursue profits by investing time and resources – in the pursuit of more government protection – the activity known as "rent-seeking".[14] This sort of competitive atrophy does not always happen, especially when the protected industry happens to be endowed with a strong entrepreneurial drive to export to world markets (the explanation often given for the development of world-class industries behind high protection in Japan). But such motivation is not very common, either in developed or in developing countries.

3. Probably the strongest misdirecting force of all is the political pressure that would-be beneficiaries exert on the intervention decisions made by governments. Import protection is a form of wealth transfer to owners, workers and related suppliers of the protected enterprise. Both efficient and inefficient enterprises can benefit from such wealth transfers. Both, therefore, have the strongest incentives to invest heavily in political efforts to secure them. Certain very large industries will have enough political power to obtain trade protection in any circumstances. Where programs for infant-industry intervention exist, however, they provide an especially vulnerable target for protection-seekers – a pre-existing commitment to take "corrective" action against market difficulties and an ongoing decision-making procedure to which any industry can address its demands. Such programs trigger a kind of political synergism because, by holding out a more visible chance of success at the outset, they induce greater investments of political capital by claimants, and the greater investment usually does increase the chances of eventual success.

To date, the experience of developing countries would suggest that their own intervention policies have suffered a political distortion of the kind just described. Governments of developing countries have not been very discriminating in the use of trade protection. Typically they have erected very high trade barriers to protect virtually all local industry. While no doubt some of this protection could be classified as rationally calculated investment, the main principle on which decisions were based seems to have been to protect whatever is in place, plus whatever new investment can be induced by offering local or foreign investors a very sheltered market.[15]

In the author's judgment, the three forces just described – the built-in ineptitude of government investment decisions, the tendencies of protected industries to misbehave and the problem of political pressure – exist in every decision-making setting and exercise an important influence. They are pervasive because they arise from basic and enduring features of most market-economy societies. It is certainly possible, of course, to imagine situations in which a government is able to control these forces to the extent necessary to conduct a successful intervention policy. Indeed, there are probably instances where governments have actually done so for certain periods of time. But the odds are that, over time and in most countries, these forces will cause governments to invest more in "losers" than can be recouped from "winners".

If this conclusion is correct, it follows that the economic assumptions underlying two of the main pillars of the GATT's policy towards developing countries – its "economic development" exceptions and its non-reciprocity doctrine – are incorrect. It will be necessary to be aware of these conflicting opinions about economic assumptions when considering the separate legal policy issues raised by these two exceptions to GATT rules.

ECONOMIC ASSUMPTIONS: PREFERENCES

Although not all the economic arguments advanced on behalf of preferences are accepted, most economists would agree that preferences can produce some economic benefit for developing countries. The main issue is not whether such benefits can be achieved, but whether the actual size of these benefits is large enough to outweigh the considerable legal costs of such a policy.

In theory, there seems to be no reason why tariff preferences cannot produce certain static economic benefits for developing countries. Three different situations may be noted. First, even if the preference has no effect at all on the volume of exports, it nevertheless involves the reduction or elimination of a tariff duty, and this should increase the return to the developing-country exporter in those cases where competition does not require the entire refund to be passed forward. Second, in the case where producers from developing countries enjoy a comparative advantage over all other suppliers, a preferential tariff reduction will have the same beneficial trade effects as a reduction in the MFN tariff; the higher rate paid by developed-country suppliers will be immaterial.[16] Finally, even where developing-country producers do not have a comparative advantage, any trade diversion caused by the preference will still be beneficial to the developing country, even though it reduces world economic welfare. From the developing country's perspective, any trade induced by a preference will necessarily represent a higher return than is otherwise available from the resources being employed. In addition, preferences in this final trade-diversion situation may also have positive long-term effects of the infant-industry sort, helping a potentially efficient industry get onto its feet.[17]

Just as in the case where trade barriers are reduced on an MFN basis, of course, the trade benefits of a preferential tariff reduction depend in part on the stability of that tariff reduction over time. If the preferential reduction were subsequently withdrawn, investments made by developing countries in the new trade opportunity could turn out to be wasteful. In the case of trade-diverting preferences, even a subsequent lowering of the MFN rate could have this effect.

Given the general acceptance of these potential economic benefits and their limits, the policy debate has tended to focus on the actual consequences of preference policies – the extent to which the theoretical welfare gains are likely to be achieved in practice, the actual cost of achieving those gains and whether the gains are likely to outweigh the costs.

There is one disagreement over basic economic issues that sometimes colors initial value preferences in this debate, although it is usually not central to it. The disagreement concerns the assumptions that are made about the benefits developing countries would receive from the alternative policy – a policy of seeking further trade liberalization on an MFN basis. Proponents of the policy of preferential treatment concede that a world economy based on MFN liberalization would be the most efficient and would thus produce the highest level of overall world income, but they argue that developing countries would not benefit very much from such market conditions because the handicaps faced by their industries render them unable to compete effectively in such a market. Critics disagree, arguing that MFN liberalization would be more effective because it would direct investment to those industries with the greatest comparative advantage, industries where developing countries have already demonstrated their ability to compete effectively.

The reason this issue is not central is that the main ground of attack against preferences is the claim that the costs of a preference system will exceed its acknowledged benefits – a claim which makes it unnecessary to argue how large the gain from MFN liberalization would be or even how much, if any, MFN liberalization can be expected. Thus, while the author agrees with the critics that further MFN liberalization would be beneficial for developing countries, nothing in the subsequent analysis will turn on that economic assumption.[18]

There is some disagreement among economists over the volume of actual and potential benefits from preferences, but even in the best case it seems reasonably clear that the volume of benefits will be limited. The low level of most MFN tariffs on industrial products obviously limits the size of the preference margins that can be created, and these tariffs are likely to decline even further. In addition, the widespread use of quantitative import restrictions on both industrial and agricultural trade makes preferences irrelevant wherever they apply.[19]

In the end, therefore, the debate over the policy of preferential treatment usually turns on questions in the realm of legal policy – the way in which discriminatory treatment policies are most likely to be implemented by the governments of developed countries and the kinds of collateral consequences that such implementation is likely to entail.

THE PLACE OF ECONOMIC ISSUES IN THE LEGAL ANALYSIS

The summary description of the economic issues in the previous three sections was intended primarily to define the economic landscape against which the legal issues are to be examined.

The major feature on that landscape is the very large possibility that, contrary to the economic premises of the GATT's current policy, trade protection in the home market is economically harmful to developing countries. The main force of that conclusion will be found in the following chapter, which deals with the impact of the GATT's legal policies on the decision-making processes of the governments of developing countries. The GATT's impact will be examined under two different economic assumptions: (i) the assumption that a policy of trade protection is harmful and should be avoided to the greatest extent possible and (ii) the contrary assumption that such protection can be economically beneficial.

Economic assumptions will not figure very prominently in the other main branch of the analysis – the examination of how GATT legal policy affects the decision-making of governments in developed countries in relation to developing-country trade. There is no disagreement at all about the economic assumption that MFN liberalization by developed countries is more beneficial than no MFN liberalization. The only issue concerning MFN liberalization is the legal policy question of how best to achieve it. Likewise, although there is some disagreement about the size of the economic benefits to be obtained from preferential trade measures, the major issue with respect to discrimination in favor of developing countries is the size of the offsetting harmful legal consequences. Here, too, it will be possible to discuss the legal policy issues independently.

NOTES AND REFERENCES

1. International Law Association, *Report of the Sixty-first Conference*, op. cit, pp. 131–32. See also the text at notes 4–14, Chapter 6.
2. See sources cited in note 10, Chapter 6.
3. For a work that demonstrates the fallacies of mercantilism and presents a lucid elementary exposition of the theory of comparative advantage, see Jan Pen, *A Primer on International Trade* (New York: Random House, 1967). See also Richard Blackhurst, Nicolas Marian and Jan Tumlir, *Trade Liberalization, Protectionism and Interdependence*, GATT Studies in International Trade, No. 5 (Geneva: GATT Secretariat, 1977); Peter H. Lindert and Charles P. Kindleberger, *International Economics*, 8th edition (Homewood, Illinois: Richard D. Irwin, 1982) pp. 112–26 and 154–59. At a more advanced level, the case is presented very clearly by W.M. Corden in *Trade Policy and Economic Welfare* (Oxford: Clarendon Press, 1974). An interesting demonstration of the internal fallacies of mercantilist doctrine is given in Kenneth M. Clements and Larry A. Sjaastad, *How Protection Taxes Exporters*, Thames Essay No. 39 (London: Trade Policy Research Centre, 1985).
4. Most professionals find the incongruence amusing, an attitude perhaps best captured by Harry Johnson's often-quoted comparison of reciprocity theory to seduction: "In each case the benefit to be received is treated as a loss for purposes of negotiations and in each case the consequence of this fiction is continual frustration and frequent non-consummation". Harry G. Johnson, *The Canadian Quandary: Economic Problems and Policies* (Toronto: McGraw Hill, 1963).
5. Anne Krueger and Constantine Michalopoulos recall that in the early years of development economics, "most analysts thought that protection . . . would be essential to foster industrial activity in developing countries. Although the static comparative advantage argument was recognized to some extent, 'infant-industry' and 'dynamic' considerations were also thought to apply." Anne O. Krueger and Constantine Michalopoulos, "Developing-country Trade Policies and the International Economic System", loc. cit., p. 42. Particularly influential in this line of thinking, especially among developing-country economists, were Raúl Prebisch, *The Economic Development of Latin America and Some of its Problems* (New York: United Nations Economic Commission for Latin America, 1949) and Gunnar Myrdal, *An International Economy: Problems and Prospects* (New York: Harper & Row, 1956). The apogee of this approach was perhaps Raúl Prebisch's blueprint for the first UNCTAD conference in 1964, *Towards a Global Strategy of Development*, Report by the Secretary-General, United Nations Document TD/3/Rev.1 (Geneva: UNCTAD Secretariat, 1964).
6. An influential work, often cited as the launching pad for the resurgence of liberal views in the thinking of professional economists about trade policy in developing countries, is I.M.D. Little, Tibor Scitovsky and M.F.G. Scott, *Industry and Trade*

in Some Developing Countries: A Comparative Study (London: Oxford University Press, for the OECD, 1970). Also quite influential has been a large study under the aegis of the National Bureau of Economic Research (NBER) summarized in two volumes: Krueger, *Foreign Trade Régimes and Economic Development: Liberalization Attempts and Consequences* (Cambridge, Massachusetts: Ballinger, for the National Bureau of Economic Research, 1978); and Jagdish N. Bhagwati, *Foreign Trade Régimes and Economic Development: Anatomy and Consequence of Exchange Control Regimes* (Cambridge, Massachusetts: Ballinger, for the National Bureau of Economic Research, 1979). See also, Bela Balassa, *The Newly Industrializing Countries in the World Economy* (New York: Pergamon Press, 1981); and Little, *Economic Development: Theory, Policy and International Relations* (New York: Basic Books, for the Twentieth Century Fund, 1982).

7. See Krueger, *Foreign Trade Regimes and Economic Development*, op. cit. For a summary of these findings, see Krueger and Michalopoulos, "Developing-country Trade Policies and the International Economic System", loc. cit., pp. 40–45.

8. In the project of the Trade Policy Research Centre on the Participation of Developing Countries in the International Trading System, the problem of relapses by countries that have attempted significant liberalization is discussed, in particular, in Deepak Lal and Sarath Rajapatirana, *Impediments to Trade Liberalization in Sri Lanka*, Thames Essay No. 51 (London: Trade Policy Research Centre, 1989); Romeo Bautista, *Impediments to Trade Liberalization in the Philippines* (London: Trade Policy Research Centre, 1988); and Roque Hernandez and Carlos Rodriguez, "Impediments to Trade Liberalization in Argentina", in Larry Sjaastad (ed.), *Impediments to Trade Liberalization in Latin America* (forthcoming). See also T.G. Congdon, *Economic Liberalism in the Cone of Latin America*, Thames Essay No. 40 (London: Trade Policy Research Centre, 1985); and Martin Wolf, "Timing and Sequencing of Trade Liberalization", *Asian Development Review*, Manila, Asian Development Bank, Vol. 4, No. 2, 1986.

9. One such market distortion often discussed is the infant-industry situation in which the return to the private investor–producer will be less than the full social benefit of the investment. Theoretically, government assistance to induce the investment in this case would produce a positive welfare effect, but the most efficient form of intervention would be a direct subsidy rather than tariff protection. See Johnson, "Optimal Trade Intervention in the Presence of Domestic Distortion", in Robert E. Baldwin (ed.), *Trade, Growth and the Balance of Payments: Essays in Honor of Gottfried Haberler* (Amsterdam: North Holland, 1965), pp. 3–34. See also Corden, *Trade Policy and Economic Welfare*, op. cit. One case in which a tariff is acknowledged to be an optimal form of intervention, purely from a national welfare point of view, is the so-called optimal tariff situation where, in certain monopsony-type market conditions, terms of trade can be improved by raising the tariff. The author has always thought the theoretical interest in this point has exceeded its practical relevance.

10. For an explanation of infant-industry arguments and related claims for developing-country trade protection, see Gerald M. Meier, *International Trade and Development*, 2nd edition (New York: Harper & Row, 1968). See also Krueger, "Trade Policies in Developing Countries", in Ronald W. Jones and Peter B. Kenen, *Handbook of International Economics* (Amsterdam: North Holland, 1984) pp. 521–27. Perhaps

a more official view would be the one in the UNCTAD Secretariat's *Protectionism and Structural Adjustment in the World Economy*, op. cit., pp. 19–20.

11. In practical terms, this means that the assisted industry must eventually be able to stand on its own feet, for an industry that requires perpetual assistance will not be contributing any improvement to the country's welfare. In addition, even short-term assistance must not cost the economy more than the discounted value of the future return to the society.

12. See Goh Keng-Swee, "Public Administration and Economic Development in LDCs", Fourth Harry G. Johnson Memorial Lecture, *The World Economy*, September 1983, pp. 229–43.

13. Support for many of the observations in this analysis can be found, more fully developed, in Little et al., *Industry and Trade in Some Developing Countries*, op. cit.

14. For a collection of works on rent seeking, see Robert D. Tollison, "Rent Seeking: Survey", *Kyklos*, Vol. 35, No. 4, 1982, pp. 575–602.

15. See Krueger, "Trade Policies in Developing Countries", op. cit., p. 525.

16. Rolf Langhammer and André Sapir estimate that the trade-creating effect of both the United States and the European Community preferences has been larger than their trade diverting effect. Rolf J. Langhammer and André Sapir, *Economic Impact of Generalized Tariff Preferences*, op. cit. A contrary conclusion was reached in relation to the United States' preferences in a 1983 study by the United States International Trade Commission, *An Evaluation of US Imports Under the Generalized System of Preferences*, Publication No. 1379 (Washington: United States International Trade Commission, 1983). The Commission's conclusions proved helpful in the 1984 legislative debate over extending the GSP law. Its conclusions were cited in the report of the House Ways and Means Committee in support of extending the law for another eight years; the conclusions proved, according to the report, that GSP was causing little harm to United States producers: " . . . increased GSP imports appear to be at the expense of imports from [other] developed countries". House Report No. 98-1090, 98th Congress, 2nd Session (1984), p. 3.

17. Unlike the case of infant-industry protection in home markets, the assistance given in the case of trade-diverting preferences comes at the expense of other countries. Thus, provided the preference remains in effect, the developing country does not stand to lose anything if the assistance is costlier than the welfare gain. The developing country gets whatever gain there is, while other economies pay the cost.

18. Helen Hughes and Anne Krueger argue that, during the 1970s, protection in developed countries did not seem to have retarded the growth of manufactured goods exports from developing countries very much because the rate of growth of those exports remained so high during this period that it would have been difficult for exports to increase any further. See Helen Hughes and Anne O. Krueger, "Effects of Protection in Developed Countries on Developing Countries' Exports of Manufactures", in Baldwin and Krueger (eds.), *The Structure and Evolution of Recent US Trade Policy* (Chicago: University of Chicago Press, for the National Bureau of Economic Research, 1984) pp. 389–418. To the same effect, see Henry R. Nau, "The NICs in a New Trade Round", in Ernest H. Preeg (ed.), op. cit., pp. 68–70.

19. For a comprehensive summary of their own and other research on the trade effects of GSP programs in the United States and the European Community, see Langhammer and Sapir, *Economic Impact of Generalized Tariff Preferences*, op. cit. Other leading work on the effects of GSP include André Sapir and Lars Lundberg, "The US Generalized System of Preferences and its Impacts", in Baldwin and Krueger (eds.), *The Structure and Evolution of Recent US Trade Policy*, op. cit., pp. 195–231; *An Evaluation of US Imports under the Generalized System of Preferences*, United States International Trade Commission, op. cit.; Langhammer, "Ten Years of the EEC's Generalized System of Preferences for Developing Countries: Success or Failure?", Kiel Working Paper No. 183 (Kiel: Institut für Weltwirtschaft an der Universitat Kiel, 1983); Tracy Murray, *Evaluation of the Trade Benefits under the United States Scheme of Generalized Preferences*, United Nations Document TD/B/C. 5166 (1980); and Robert E. Baldwin and Tracy Murray, "MFN Tariff Reductions and Developing Country Trade Benefits under the GSP", *Economic Journal*, Cambridge and York, Vol. 87, March 1977, pp. 30–46.

9

Impact of GATT Legal Policy on Internal Decision-making

THE PRESENT chapter examines the effect that GATT legal policy has on the decision-making process of the governments of developing countries. The reason for beginning here is the author's conviction that a government's own trade-policy decisions are the most important determinant of its economic welfare. It is here that the GATT's legal policy can make its most important contribution to developing-country welfare or do the greatest harm.[1]

The chapter begins with what might be called a model – a rather lengthy analysis of how the decision-making process of the governments in developed countries is affected by the GATT legal obligations they have accepted. This model is then used to consider how decision-making processes in developing-country governments would be affected by either of two GATT legal policies – (i) the GATT's current no-obligations policy towards developing countries and (ii) an alternative GATT legal policy that would require developing countries to accept roughly the same obligations as developed countries, the alternative sought by most critics. The impact on developing countries will be considered under each of the two contending economic assumptions in this area: that intervention policies are harmful and that they are helpful.

The chapter concludes that the GATT's current policy is harming developing countries more than it is helping them, even under the assumption that developing countries can be helped by infant-industry policies.

DEVELOPED-COUNTRY MODEL

GATT law appears somewhat anomalous. If liberal trade policy is in every country's self-interest, why do the governments of developed countries consider it necessary to enter international legal commitments requiring it? The most likely answer is because they find these self-imposed "chains" helpful in obtaining political support for such a policy.

To understand this internal function of GATT law, the general political setting in which trade-policy decisions are made has to be understood. The first element of that setting is the political opposition. Even if it were always true that liberal trade policies are in the overall national interest, there will always be individual economic interests that do not benefit from trade liberalization. Individuals in import-competing industries are usually made worse off economically when trade barriers are lowered, and they usually gain economically when trade barriers are increased. These perceptions of self-interest are by no means illusions based on the seductive logic of mercantilist ideology. For these individuals, self-interest is simply different from the national interest. Consequently, their opposition to liberal trade policy can be expected to be a normal, permanent and quite vigorous part of the political scene. It is not something that will go away with greater education and understanding about the theory of comparative advantage.

Those whose self-interest is opposed to liberal trade policy tend to exert a political influence disproportionate to their numbers or to the total value of their interests. This is because the losses to them from trade liberalization, or their gains from increased protection, tend to be of significant magnitude for the individuals involved – usually the loss or saving of a job or significant changes in income. The relative magnitude of such losses and gains make them worth the expenditure of considerable political energy. By contrast, the benefits of liberal trade policy tend to be dispersed among many more individuals and in smaller amounts. The largest part of the benefits from trade liberalization are usually the small gains to consumers of which the consumers themselves are scarcely aware. More concentrated benefits do exist for commercial consumers and for exporters who prosper from trade liberalization, but even these benefits are often not clearly defined because of their prospective and often indirect character. Thus the prospective benefits from trade liberalization tend not to elicit the same intensity of political effort.

There exists, then, a built-in political opposition to liberal trade policy within most governments and the power of this opposition is usually amplified by the relatively more concentrated nature of its economic interests. Such forces exist in all market economies, wherever there are private economic interests threatened by liberal trade policy. So long as those interests have some way of making things unpleasant for government officials, they can create effective pressure.

It would be incorrect to say that GATT legal obligations are always needed to overcome such opposition. There will be a natural coalition of political forces in favor of liberal trade policy and, despite their dispersion, these forces will often be strong enough to be effective, even without assistance from international obligations.

It is important to have a clear understanding of just how many different interests there are on the side of liberal trade policy. To begin with, of course, there are all those with direct economic interests in lower trade barriers – importers, consumers (especially commercial consumers such as large retail merchants) and the various allied services connected with trade. Next, there are the many other economic interests that are affected by the general conditions of foreign trade, such as those who have lending or investment interests in the foreign countries involved and, of course, those who export to them.

Finally, broader policy preferences exert considerable influence. There are convictions that liberal trade policy is needed for a strong national economy. There are convictions that such a trade policy is necessary for international political stability. With respect to trade policy towards developing countries, there are convictions that liberal policies are morally obligatory. Views of this broader kind exercise a more substantial influence than might be expected among leaders in the private sector. They are even more influential, of course, among government officials who are, let it be understood, an important force in themselves. Such officials have personal convictions, they tend to hold them strongly (public policy is, after all, the life's work they have chosen) and they are the persons closest to the locus of decision.

The role that GATT obligations play is to augment the political power of these interests. The expectation is not that GATT obligations will enable these interests to prevail in every case, but that they will make a difference at the margin – that they will help to achieve some greater degree of liberal trade policy behavior (or avoid some greater degree of trade restriction) than would exist without them.

GATT obligations can influence the processes of government decision-making in two major ways. The first is the direct impact of such obligations in blocking opposing pressures for protection. The second is their contribution to rounding up additional political support for liberal trade policies.

GATT legal obligations can act directly on actors in the decision-making process in several ways:

(a) Respect for international legal obligations can be a force sufficient by itself to dictate the position of some government officials, especially those new to the process or otherwise undecided. International obligations evoke respect not only out of deference to norms that carry the title "law", but also out of more self-interested concerns to avoid unpleasant and damaging public controversy.

(b) International legal obligations can serve as an acceptable public explanation of decisions taken for other reasons, in cases where the other reason (for example, convictions about correct economic policy) would itself be difficult to defend politically. The prospect of having to suffer economic retaliation for breach of obligations is a particularly effective justification in this regard. Injury to other citizens (those who would suffer from retaliation) is often the only really viable excuse a politician can give for declining to help constituents who are themselves suffering economic harm from imports: Legal obligations make the threat of injury credible and help to remove some of its provocative qualities by making it appear a regular and lawful response to wrong behavior. Law is usually thought of as a source of compulsion, but in reality law often plays the opposite role of permitting government officials to do things that could not otherwise be done.

(c) International legal obligations are a concise way of defining policy for government officials. Liberal trade policy would not fare very well if every new generation of officials were permitted to rethink the case for free trade, especially if they had to do so in the process of resolving ad hoc problems one-by-one as they come across the desk.

(d) International legal obligations can serve as a forceful warning to the public not to build up an investment in, or an expectation of, certain trade-distorting measures. Often the best way to defeat a demand for protection is to stop it before it gets going.[2]

In addition to these four kinds of direct impact, GATT obligations also impose a legal structure on international trade relationships which, although somewhat artificial, does help to enlist the economic interests of the export sector in support of liberal trade policy. The key concept of the legal structure is the idea of reciprocity – the idea that governments will be willing to lower foreign trade barriers, but only if other governments "pay" by lowering their own trade barriers. A consequential proposition is that governments who increase trade barriers above the agreed level will be met by a reciprocal raising of barriers abroad. Since exporters do, in fact, gain when foreign trade barriers are lowered and do, in fact, suffer losses when foreign barriers are raised, the reciprocity link gives them a clear economic interest in making sure that their own government follows trade policies that are as liberal as possible.

The reciprocity doctrine works, but its workings are not quite as straightforward, nor as costless, as might be suggested by the conventional description just given. The complicating factor is that the reciprocity doctrine does not make sense as economic policy. While nations do, in fact, gain more from reciprocal trade liberalization than they do when only one side reduces trade barriers, they do not gain from following the negative precepts of the reciprocity doctrine – refusing to reduce trade barriers when reciprocity is not given and retaliating when others raise trade barriers. Unilateral, unreciprocated trade liberalization generates more economic benefit than no trade liberalization at all. Likewise, retaliation usually harms the retaliating country as much as it harms the country retaliated against. There may be times when current losses from the reciprocity game would be justified by future gains – for example, if retaliation were to induce other governments to join future liberalization exercises. But such instances would be a minority of the cases at issue.

The trick in using the reciprocity doctrine, therefore, is to obtain its political benefits without paying the costs of following its mercantilist precepts to the letter. Governments of developed countries have been surprisingly successful in doing so in day-to-day policy. Their technique is the time-honored practice of speaking more forcefully than they act. Governments do, of course, make every effort to obtain the reciprocity they promise because reducing foreign trade barriers really is good for all concerned. But when equivalent reciprocity is not forthcoming, governments usually try to go ahead with their own liberalization anyway. Likewise, although governments are usually quick to threaten retaliation when reciprocity doctrine calls for it, they tend to be exceptionally slow in carrying out those threats.[3]

The gap between promise and performance has less effect than might be supposed. Several factors help to obscure the inadequacy of the performance. In the first place, governments have considerable ability to "enhance" any package of value they receive by (i) artfully defining the respective starting points of the parties involved, (ii) identifying lots of trade advantages as reciprocal benefits even if they were not actually part of the bargain and (iii) rearranging the numbers until they prove maximum trade gains. In addition, the time at which political support must be given is usually in advance of the time the actual bargain with foreign governments is struck, so that failed promises do not become relevant until next time, when the new promises, made by new actors in new circumstances, help to blunt the force of remembered disappointments. Even these factors, however, do not fully explain how governments of developed countries retain credibility in the face of so much non-delivery. It is as though exporters want to continue believing in these artificial benefits, perhaps because they perceive intuitively what many economists have been saying for some years: that exporters do benefit even when liberalization is unilateral.[4]

It is more difficult to say whether the governments of developed countries have succeeded in avoiding the long-term costs of adopting a legal policy based on mercantilism. The reciprocity doctrine could be called a bargain with the devil. Governments receive political support for liberal trade policies, but at the cost of endorsing mercantilist concepts that clearly undermine whatever chances they might have of building truly stable support for such policies based on a correct appreciation of the gains from international trade. The bargain is clearly not a good one. The real issue, however, is whether any better bargain is possible – whether there is any alternative legal policy that will produce better results in the political world where trade policy is made. Politicians tend to believe there is not. Recent history has not supplied much evidence[5] that they are wrong.

Added together, the political support generated by the reciprocity doctrine and the more direct legal effects described earlier constitute the counter-weight that GATT legal obligations contribute to the decision-making process. Although it is not possible to quantify these effects, the author is convinced that they are substantial. Both legal norms and reciprocity considerations usually appear prominently in all public defences of the liberal position, supplying not only their own persuasive power, but also serving as a point of focus for all other interests and policy preferences seeking the same result.[6] Perhaps the best test of the GATT's impact would be to ask trade-policy officials in developed countries to predict the effect of removing GATT obligations from the domestic political equation. In the author's view, such officials would agree that, while there is much that GATT obligations cannot prevent, the trade policies of developed countries would become measurably more protectionist without them.

IMPACT IN DEVELOPING COUNTRIES

The impact of the GATT's current, no-obligations legal policy for developing countries can best be examined against the background of the model just presented. The first step is to ask whether the model fits – whether being bound by GATT legal obligations would have the same impact on decision-making in developing countries as in developed countries. If so, then the next step is to compare that impact with the impact of the current no-obligations policy. In order to take account of conflicting views about the economic effects of trade barriers, the impact of these two legal policies will be compared under two sets of economic assumptions:

(a) The case of a developing-country government that agrees with the liberal trade policy objectives stated in the GATT's current obligations and wishes to pursue the most liberal trade policy possible.

(b) The case of a developing-country government persuaded that trade inter-vention can be economically beneficial and which therefore wishes to conduct an active interventionist policy.

FOLLOWING LIBERAL TRADE POLICIES

It is certainly not impossible for developing-country governments to follow liberal trade policies without compulsion from the GATT. Hong Kong and Singapore have followed what are probably the most liberal trade policies in the world during a time when their GATT obligations were, in practical terms, zero. Are the Hong Kong and Singapore examples typical of developing countries in general? Or do most developing countries have the same political difficulties that developed countries encounter in trying to follow liberal trade policies? If the latter, would GATT obligations provide the same kind of assistance to developing-country governments? Would they achieve the same results? Would they entail the same costs?

For most developing countries, there would appear to be no a priori reason why political opposition to a liberal trade policy should be any weaker than it is in the average developed country. Nor is there any a priori reason to believe that the average developing-country government is any better able to overcome such opposition than its developed-country counterpart. If anything, the balance of underlying political forces should generally tilt more towards the protectionist side. While developing countries often do have a vigorous export sector that would support liberal trade policy, many of the other liberal trade forces found in developed countries, such as foreign investors and lenders, have no counterpart in the typical developing country.

The effect of IMF requirements on the process of government decision-making in most developing countries tends to confirm the need for some outside assistance in taking decisions that involve economic hardship for significant interests. In case after case, the IMF is used as an excuse for taking unpopular economic measures that governments seem unable to manage on their own political responsibility.[7] Political justification in terms of external compulsion seems essential to such decisions.

Given the need for outside assistance, would GATT obligations provide it? It is the author's view that they would, although not in quite the same way that they assist the governments of developed countries. There are differences in the situation of developing countries that would create somewhat different problems and different results.

The initial problem for developing-country governments will be to establish a reciprocity relationship that will induce their exporters to undertake GATT legal obligations. A case has to be made that acceptance of legal obligations will earn better trade opportunities than would exist otherwise. To make such a case, governments of developing countries must be able to identify new trade opportunities created by these new legal undertakings, or to demonstrate that existing opportunities for market access have been preserved as a result of those undertakings.

Identifying new improved trade opportunities will not be easy. In the following chapter, the likely response of developed countries to an offer of reciprocity by developing countries is examined in some detail. The conclusions are (i) that developed countries are likely to continue roughly the same pace of gradual trade liberalization with or without reciprocity and (ii) that the existing pace of trade liberalization is not likely to be increased by an offer of reciprocity from developing countries.

Developing countries should be able, however, to arrange matters so that they can claim reciprocity credit for whatever modest new liberalization does take place even if such liberalization is not, strictly speaking, in exchange for their own legal undertakings. Reciprocity is not a fact but a perception about motivation. If governments of developed countries say that new liberalization by them depends on reciprocity and if governments of developing countries say they believe the threat, any new liberalization that occurs becomes' a reciprocal payment.

Because new liberalization is likely to be quite limited, however, an important part of the reciprocity demonstration will probably have to come on the negative side, that is, by demonstrating that existing levels of market access have been protected against new trade restrictions. The following chapter concludes that the "graduation" doctrine constitutes a threat of such new trade restrictions for advanced developing countries who do not offer liberalization. The Tokyo Round negotiations also gave a certain degree of credibility to the threat of conditional MFN treatment by developed countries. The tone of trade diplomacy in the years since the Tokyo Round negotiations has become even more bellicose. In sum, there should be no shortage of credible threats, and developing countries wishing to liberalize trade restrictions should be able to use these threats as a plausible justification for doing so. If GATT legal obligations can become established in developing countries, they will very likely exercise a stronger direct impact on the decision-making process than they do in developed countries. The reason is that GATT legal discipline will tend to be viewed in much the same way that the IMF is now perceived in developing countries, as an external bogeyman. Like the IMF, the GATT has always been perceived as an alien enterprise managed by the rich countries. And, like the IMF, the GATT has the power to do real harm to individual developing countries, by retaliation, if they do not cooperate.

While this bogeyman quality will make GATT obligations more effective, it will unfortunately also make the political cost of agreeing to them a lot higher for politicians in developing countries. In most developing countries, sensitivity to colonial-type relationships remains quite high. Any policy that appears to involve submission to compulsion from the developed countries will provoke strong reactions.

The political cost will be even higher if, as is not unlikely, the actual enforcement of GATT obligations proves to be more strict for developing countries than for developed countries. Developed countries enjoy a certain leeway in the enforcement of their own obligations because other governments respect their economic power and so tend to temper legal claims against them with "understanding". On the other hand, most developed countries, in spite of their general policy of benevolent inattention, are capable of acting in a very peremptory fashion towards smaller countries who cannot really hurt them in return. Rather strict enforcement demands were common during the early years of the GATT[8]; even during recent years when laissez-faire attitudes have been prevalent, there have been quite clear examples of differential enforcement, such as the requirement of the GATT waivers for balance-of-payments surcharges.[9]

More severe enforcement pressures would not be all bad. If it is true that less government intervention is better than more intervention, it follows that developing countries will actually gain economically from stronger GATT discipline. But the economic benefits will not do much to diminish the short-term political cost.

It seems fair to conclude that, in most developing countries, the governments wishing to follow a liberal trade policy have essentially the same internal needs for political assistance that governments of developed countries have and that acceptance of a reciprocity-based GATT legal relationship would also work for them in generating the kind of additional political support needed. There will be problems in obtaining (or creating) the kind of reciprocity needed to win initial support, and this problem must be overcome for the policy to work at all.[10] There will also be problems in withstanding the political costs of GATT discipline once it exists. But if governments want to create political support for following a liberal trade policy, GATT legal relationships have the capacity to provide it. The GATT's current legal policy, by comparison, has a far different impact. In the case of the developing country wishing to pursue a liberal trade policy, the current no-obligations policy is certainly providing no assistance and is probably an active political impediment.

The distinctive character of the current policy is not that it permits import protection but that it makes no real effort to limit or to control such protection. Instead of providing politicians and officials with grounds to oppose trade barriers, the GATT's current policy constitutes an authoritative blessing for them. It tells every participant in the decision-making process that trade barriers can be "necessary to economic development". More important, instead of trying to enlist the support of the export sector for liberal trade policy, the GATT's current policy seeks to insulate the export sector's economic interests from the trade-policy decisions taken by its government. The whole point of the non-reciprocity doctrine is to protect developing-country export markets from any negative effects caused by protectionism at home. To the extent that it is successful, the non-reciprocity doctrine tends to remove the major incentive that export industries have (or at least the major incentive they can see and understand) for opposing protectionist trade policies at home. The overall effect of the GATT's current policy, then, is to intensify the political forces pressing politicians to use import protection as a solution to most problems. It is not an exaggeration to say that developing countries wishing to pursue a liberal trade policy would be better off leaving the GATT entirely than trying to conduct policy on the basis of the GATT's present policy.[11]

FOLLOWING INFANT-INDUSTRY POLICIES

The case that remains to be considered is the one which rests on the contrary economic assumption that trade intervention policies can be economically beneficial. The question to be asked is whether acceptance of GATT obligations would make it possible for governments to pursue such policies more effectively, or whether the current no-obligations status would be more advantageous.

It is difficult to answer this question in a way that will cover all possible variations of the assumption. For example, if intervention is justified under the assumption that absolutely every case of intervention is beneficial, it would have to be conceded that the current no-obligations policy would be superior, for it would impose no constraint on protectionist policies. On the other hand, if intervention is being justified under the more sophisticated assumptions of the infant-industry argument presented in the previous chapter, the benefit of the no-obligations policy is far less clear.

The infant-industry argument accepts the general tenets of comparative advantage theory, but it argues that markets are imperfect and that government intervention policies can improve on the outcomes that markets would produce if left alone. To make sound investment decisions overall, however, governments must still be able to refuse to undertake wasteful investments. Thus governments seeking to operate such an interventionist policy actually need the same sort of powers to resist protectionist demands that are needed under liberal trade-policy regimes.

There is nothing in the infant-industry economic assumptions to change the likelihood that political pressures will favor wasteful intervention. The political behavior of import-competing industries is a constant, as is their ten-dency towards disproportionate strength. Indeed, their strength will probably be even greater in the interventionist milieu being assumed here, for once gov-ernment undertakes an active program of intervention, every failing industry in the country will seek to invoke government aid. Given the tendency in many developing countries to accept few, if any, of the world's economic disadvan-tages as natural, most will be entitled to consideration. In short, developing-country governments following active interventionist policies are going to need all the outside help they can get in order to contain such forces.

Nor is there anything in the infant-industry economic assumptions that would change the kind of assistance GATT obligations could give. External threats can still provide the kind of bogeyman justification described earlier, as can affirmative support from exporters.

One set of GATT obligations could be applied fully without causing any interference with interventionist policies, namely those obligations that pro-hibit especially pernicious protective devices such as arbitrary technical and safety standards, arbitrary customs valuation or quota-licensing procedures and so forth. Governments following trade intervention programs have no need to use such crude policy instruments and should welcome GATT assistance in rejecting them.[12]

An interventionist policy presumably would require greater freedom under the key obligations regarding tariffs and quantitative import restrictions, those that control the basic level of protection. The GATT, however, already con-tains such a provision. Article XVIII permits special infant-industry protection, but it requires a GATT review of the economic justification, together with subsequent monitoring to make sure that the special protection is temporary. This procedure is just the kind of outside pressure a government official would need to help turn away claims from inefficient industries: "Sorry, but we have to clear these protectionist measures in the GATT, and 'they' (the bogeymen developed countries) would never accept this."

Article XVIII has lain rusting and unused for several decades. Developing countries have stopped asking for permission to impose new trade barriers under Article XVIII, mainly because developed countries have stopped chal-lenging them. The reason for developed-country disinterest has been the seem-ing impossibility of the task, given the almost perpetual balance-of-payments problems and other development excuses.[13] If a new GATT is assumed, how-ever, where developed countries begin to increase regulatory pressure, Article XVIII would still be there as a legal defence for infant-industry policies.

Would Article XVIII give the right balance of pressure and freedom? The developing countries did complain in 1954–55 about the procedure under Article XVIII, arguing that it was too difficult for developing countries to obtain permission for new import protection in deserving cases.[14] It is certainly true that the GATT reviewers did look carefully at the efficiency prospects for the infant-industry investments submitted under Article XVIII, and they did, on occasion, force applicants to trim some projects from their requests. On the other hand, the author has seen no evidence that developing countries were ever really interested in using Article XVIII as a restraining force in their own policy-making processes. In 1955 the objective of developing countries was not to reform Article XVIII, but to escape it.

At the present time, the degree of rigor in Article XVIII would probably raise concern in both directions. The substantive criteria of Article XVIII have been considerably loosened in recent years to a degree that most advocates of liberal trade policy would find excessive. Article XVIII now appears to allow developing countries to set aside tariff bindings and the prohibition of quantitative import restrictions (i) with little or no compensation, (ii) with little or no control as to the purpose of measures taken and (iii) with only a power to disapprove of such measures after they are taken – a power that looks as though it could easily be blocked by the developing-country majority in the GATT.[15] On the other hand, the procedure still provides the developed countries with the opportunity to interrogate developing countries about economic necessity and thus provide an occasion for bullying and other kinds of ad hoc pressures. If the procedure stimulates developed-country interest in stopping a measure, the legal loopholes of Article XVIII will not necessarily prevent them from doing so.

In the final analysis, there is probably no solution that does not require some degree of trust. If nothing were to be gained, of course, there would be no reason to ask the governments of developing countries to take such a risk. But, if the observations which have been made earlier about the difficulty of controlling interventionist policies are correct, then GATT obligations do offer a positive gain for any government pursuing an interventionist policy that involves some judgment about where to intervene. Such governments can acquire substantially greater control over policy, and thus substantially greater welfare gains from it, with the aid of the restraints created by the type of procedure established by Article XVIII. Far from diminishing sovereignty, such legal restraints would increase it.

NOTES AND REFERENCES

1. For other works stressing the importance of GATT law in internal decision-making, see the sources cited in note 2, Chapter 7. For a detailed study of domestic legal and governmental structures on foreign trade matters in the European Community, Japan and the United States, see John H. Jackson, Jean-Victor Louis and Mitsuo

Matsushita, *Implementing the Tokyo Round: National Constitutions and International Economic Rules* (Ann Arbor, Michigan: University of Michigan Press, 1984). For studies of the decision-making process in the administration of United States trade laws, see the works of Stephanie Lenway, Robert E. Baldwin and J. Michael Finger cited in note 2, Chapter 7.

2. For a more detailed view of these various forms of direct impact in the United States, see Robert E. Hudec, "GATT or GABB?", loc. cit.

3. Prior to the more heated times of the 1980s, recorded instances of GATT retaliation were quite rare. From 1947–77, the author's research has uncovered only one instance when a government used its authority to retaliate in response to a legal violation and only six cases in which a government used its right to terminate legal obligations as a form of "compensation" for new trade barriers imposed legally (for example, safeguard measures under GATT Article XIX). See Hudec, *Adjudication of International Trade Disputes*, op. cit., pp. 82–83. The period since 1977 has seen approximately eight to ten such instances, depending on classification. Even in this period, the retaliation has often been largely symbolic; governments will often exercise their right to suspend or terminate a legal obligation owed to the offending party but then will not actually raise any trade barriers.

4. See Kenneth W. Clements and Larry A. Sjaastad, *How Protection Taxes Exporters*, op. cit.

5. The bargain-with-the-devil aspect of the current legal policy deserves a great deal more thought. Final judgment is elusive because it involves judgments about the political success of alternative legal policies that have not been attempted very widely in the political climate of the recent past. In thinking further about such alternatives, two points should be kept in mind:

   (a) The key problem governments confront in trying to follow liberal trade policies is the core of strong opposition from import-competing industries. That core opposition is not something created by misguided mercantilist thinking, nor is it something that can be dissolved by better education in economics. It is a totally rational response based on a completely accurate perception of individual economic interests. The only way to overcome such opposition is to overpower it. The ultimate test of any legal policy, therefore, is its ability to assemble a coalition of interests stronger than the other side and to induce that coalition to act as vigorously as the other side.

   (b) While it cannot be denied that the miseducation generated by the reciprocity doctrine makes it more difficult to educate the political electorate about the actual benefits of trade, it would be a mistake to attribute the overpowering influence of mercantilist thinking to this one source. There are many other sources of mercantilist teaching in most societies, not the least of which is the dedicated and persistent pedagogy of the core protectionist interests. Given the seductive logic of mercantilism to begin with, it is quite possible that the vast majority of the electorate will end up accepting the mercantilist view of trade whatever governments say. Moreover, to the extent that government teaching can have influence, it should not be assumed that the sponsorship of reciprocity doctrine forecloses all other efforts by governments to establish a better understanding of trade. Government officials are usually quite adept at delivering different messages to different audiences, and nowhere is this more true than in the area of international trade policy. In the author's experience, off-the-record advocacy with business and political leaders rises to a considerably more rational level than the table-thumping reciprocity rhetoric usually addressed to the general public. In short, while the reciprocity doctrine does involve a concession to irrational dialogue with voters (who, it must be remembered, have the last word), it does not prevent efforts to establish a more rational policy orientation on the part of leaders who frame the issues. In the author's experience, the number of well-informed leaders is significantly greater today than it was twenty-five years ago. Unfortunately, so is voter interest in international trade issues.

6. Examples can usually be found in the newspaper accounts of almost any debate over proposed trade restrictions. The following statements pertaining to footwear restrictions are typical.

   (a) Statement of the President of the United States, Ronald Reagan, declining to impose import restrictions on footwear imports in spite of a positive escape-clause ruling by the United States International Trade Commission, *Federal Register*, Washington, Vol. 50, 26 August 1985, p. 35205: "Second, import [restrictions] would result in serious damage to US trade in two ways. If the ITC global remedy were imposed US trade would stand to suffer as much as $2.1 billion in trade damage either through compensatory tariff reductions [made by the United States] or retaliatory actions by foreign suppliers. This would mean a loss of US jobs and a reduction in US exports."

   (b) Statement of the Canadian Minister for International Trade, then James Kelleher, on 20 November 1985 explaining the decision to remove footwear quotas, quoted in *International Trade Reporter*, Vol. 2, 1985, p. 1490: "The imposition of quotas invariably raises demands for compensation by countries whose exports are affected. These demands are neither unfair nor unrealistic. They are provided for by the rules of the international trading system which Canada supports. But they are very expensive."

7. See Stephan Haggard, "The Politics of Adjustment: Lessons from the IMF Extended Fund Facility", *International Organization*, Vol. 39, No. 3, 1985, pp. 505–34.

8. See text at notes 7–12, Chapter 2.

9. See text at notes 24–27, Chapter 2.

10. If developing countries adopt a legal policy based on reciprocity and are then unable to demonstrate the requisite reciprocity, the policy will produce exactly the opposite effect from the one intended. Protectionist interests would then be able to seize on the absence of adequate reciprocity as a new justification for retaining trade barriers.

11. It should be noted that the alternative legal policy recommended in this chapter – acceptance of reciprocal GATT legal obligations – will not represent an escape from mercantilist ideas. As was pointed out in the previous section, the GATT's "reciprocity" doctrine is itself a thoroughly mercantilist concept, resting on the premise that trade liberalization is harmful and therefore must be paid for. Thus, while a legal policy based on reciprocity should help governments in developing

countries to generate greater political support for trade liberalization than is possible under the present policy, it will not free their trade policy from whatever negative effects arise from government sponsorship of mercantilist ideas. A reciprocity-based policy remains a bargain with the devil – albeit, it is hoped, a better one than the one developing countries are now committed to. It could be argued, of course, that the bargain will not necessarily be a better one for free-trade entities like Hong Kong or Singapore because the current no-obligations legal policy has evidently not been persuasive enough to interfere with their ability to think rationally about trade policy, whereas the seductive teachings of GATT reciprocity doctrine might persuade them to withhold trade liberalization until they get reciprocity. In the author's view, however, it will be a cold day in Hong Kong before that happens. For further discussion of the possible negative effects of a legal policy based on reciprocity, see note 5.

12. As pointed out in notes 37–40, Chapter 5, this approach to such trade barriers was already evident in the Tokyo Round codes on these subjects.

13. See the discussion at notes 17–22, Chapter 2.

14. See the discussion at notes 7–11, Chapter 2.

15. Two liberalizations of Article XVIII criteria have been made following the amendments made at the 1954–55 Review Session. Both were accomplished without amending the text of Article XVIII itself. The first was a little-noticed footnote called an Ad Article slipped into the Part IV non-reciprocity provision in 1964. The second paragraph of Ad Article XXXVI(8) states that the non-reciprocity principle applies to Article XVIII(A), thereby effectively removing the duty to compensate for increases of bound tariffs under this section. (Compensation rights for Article XVIII(C) quotas were already limited by the 1955 amendments.) The second liberalization was a "decision" taken as a part of the 1979 Tokyo Round Framework Agreements package. "Safeguard Action for Development Purposes", Decision of 28 November 1979, *BISD*, 26th Supplement 209 (1980). The decision made two major changes. It substantially expanded the purposes for which trade barriers can be used to improve existing industries, effectively removing the issue of purpose as a criterion. Then, even more important, it eliminated the requirement of prior approval, replacing it with the same permission for advance implementation of trade barriers that exists in the provisions for "safeguard" measures in Article XIX and which is in fact taken advantage of in every action under Article XIX. The difference is important because, so long as prior approval is required, opponents can block the measure by blocking approval. Where the measure can go into effect first, however, the burden is on opponents to obtain a decision disapproving it – something impossible to do if the developing-country bloc chooses to stop it.

10

Impact on Decisions in Other Governments:
Non-reciprocity

THE FOLLOWING two chapters examine the extent to which the GATT's current policy towards developing countries is likely to be effective in persuading the governments of developed countries to reduce trade barriers or otherwise improve the market access for the exports of developing countries. The present chapter considers the effectiveness of the non-reciprocal legal relationship sought by developing countries. The following chapter will consider the effectiveness of the commitment to obtaining preferential terms of market access.

One general caveat must be entered as to the analysis in both chapters. In principle, the legal policies being advocated by developing countries are meant to apply to all sectors of trade, agricultural as well as industrial. In practice, most of the debate about the effectiveness of those legal policies tends to focus on their effectiveness in lowering trade barriers in the industrial sector. It is usually taken for granted that trade barriers on the agricultural side are more deeply rooted and that more basic reforms may be needed before this or any other legal policy is going to have much chance of success. The analysis in the following two chapters is subject to the same reservation about trade in agricultural products.

BASIC POSITIONS REVIEWED

The debate over the effectiveness of the current non-reciprocal legal relationship between developed and developing countries is essentially a legal debate. All sides would agree that the objective – reduction of trade barriers by developed countries – is economically beneficial for developing countries. Every economic theory from mercantilism to comparative advantage teaches that developing countries would benefit from such liberalization.[1] The issue is one of means – whether a non-reciprocal legal relationship will be more, or less, effective in eliciting such liberalization than a legal relationship based on reciprocity.

Not surprisingly, those who support the GATT's current policy argue that reciprocity is not only wrong in principle but is also ineffective in negotiations between developed and developing countries. More will be gained, they contend, if developing countries focus all their efforts on what will be called "the welfare obligation" – the idea that rich countries have a moral duty (and possibly a legal duty) to assist the development of poorer countries.

Critics of the current non-reciprocal relationship claim that the governments of developed countries will never make significant trade concessions without reciprocity. They acknowledge that some token concessions may be granted in response to welfare demands, but they insist that such concessions will be neither meaningful nor legally secure. Some of the critics predict that the absence of reciprocity will actually make things worse for developing countries because, without reciprocity, developed countries will also have less incentive to observe those GATT obligations already in force.[2]

EXPERIENCE OF THE GATT TO DATE

After years of debate and of gradual compromising, all the key ideas advanced by developing countries – non-reciprocity, preferences, special and differential treatment – were accepted at the formal level during the 1970s. They now appear in several GATT legal texts and in countless declarations. They have also become part of the GATT's daily working life. Delegates from developed countries and GATT officials in the Secretariat now routinely anticipate the policy demands of developing countries when planning for any initiative and, whether or not they agree with such positions, their proposals usually include something to satisfy them.

Demands from developing countries for unilateral liberalization have also produced more than a few tangible responses by governments of developed countries. As early as 1962, the United States Congress granted the President authority to eliminate duties on tropical products on a non-reciprocal basis. Although this 1962 initiative failed when the European Community refused to go along with it, it was an early demonstration that the governments of developed countries were, in some cases, willing to act without reciprocity. Later, in the Kennedy Round negotiations, governments of developed countries made significant and essentially unreciprocated tariff reductions on products of interest to developing countries. They did so again in the Tokyo Round negotiations. Finally, however limited existing GSP programs may be, they do constitute yet another set of unreciprocated tariff reductions on developing-country trade.[3]

So far, the overall improvement in trade opportunities as a result of these by developed countries actions has been mixed. On the positive side, under the MFN clause, developing countries have been granted virtually all GATT tariff reductions since 1947. For industrial products, world markets have generally been open enough to provide market incentives for the development of significant new industries. Indeed, for much of the period, exports of manufactures from developing countries have grown at a rate higher than the trade of developed countries.[4]

On the negative side, however, a disproportionate number of barriers still limit developing-country trade – both existing barriers that have not been lowered and, more important, a growing number of new ones. The major area where existing barriers have remained high is trade in temperate agricultural products, where restrictions generally affect both developed and developing countries alike. In the area of industrial trade, the post-war level of tariffs has been lowered very substantially,[5] but selected high spots do remain, and these high spots tend to be concentrated on labor-intensive products, such as textiles which are made chiefly by producers in developing countries.[6] In addition, the long-standing problem of tariffs that increase progressively according to the degree of processing continues to create fairly high de facto protection against processing industries, another form of protection that particularly affects industries in developing countries.[7]

The most ominous barriers on the industrial side are the growing number of new quantitative restrictions, often in the form of voluntary export restraints, that developed countries are erecting against the most competitive products from developing countries – textiles, shoes, consumer electronics and so forth. The restrictions commonly apply only to exports coming from the developing countries. The Multi-fiber Arrangement, for example, has been used to restrict textile imports from virtually every developing country, but since the beginning there has been a gentlemen's agreement between the United States and the European Community not to restrict each other's trade. Even though these restrictions sometimes permit large volumes of imports to continue, and even to grow a bit, they are capping the most dynamic growth possibilities.[8]

Does the disproportionate number of trade restrictions on industrial exports from developing countries prove that the GATT's current policy of non-reciprocity is actually making things worse? There are two difficulties in accepting that hypothesis. First, it is difficult to know whether the new restrictions are in fact disproportionate to the actual economic dislocation being caused in developed countries. Exports from developing countries consist primarily of labor-intensive products; developed countries usually have the greatest comparative disadvantage in this type of product and thus the industries producing these products are most exposed to damage from import competition.

Second, even if exporters of developing countries are being treated worse than others, it is not at all clear that non-reciprocity is the cause. Developing-country exporters tend to be the new producers in the market, as well as the producers with the lowest prices. As a consequence, they are immediately identified by established producers as the source of any new competitive discomfort. Placing the blame, and most of the burden, on newcomers is not a reaction reserved for newcomers from developing countries. Developed countries had exactly the same reaction when Japan, the first post-war newcomer, began to "disrupt" markets in developed countries in the 1950s and 1960s (after having done so to some extent in the 1920s and 1930s).

If the enquiry is shifted from trade barriers to the more technical question of enforcing GATT legal rights, a similar pattern of results will be found. Once again, it appears that developing countries are doing rather well in terms of formal recognition, but less well in terms of actual results.

Developing countries have begun to use the GATT's adjudicatory, or "dispute settlement", procedures with greater frequency in recent years.[9] The outcomes in the cases actually prosecuted have been reasonably satisfactory. This in itself is something of an accomplishment because complaints by developing countries could well have inspired a chilly reception when claiming a right to enforce legal obligations which the complainants did not regard as binding on themselves. That did not happen. Most delegations from developed countries were not only correct, but were also quite supportive. In most of the cases carried to a formal decision, the developing-country plaintiffs won clear legal decisions in their favor. Moreover, while none of the decisions produced any dramatic changes, plaintiffs in the non-political cases reported that vindication of their legal right had eventually resulted in a worthwhile improvement in treatment.

Unfortunately, these dispute-settlement cases are still quite few when compared with the number of questionable trade restrictions that at present affect exports from developing countries. Most of the discriminatory restrictions against such exports would be in violation of the GATT if imposed directly. For the most part, however, developing countries have agreed to impose these restrictions on themselves, in exchange for market access somewhat more favorable than would be granted if the importing government imposed the quotas. Such agreements are based, obviously, on the belief that the threat of more restrictive quotas is credible – in other words, that GATT law is not capable of deterring the importing-country government from imposing such quotas in the first place. Taken as a whole, the GATT's current policy towards developing countries cannot be graded as either a success or a failure. It does seem to have generated at least enough pressure for trade liberalization to assure what might be called minimally adequate treatment, roughly parallel to what has been given to other newcomers in the past. Given the political and economic weakness of developing countries generally, obtaining even this degree of access in the markets of developed countries is an achievement not to be taken for granted. In terms of what both sides claim to want, however, it cannot yet be called a success.

FRAMEWORK FOR ANALYZING FUTURE IMPACT

The critical issue is the question of future impact. Is it likely that continued assertion of the welfare claims of developing countries will bring about significant improvement in the market access granted by developed countries? Or, on the other hand, would developed countries provide greater trade opportunities if developing countries accepted equivalent GATT legal disciplines?

The answer to these questions depends primarily on understanding the manner in which trade-policy decisions are made in developed countries. As pointed out in the previous chapter, the process of persuading governments to reduce trade barriers is not a process that involves bending the will of some monolithic entity. Rather, it is a process of persuasion built on the recognition that the political landscape in most countries already contains significant forces favorable to liberal trade policy and that the way to induce governments to adopt more liberal trade measures is to supply those allies with additional sources of political power. To evaluate the effectiveness of any GATT legal policy, therefore, it is first necessary to identify the favorably disposed forces already on the scene and then to determine how much the legal policy in question is likely to augment the power which those allies already have.

PROBABLE IMPACT OF A NON-RECIPROCITY POLICY

Proponents of the GATT's current welfare-based legal policy argue that it already generates considerable political support for improving market access for the trade of developing countries. They also argue that it is likely to generate even more support if developing countries keep hammering away at it. This argument has two dimensions: one legal, the other political.

The Issue of Legal Force

As noted in Part I of this study, the effort in recent years to define a new "international law of economic development" has included, as one of the new obligations to be recognized, a duty of preferential and non-reciprocal treatment towards developing countries.[10] If such a duty were recognized as an obligation of customary international law, binding on all governments, this would obviously make a major contribution to the success of the non-reciprocity policy.

There can be no disagreement about the number of formal endorsements given to welfare obligations in the past two decades in resolutions, declarations, legal texts and government practice. Developed countries have viewed formal acts of recognition as an inexpensive way of responding to demands from developing countries for trade liberalization, and they have spent this form of currency rather lavishly. As noted before, the number of quasi-commitments has already persuaded many legal scholars to characterize the welfare concept as a sort of quasi-law, using various labels such as "soft law", "legal principle", "law-in-the-making" and "obligation of good faith".

In the author's view, however, this is as far as the legal force of the welfare obligation can ever go. Governments can, of course, undertake voluntary contractual obligations providing for whatever preferential and non-reciprocal treatment they choose. But, however much endorsement it receives, the welfare concept itself is incapable of being defined with the kind of specificity needed to establish a meaningful obligation of customary international law, applicable to the governments of all developed countries. There is no general principle of legal theory that can be used to determine the specific rights and duties such legal obligations would entail: No legal theory can tell us how much a particular disadvantaged party is entitled to receive from any particular advantaged party, or how much a particular advantaged party is obliged to give.[11]

The examples of redistributive justice found in national tax and welfare laws do not supply such a principle. Such laws do not create citizen-to-citizen rights and duties. They are always structured as public law – the extra duties of the rich (for example, paying higher taxes) are owed to the sovereign rather than to particular deserving claimants; the rights of the deserving poor (for example, rights to welfare payments) are recognized as an obligation owed by the sovereign rather than by any individual taxpayer.[12] In order to establish preferential legal relationships between individuals, an entirely different legal structure would be needed – one that defined the relative status of each participant, in a manner at least as elaborate as medieval feudalism. Feudal law did manage to define such an intricate system of status gradation and thus was able to enforce status-defined rights and duties. Neither national nor international legal systems of the modern era possess the tools needed to take that first step.

In the absence of a principled basis for defining specific obligations, the "law" of the welfare concept will never be able to answer any operative questions. It will be unable to state authoritatively whether or not a particular developing country does or does not have a legal right to some specific kind of treatment that it wants. Indeed, since it cannot even furnish a principled definition of "developing country", such a law will never be able to say whether advanced developing countries have any rights at all.[13] To put the matter concretely, if developed countries were to exclude the top fifteen developing countries from the GSP tomorrow and were to demand full reciprocity from them on pain of retaliation, there would be no basis on which a tribunal could adjudicate the legal correctness of that action.

In sum, the emerging international law of economic development will not be able to add any legal force to the demand of developing countries for non-reciprocal liberalization by developed countries. The only source of additional liberalization will be the same source developing countries have always looked to – liberalization by negotiation. The only form of legally binding welfare rights they can hope to achieve will be the contractual rights that emerge from this process. For concessions on an MFN basis, the non-reciprocity strategy will continue to require the one-sided negotiating practices used in the Kennedy Round and Tokyo Round negotiations. Such negotiating practices would also be the exclusive route to any legal binding of preferences, if that should ever happen.

The Issue of Political Force

Once the legal mirage disappears, it becomes clear that the effectiveness of the GATT's current non-reciprocal legal relationship, in terms of its impact on decision-making in developed countries, will depend on the sum of the political forces that can be mustered to support unilateral liberalization. The number of different political forces supporting this policy is quite substantial. In the previous chapter, what might be called the bedrock sources of such support were described – the economic interests and the policy preferences that tend to support liberal trade policy in nearly every instance. In addition to these bedrock sources, there are also many other sources of support that can be counted on when developing-country trade is involved.

The most visible, of course, is the moral force of the welfare obligation itself. The political strength of this idea has been demonstrated repeatedly in the post-war world, not merely in trade-policy actions but in dozens of other areas where some form of unilateral economic assistance has been provided. It is sometimes said that such assistance is never genuinely altruistic; it occurs only when it is beneficial to domestic interests in the donor country. The author believes such assertions under-estimate the independent influence of moral convictions held by government officials, but, even if the assertion is true, it does not mean the welfare idea is politically ineffective. On the contrary, the fact that local interests use the welfare idea to advance their own well-being means that they believe it helps them. Thus it does not matter that the welfare obligation will be most fervently advocated by importers, bank creditors and other domestic interests that benefit from a liberal trade policy. If it works for them, it will also be working for developing countries.

A second added source of political support for a liberal trade policy towards developing countries is the "tinder box" phenomenon. The general vulner-ability of developing countries to political and economic instability tends to magnify the risks of adopting policies that are economically harmful to them. This, in turn, magnifies the political attention given by those interests in devel-oped countries who stand to be injured if adverse trade-policy actions cause harm. Concern over the potentially destructive effects of the debt burdens of developing countries, for example, currently exercises a major influence in favor of liberal trade policy towards developing countries.

A third special source of political support for the liberalization of developing-country trade is a phenomenon that might be called "built-in reciprocity". Developing countries typically need many more imported goods than their currency earnings can pay for. Increased earnings, therefore, usually mean increased imports, even where no legal promise of reciprocity has been made. Many exporters in developed countries will thus find it in their economic interest to support liberal trade policies towards the exports of developing countries (as well as grants, loans and anything else that increases purchasing power). They will stand to benefit from such policies whether or not the developing country offers legally binding reciprocity in return.

Finally, GATT law itself should probably be counted as a source of support for the interest of developing countries. After almost forty years, the GATT's code of legal obligations has begun to acquire the respect of a legal system built right on norms that command respect, not merely because they have been paid for, but also because they define correct and responsible government behavior. Time has also endowed GATT obligations with a quality of law in the institutional sense, so that GATT obligations now possess a certain amount of respect-for-law force independent of their substance. This larger perception of GATT law can already be seen in the handling of legal complaints brought by developing countries. GATT law may be of only limited force, but it does seem to cover the non-paying member.

These various factors ensure that, reciprocity apart, the political structure in most developed countries will contain substantial forces favoring improved market access for the exports of developing countries. These are the polit-ical forces that have produced the not insubstantial degree of unilateral liberalization achieved so far. They will be the foundation of whatever future impact a legal policy built on the welfare obligation will have.

What, then, can be said about the probable future impact of these forces, assuming continued assertion of the current non-reciprocity policy? One factor which is likely to become a source of increased political support for unilateral liberalization is the "tinder box" phenomenon. In the author's view, the rate of political and economic crises in developing countries seems likely to accelerate in the decades ahead. If this is so, there should be more pressure to avoid adding to the problem with adverse trade policies.

On the other hand, it seems doubtful whether the basic welfare obligation can contribute any more to the political balance than it has already. In the first place, there are limits on the amount of political force that the welfare idea can generate. The moral obligation to poor countries may be felt very strongly, but it is often difficult to demonstrate that a meaningful share of the trade benefits are going to the poorer developing countries, or that benefits of any kind are going to poor people in any country. In addition, welfare benefits given through trade liberalization tend to involve a rather inequitable way of distributing the cost. Trade opportunities given to other countries are paid for, in large part, by the economic suffering of those who look like the domestic poor – the domestic workers being injured by increased imports.[14] Nothing blunts a sense of duty to the poor as effectively as a competing sense of duty to another poor person closer to home.

In the second place, the campaign itself is already beginning to show signs of having peaked. It is now more than ten years since the declaration of the New International Economic Order, which constituted an almost totally unqualified endorsement as far as trade issues were concerned. Subsequent efforts to make the political consensus even stronger seem to have lost conviction and to have fallen into something of a formalistic rut. The word "rut" would also describe the pattern of responses by developed countries during the past decade.

In the author's view, the reason why the non-reciprocity policy appears to be at a standstill is that it is increasingly confronting a type of trade problem that it is not strong enough to deal with. The trade problem in question is the "safeguard" situation – the demand for new trade restrictions because of damaging foreign competition. Political support built on general policy preferences can be fairly effective in orienting overall policy towards a goal of trade liberalization. It is considerably less effective, however, when it comes to dealing with the problem of those whose economic interests are being threatened by competition and who are therefore demanding emergency protection.[15] In those cases, effective opposition to new trade barriers usually requires having enough economic power to threaten other equally important economic interests. A legal relationship based primarily on the welfare obligation is not capable of generating such power.

The bottom line on the non-reciprocity policy, then, is that it does not seem likely to produce any significant improvement in the trade policies of developed countries. On the other hand, the policy does seem to enjoy considerably more political support than most observers give it credit for – enough, it appears, to keep alive the more general commitment to the liberalization of trade with developing countries that was witnessed in the 1960s and 1970s. This is an impact not to be dismissed lightly. It remains to be proved that a legal policy based on reciprocity will do better.

PROBABLE IMPACT OF A POLICY BASED ON RECIPROCITY

In the previous chapter, some general observations were offered about the influence of reciprocity on decision-making in the governments of developed countries. It was noted that, although the political forces in most developed countries would generate significant support for a liberal trade policy even without reciprocity, a legal framework based on reciprocity adds important strength to such forces. It was then suggested that reciprocity would have a similar impact on the decision-making process in the governments of developing countries as well, and for that reason the adoption of reciprocal GATT obligations was recommended as an aid to more effective decision-making. The present section addresses the question of whether these general conclusions hold true in the specific case at issue – whether reciprocity from developing countries in particular will make it easier for the governments of developed countries to follow a more liberal trade policy towards them.

In theory, the same phenomena would seem to exist in this case as in others. If developing countries were to offer additional market opportunities for exporters in developed countries, contingent on reciprocity, that offer should give exporters an added reason to support liberal trade policies by their own government in return. Moreover, two recent cases seem to offer tangible proof that the theory works. In 1984, the Peoples' Republic of China appeared to be successful in enlisting the support of agricultural exporters in the United States in opposing new textile restraints by threatening to cut off projected grain purchases.[16] At about the same time, Malaysia persuaded Sweden to withdraw restrictions on rubber boots by threatening to cut off purchases of trucks.[17] Nonetheless, when the question is posed in terms of the actual situation in the world today, the theoretical answer seems unpersuasive. The issue might be posed in practical terms as follows: "Compared with the trade policies they are presently following, would governments in developed countries really be able to follow a more liberal trade policy towards developing countries if the latter were to offer reciprocity?" Intuitively, the answer would seem to be: "No, developed countries are already doing a certain amount, with difficulty most of the time, and it is hard to believe that reciprocity from developing countries will help overcome the forces now preventing further liberalization."

Further reflection suggests several reasons for this scepticism. In the first place, as the preceding section has pointed out, there are already many special political forces working on behalf of liberal trade policies towards developing countries in particular. This means that developing countries already have the benefit of many kinds of political support not available on general trade issues. Some of the support that reciprocity might add is already in place.

Second, there are a number of reasons why exporters in developed countries will be reluctant to expend very much political effort in exchange for new trade commitments by developing countries:

(a) The markets in a majority of developing countries, unlike the market in China, are still quite small. Moreover, even in those developing-country markets that are becoming significant,[18] the long history of balance-of-payments problems and other trade-restricting crises in developing countries will often lead exporters to discount the future value of whatever new market opportunities are offered. The drastic import cutbacks by many developing countries during the early days of the recent debt crisis are the most immediate reminder of how quickly things can change.

(b) It must be recognized that commitments by developing countries to reduce trade barriers do not appear to make much difference to the amount of market access that exporters can expect. Most developing countries already import as much as their foreign-exchange earnings permit, without any legal commitments at all. Consequently, exporters already have very significant incentives to press their own governments for any trade liberalization that will improve the earning power of developing countries. The prospect of legal commitments is not likely to make them do more. (The fact that lower trade barriers would eventually permit developing countries to export more, and thus to earn enough to import more, is seldom perceived.[19])

(c) There is also reason to wonder whether developing countries can do much to influence exporters in developed countries by threatening to close their export markets. Threatening large countries can be dangerous. To be sure, the examples just cited of threats by China and Malaysia demonstrate that such threats can sometimes be made without triggering a warlike response. Indeed, there will also be many cases where the governments of developed countries will actually welcome such threats as an aid to resisting protectionist forces at home. Still, most developing countries operate in an environment where developed

countries hold many other interests hostage, so that developing countries always have to be careful about not jeopardizing such interests.
There is always next year's textile quota to worry about. In this situation,
even threats welcomed by the governments of developed countries are
not always risk-free. Moreover, even where threats are feasible, developing countries do not necessarily need a legal relationship based on
reciprocity in order to make them. Developing countries already have
fairly broad powers to close their markets because, under the GATT's
current legal policy towards developing countries, they are reasonably
free to raise trade barriers as they wish. Neither the Chinese nor the
Malaysian cases already mentioned involved threats based on GATT
retaliation rights.

(d) Finally, the fact that many exporters in developed countries seem quite
content with the present situation raises the question of whether there
may not be factors which make exporters prefer not to have GATT-
bound obligations on their side. One factor which might explain these
attitudes is that the import markets in developing countries are controlled, typically, by quantitative restrictions and that the officials who
administer these restrictions have considerable discretion as to whom
access is given. In cases where government control over markets is
extensive, the key to selling successfully is, usually, skill in dealing with
bureaucrats and others in power, rather than lower trade barriers or
lower prices. Those who know how to manipulate the system do not
necessarily want to see the system changed.

In brief, it is possible to sympathize with the scepticism expressed by many
officials in developing countries concerning the effectiveness of legal policies
based on reciprocity. To be sure, it can never be said that an offer of reciprocity will have no effect whatsoever. Moreover, it seems likely that China
and probably a few other advanced developing countries will one day soon
reach a position where reciprocity matters. But for most developing countries,
including most of the larger ones, reciprocity is not likely to have much impact
on the number and size of new export opportunities. Given this forecast, it
can be understood how developing countries, having got this far on the basis
of the non-reciprocity doctrine, might believe it wisest (not to mention easiest)
to keep following that same path.

SIGNIFICANCE OF THE GRADUATION DOCTRINE

The recent "graduation" doctrine advanced by the United States would appear
to be evidence contrary to the author's general scepticism about the value of

reciprocity for developing countries.[20] According to the graduation doctrine, reciprocity will now be expected of advanced developing countries, and the market access they receive will henceforth depend on whether they do in fact make reciprocal concessions. Taken literally, the doctrine means that a non-reciprocity policy is no longer viable.

To begin with, it should be emphasized that the graduation position of the United States demands reciprocity only from the more advanced developing countries. The not-so-prosperous developing countries are not included. For them, the graduation policy is actually an official confirmation that reciprocity is neither expected nor wanted. In the view of the United States Administration, presumably, reciprocity is not very relevant to its ability to maintain liberal trade policies towards such countries. This often-neglected side of the graduation doctrine should be underlined. It is a quite important statement of policy; it covers most developing countries.

With respect to the more advanced developing countries, it is obvious that their refusal to give reciprocity is causing some kind of problem. It is less clear just what the problem is, or how serious it is. There are actually several different kinds of demand for graduation in the policy of the United States and also several different explanations of the policy objectives behind the doctrine.

The graduation concept is sometimes used to describe a reciprocity requirement for new liberalization in future trade negotiations. The idea is that advanced developing countries will have to offer reciprocity or else developed countries will not grant any further trade liberalization on products of interest to them. A further threat is sometimes also implied. Contrary to the traditional reciprocity rule for trade negotiations, where all concessions are made or withdrawn on an MFN basis, the United States' demands for graduation occasionally threaten a discriminatory denial of benefits (the so-called conditional MFN approach). Indeed, in the Tokyo Round negotiations, the United States actually has discriminated by denying the trade benefits both of the Subsidies Code and of the Government Procurement Code to any country which has not signed.[21]

Graduation has also been mentioned in the context of emergency safeguard measures that are imposed when imports of a particular product cause injury to a local industry. The suggestion here is that it will be more difficult to protect developing countries against unwarranted or excessive restrictions if they have not paid for the market access that is being objected to. Given the large number of such restrictions that have already been imposed against developing countries, many of them discriminatory, the reference to reciprocity in this context sounds rather like rationalization of a situation that already exists.

Finally, graduation comes up in the context of taking away special benefits like GSP. In this area, the term seems to have two different meanings. The first, which might be called "pure graduation", lays down that since the advantages of the GSP are unilateral concessions granted to help poor developing countries, GSP must lose its justification when countries reach a certain level of economic development; at that point, GSP treatment should be withdrawn entirely. The GSP legislation in the United States does provide for such absolute termination of GSP benefits when certain thresholds of per capita income are reached. On the other hand, the same legislation also provides for what might be called "quasi-graduation", under which advanced developing countries with a somewhat lower per capita income are permitted to retain GSP benefits, but only if they pay for them by adopting more liberal commercial and investment policies.[22]

The official justification for the graduation demand makes no economic sense. It is simply an extension of the same discredited mercantilist concepts that were used to justify the non-reciprocity doctrine in the first place – the view that trade liberalization is a form of payment that transfers economic benefits from the government making it to the government receiving it and that poor countries should not be asked to pay. The graduation doctrine merely carries these ideas one step further, declaring that advanced developing countries are rich enough to pay like everyone else.

When pressed for a better explanation, government officials usually respond with one of three answers. Some officials readily admit that the explanation is economic nonsense but they nonetheless justify the demand for reciprocity as a form of coercive altruism. Developed countries, they say, should coerce advanced developing countries into adopting policies that are in the long-term self-interest of the latter. While this seems a bit rough, they admit, most developing countries actually need this kind of extra push after decades of being nourished on GATT doctrines which affirm the need for protectionist policies in developing countries. *In terrorem* threats of retaliation by developed countries, they contend, are about the only political justification powerful enough to permit governments in those countries to adopt more liberal trade policies.

At the other extreme is a second group of officials who appear honestly to have taken the GATT's mercantilist economics to heart and to be genuinely upset by the refusal to pay. This kind of self-indoctrination is not supposed to occur, but the average GATT trade-policy official has so much daily contact with the idea of reciprocity, in various forms, that it often does become internalized. There is, first of all, the constant dialogue with individuals representing business interests where there is genuine economic interest in reciprocity. Next, there are the dealings with political leaders, who have a mercantilist-type concern over equitable sharing of political burdens and who become irritated when officials in other governments transfer more than their fair share of political problems to others. Finally, there is the daily practice of diplomacy itself, where reciprocal effort is simply a basic expectation. It is the rare GATT diplomat who has never become angry with the French.

Somewhere between the first two groups is a third group of officials who say that, while they themselves do not swallow the mercantilist logic of graduation, they are forced to take that position because there are powerful business and political interests in their countries that do believe it very strongly. The graduation concept, in other words, comes from the legislators and their business constituents. Right or wrong, these officials say, such demands for graduation are a political reality and governments must respond to them if they wish to retain support for their trade policy. This third explanation of the graduation doctrine is the only one which gives reason to believe that reciprocity will in fact have some impact on the political viability of liberal trade policies towards the exports of developing countries.[23]

If the reciprocity complaints underlying this third explanation are probed further, however, it is evident that they rest on something a little different from the normal economic interest in reciprocity. It is interesting, for example, that complaints against advanced developing countries tend to describe those countries, not in terms of per capita income levels but in terms of export volumes to the United States. They are, in the main, complaints from the United States' industries affected by that import competition. The performance of these developing-country exporters is used to argue that they are equals in a business sense. If they are big enough to market effectively in the United States, the complainants are saying, they are certainly big enough to accept the risks of competitive discomfort in their home markets.

This type of reciprocity concern is primarily defensive in character. Although there have been some complaints in product sectors where two-way trade is a possibility (for example, trade in commuter aircraft between the United States and Brazil), most of the complaints are from domestic producers who have no illusions about being able to compete in the home market of the developing-country producers. The complainants are not really interested in lowering trade barriers abroad. They are mainly interested in reciprocity or, rather, the lack of it as a justification for more protection at home.

Given this configuration of domestic economic interests behind the graduation doctrine, it follows that the primary political consequence of developing-country reciprocity would be to supply government officials with a counter-argument against these somewhat disingenuous demands for more protection. Such reciprocity will have political value because it will in fact help government officials to justify resistance to protectionist demands. It will not, however, change anything in the basic alignment of economic interests.

In particular, it will not create any greater involvement of the export sector. The basic perception here – and it is an empirical one – is that the export sector is neither behind nor much affected by the demand for reciprocity inherent in the graduation doctrine.

So far, action by the United States under the graduation principle has tended to confirm this view. Much has been demanded, but when strong resistance has been encountered, the government of the United States has usually been willing to settle for just enough to hold off Congressional criticism. The United States did extract somewhat more reciprocity from developing countries in the Tokyo Round negotiations than in previous negotiations. It also adopted a fairly harsh conditional MFN policy when implementing the Subsidies Code and the Procurement Code, but then most of the significant discriminatory exclusions were later cancelled in practice.[24] The 1984 legislation renewing GSP authority ordered the President to withdraw GSP from quasi-graduated countries who do not grant reciprocity, but no action was required for two years. More vigorous action may be expected during the period when the Administration is seeking legislative authority for a new round of trade negotiations, but it remains to be seen whether it will endure.

In sum, reciprocity has become more important in trade policy towards advanced developing countries, but not in the usual sense. The United States Administration will no doubt continue to answer protectionist demands at home by promising to obtain some kind of reciprocity from developing countries. Failure to honor these promises in some fashion will be dangerous and could result in denial of benefits in future trade negotiations, in GSP matters and possibly in the administration of safeguard measures. But, without the involvement of the export sector, this new reciprocity game is unlikely to offer any prospect of positive gain for developing countries.

Moreover, if the graduation game continues to be played at its present level, the reciprocity stakes are unlikely be raised very high. It will be more a game than a negotiation, a game that involves assembling symbolic kinds of reciprocity to counter disingenuous reciprocity demands by industries seeking protection. The situation is reminiscent of the Royal Air Force practice, during World War II, of dropping wooden bombs on cardboard aerodromes.

SUMMARY AND CONCLUSIONS

The preceding analysis can be summarized in three propositions:

(a) The non-reciprocity doctrine of the GATT's current policy has demonstrated a considerable degree of political effectiveness in assembling support within developed countries for liberal trade policies towards developing countries. That support is probably strong enough to sustain a continuing policy attitude favorable to unilateral trade liberalization for developing countries. It has not been strong enough, so far, to protect developing-country trade from a growing number of discriminatory trade barriers. Nor is it likely to become strong enough in the future to prevent the continuance of this sort of trade-limiting behavior.

(b) It is unlikely that a legal policy based on traditional GATT reciprocity would generate significantly more political support. The political consequences of reciprocity from developing countries are simply not the same as those in the usual situation where reciprocity matters. The United States' graduation doctrine requires only a partial qualification to this conclusion. For the majority of developing countries, the graduation doctrine actually affirms that reciprocity will make no difference at all in their treatment. For the others, it is primarily a threat to existing access, not a promise that reciprocity will earn something better.

(c) The graduation doctrine means that advanced developing countries may have to offer some degree of reciprocity if they wish to avoid a deterioration of their trade position. As the graduation game is at present constructed, however, it would appear that these threats can be avoided by making rather limited concessions that would not, by themselves, require any overall change in trade policies of developing countries.

If market access were the only economic gain at issue, the lesson to be learned from the preceding three conclusions would be rather clear. Developing countries would have no reason to abandon the non-reciprocity doctrine of the GATT's present policy. The current policy may not be capable of improving market access as much as developing countries would like, but a policy based on reciprocity is unlikely to do much better.

This is not, of course, the final answer, because access to foreign markets is not the only economic benefit that a policy based on reciprocity can achieve. The previous chapter has pointed out that GATT legal obligations can achieve economic gains simply by assisting a government to follow a more rational trade policy at home.

Such policies can work only if governments are able to demonstrate enough reciprocal benefits to enlist the support of exporters. The fact that reciprocity appears unlikely to increase the present pace of trade liberalization will clearly present difficulties in this regard. As pointed out in the previous chapter, however, reciprocity can be found in whatever modest gains in market access do occur and can credibly be linked to the maintenance of existing market opportunities as well. In the author's view, therefore, the internal gains from a legal policy based on reciprocity are ultimately attainable.

NOTES AND REFERENCES

1. There would, of course, be disagreement over the economic desirability of MFN tariff liberalization that reduced margins of preference under GSP. The issue of preferences is treated as a separate, sequential question in Chapter 11.
2. See sources cited in note 1 of the introduction to Part II and note 1 of Chapter 7.
3. These measures are discussed in Chapters 3, 4 and 5.
4. The percentage share of total world exports by developing countries increased only negligibly between 1963 and 1984 – from 16 percent to 16.5 percent of trade excluding fuels, *International Trade 1984–85* (Geneva: GATT Secretariat, 1985) p. 6. For manufactures, however, the share of developing countries grew from 7.5 percent of world manufactured exports in 1965 to 15.9 percent in 1983, according to World Bank statistics. Anne O. Krueger and Constantine Michalopoulos, "Developing-country Trade Policies and the International Economic System", loc. cit., p. 47. For more detailed analysis of the rather high growth rates involved, see Helen Hughes and Anne O. Krueger, "Effects of Protection in Developed Countries on Developing Countries' Exports of Manufactures", loc. cit., and Donald B. Keesing, "Manufactured Exports from Developing Countries", in Khadija Haq (ed.), *Equality of Opportunity Within and Among Nations* (New York: Praeger, 1977) pp. 98–103.
5. Most estimates place the 1947 tariff rates at between 30 and 60 percent *ad valorem* and the current post–Tokyo Round rates at between 4 and 8 percent for the United States, the European Community and Japan.
6. See Alexander J. Yeats, *Trade Barriers Facing Developing Countries* (London: Macmillan, 1979) pp. 64–79. See also Hughes and Krueger, "Effects of Protection in Developed Countries on Developing Countries' Exports of Manufactures", loc. cit., pp. 392–97.
7. For a detailed description and analysis of the escalation phenomenon, see Yeats, op. cit., pp. 79–100.
8. For an overview of all the major (and acknowledged) non-tariff barriers affecting the exports of manufactures of developing countries, see Hughes and Krueger, "Effects of Protection in Developed Countries on Developing Countries' Exports of Manufactures", loc. cit. On the structure and effects of the Multi-fibre Arrangement, see Donald B. Keesing and Martin Wolf, *Textile Quotas Against Developing Countries*, Thames Essay No. 23 (London: Trade Policy Research Centre, 1980). It must be acknowledged that the effect of such restrictions is not always to bring export growth to a halt: GATT data for textile and apparel imports shows a very substantial 58 percent growth in imports into the United States for the years 1981 to 1984. The same data shows nearly flat, or negative, growth in the markets of other developed countries. *International Trade 1984–85*, op. cit., Appendix, Table A-15.
9. See notes 13 and 14, Chapter 5.

10. See the text at notes 4–13, Chapter 6, and the sources given in note 10 in the same chapter.

11. This appears to have been the conclusion of the UNITAR study, see note 4, Chapter 6. Also of the same view is Damien Hubbard, "The International Law Commission and the New International Economic Order", loc. cit.

12. The GATT may be playing a very small role as a redistributing sovereign, for it collects member-country dues and then spends the funds on GATT projects. If Secretariat expenditures devoted to special programs for developing countries in the GATT are larger than the receipts from those countries, the GATT is redistributing.

13. The GATT itself has never succeeded in defining "developing country" for the purposes of administering various GATT legal provisions that use that term (or its predecessor, "less developed country"). For example, the author knows of at least two cases when the Balance of Payments Committee was unable to come to agreement over whether a particular country was entitled to the special review procedures for developing countries under Article XVIII, or whether the procedures under Article XII, applicable to everyone else, were called for. The countries were Portugal and Israel. In both cases, it was agreed that the Committee would simply conduct the review without deciding what kind of review it was.

14. As is usually pointed out in such debates, the industries in developed countries with the greatest exposure to competition from the developing countries are the labor-intensive industries such as clothing and apparel, where employees tend to be the least skilled workers, with the lowest earning power and the greatest problems in adjusting.

15. J. Michael Finger makes the point that the same distinction is also important in terms of how the general public perceives trade issues:

> We have a different view of trade when we view it as a global issue and when we view it as an industry by industry matter. Our global view is probably more political than economic, relates to our individualistic, laissez-faire traditions and mentality, and in any case, emphasizes the gains from such an arrangement over its costs. Our micro view is probably more economic than political and emphasizes the costs, or injury, from trade. It concentrates on the benefits of restricting imports on individual products without paying attention to the costs of that restriction.

> J. Michael Finger, "Ideas Count, Words Inform", in R.H. Snape (ed.), *Issues in World Trade Policy: GATT at the Crossroads* (London: Macmillan, 1986). Finger's "we" is arguably the same group of citizens as those described in the preceding pages – those who support unilateral trade liberalization for developing countries on grounds of general policy convictions, moral obligations and the like. This study has suggested that the power of this "we" tends to be ineffective when confronting specific industry requests for protection. Finger is adding the important point that the supporters themselves have diminished convictions in this micro setting. Quite so.

16. See "House Republicans Write Baldridge, Citing Threat to Exports in PRC Textile Case", *Import Weekly*, Bureau of National Affairs, Washington, Vol. 9, 1984, p. 358.

17. Interview with the GATT official involved.
18. Korea, Singapore, Hong Kong, China and Taiwan are now among the top twenty importers in the world, *International Trade 1984–85*, op. cit., p. 11. Singapore and Hong Kong probably should not be listed in this context, however, since their markets are already open. Commentators today in the United States frequently make the point that almost 40 percent of United States exports now go to developing countries; these exports are fairly evenly distributed among all major producing sectors. See, for example, the United States Commerce Department data in Ernest H. Preeg (ed.), *Hard Bargaining Ahead: US Trade Policy and Developing Countries*, op. cit., Annex B-5, p. 205.
19. If exporters were aware that lower trade barriers in developing countries would produce even more export earnings (see Krueger, *Foreign Trade Regimes and Economic Development*, op. cit.) and thus even greater market opportunities, they would probably be more interested in persuading developing countries to give GATT-type reciprocity.
20. For a description of the origin of the graduation doctrine and the GATT Framework decision accepting its principle, see text at notes 1, 2 and 34, Chapter 5. With apologies to several speechwriters, the author knows of no definitive statement of the graduation policy of the United States because its description tends to vary depending on the official involved, the setting and, most of all, the audience. The speech prepared for the United States Congress is usually not the one delivered to the Group of 77. The description and analysis of the graduation doctrine in this work is based on interviews with American officials, leavened with some interpretation and on the record of United States' actions.
21. See text at notes 41–46, Chapter 5.
22. See Chapter 6. The absolute exclusion applies to countries with a per capita GNP of US$8,500 adjusted for inflation as measured by the dollar value of United States gross national product. The discretionary exclusion authority cuts in at US$5,000, similarly adjusted, or at 10 percent of GSP imports, as measured by a special statutory formula far too complex to be described here. Trade and Tariff Act of 1984, Section 505 (b) and (c), 98 Statutes at Large 2948, 3020–3023, 19 USC 2464 (c), (d) and (f).
23. The first two explanations describe attitudes of government officials. By themselves, attitudes of government officials do not change the political acceptability of a policy to liberalize trade. Of course, if angry officials keep telling legislators and constituents that developing countries are going to suffer if they fail to give reciprocity, they may eventually create a political climate in which they will be forced to make that happen.
24. See Chapter 5 and, in particular, note 43.

11

Impact on Decisions in Other Governments: Preferences

THE legal policy currently advocated by developing countries in the GATT contains two seemingly contradictory demands with respect to MFN treatment. The primary demand, reflected in the Enabling Clause, is that the MFN obligation should be set aside to permit preferential terms of entry for the products of developing countries – GSP preferences given by developed countries, GSTP preferences given by developing countries to each other and as much other preferential treatment as may be possible. The second demand, for those areas where preferential access is not given, is strict observance of the MFN obligation by developed countries – in other words, no discrimination against developing countries.

Developing countries argue that the two demands are merely different expressions of the same over-riding obligation to assist developing countries. The governments of developed countries appear to have accepted this position. They have subscribed to the Enabling Clause permitting preferential treatment, but they have never claimed that this exception weakens, in any way, their remaining obligations under the MFN clause.

As policy instruments to promote better market access, both demands made a good deal of sense. Political opposition to trade liberalization tends to be less when it is done on a preferential basis. Domestic industries have no reason at all to oppose so-called "trade-diverting preferences" (those that permit exports from developing countries to displace exports from other countries) because by definition such preferences have no competitive effects on domestic producers. As for other preferential tariff reductions that do cause increased competition with domestic producers, the preferences are still less threatening than MFN tariff reductions, for they confine the new competition to producers from developing countries.

The value of prohibiting developed countries from discriminating against developing-country trade does not need to be explained. Increased enforcement of such a rule would be extremely beneficial at the present time because developed countries are imposing an increasing number of discriminatory safeguard restrictions against exports from developing countries, and the effects are very damaging. While developing countries would obviously prefer exactly the opposite treatment – preferential treatment that excluded them from safeguard restrictions altogether – strict observance of the MFN obligation would be a great improvement on the treatment they are currently receiving.

Critics of the GATT's current policy towards developing countries have no objection to the MFN demands as such. They support vigorous enforcement of the MFN obligation wherever possible, both as a matter of economic policy and as a matter of legal policy. The controversy is over the priority demand of the developing-country policy – the demand for preferential treatment.

The economic criticism of preferences was reviewed in Chapter 8. There is, of course, the general objection to trade diversion *per se* because it reduces world welfare overall. But when the issue is narrowed to whether preferences are beneficial or harmful to developing countries, the critics tend to concede that the net welfare effect of something like GSP preferences is positive, though not very large.

The primary criticism of the preferences policy is the criticism from the legal side. It stands largely independent of the economic criticism. The legal criticism has two parts. First, it argues that government programs of preferential treatment tend to operate in a similar way to the sorcerer's apprentice generating more and more discrimination until the system finally breaks down under its own weight. Second, it argues that policies involving preferential treatment will undermine respect for MFN obligations generally, thereby intensifying the tendency of developed countries to discriminate against exports from developing countries.

Analysis will show that the second criticism is too simple. It is true that respect for the MFN obligation is in decline, and it is probably also true that policies of preferential treatment are contributing to this problem. But the overall decline of the MFN obligation rests on a number of more basic factors, and it is unlikely that changes in the legal policies of developing countries would have much impact by themselves. Consequently, treatment of this second criticism may be deferred until the alternative legal policy improving MFN discipline generally is examined.

The strongest case against preferences is the first branch of the legal criticism – the tendency of preferential treatment programs to destroy themselves.

THE CASE AGAINST PREFERENTIAL TREATMENT POLICIES

So far the experience with the policy of preferential treatment for developing countries has not been very encouraging. Some aspects of the overall GSTP design (developed under the auspices of UNCTAD) have become so refined that the whole scheme is in danger of collapsing because of its complexity. Developed countries have also managed to introduce a bewildering array of complexities and "refinements" into their laws implementing the GSP program. The overall picture is of a web of discrimination becoming so entangled that it is almost impossible to make sense of it anymore.

Proponents of the policy of preferential treatment would argue that the basic concept has been sound and that the current problems are due to inadequate implementation, especially on the part of developed countries. The critics, on the other hand, consider that the current breakdown was inevitable because any trade policy based on preferential treatment carries the seeds of its own destruction. The following paragraphs attempt to describe that inherent flaw.

The current policy of preferential treatment can be said to rest on three major premises which might be labelled efficacy, costlessness and the welfare obligation. Efficacy is the premise that economic outcomes can be manipulated rationally by discrimination by altering the relative impact of trade barriers on various trade participants. All trade protection involves this premise, for even the most ordinary trade barriers are imposed in the belief that they will be advantageous to one body of producers (the domestic producers) by imposing disadvantageous conditions on others. But discrimination is a tool that invites infinitely more complex objectives. Given all the trade barriers of all the countries in the world to work with and a licence to apply them in whatever discriminatory patterns are needed, it would be unrealistic to expect anything except an orgy of fine-tuning. It is an old bureaucratic axiom that the greater the power, the greater the belief that it can be used effectively.

The premise of costlessness is likewise an extension of a basic premise underlying all trade protection. As one author describes it, government officials tend to view ordinary trade protection as a "victimless crime" because those most immediately affected are foreign producers not represented in the political system. Discrimination is even more appealing on these grounds because it is entirely in other countries that immediate harm is caused. Discrimination is, in a sense, the ultimate refinement in the art of making someone else pay. The perception that discrimination is both an effective and a costless tool makes it an all but irresistible instrument for solving problems. All that is needed is the problem. The third premise, that discrimination should be used to satisfy the welfare obligation, supplies such a motive force. Unfortunately, it is a motive force that makes the instrument truly impossible to contain. Once discrimination is legitimized as a proper response to one morally deserving claim (for example, the duty to assist poor countries), it becomes legitimized as a way of responding to other deserving claims as well (for example, the duty to help the very poorest countries a little more). There will always be additional deserving claims waiting their turn. While all of the claims may, in fact, be meritorious, attempting to rewire market forces in order to take care of them all will sooner or later overload the circuit.[1]

The developing countries themselves have had difficulty in keeping the concept of discrimination within bounds. In Part I of this study, a description was given of how far the concept has been allowed to travel. The first extension of the GSP idea seemed harmless enough – the granting of extra discrimination in favor of least developed developing countries (LDDCs). But then, in the planning of the GSTP preferences between developing countries, the planners began to include increasingly complex kinds of discrimination. First came the demand for a more finely tuned distribution of benefits, a claim which required adjusting the level of discrimination in each country so that actual trade results would be equitable. Then, customs unions and other regional groupings asked for special refinements to preserve the economic benefits of the discrimination they were already practicing; this required several more tiers of discrimination. Depending on how many tiers of LDDC discrimination a regional grouping might have, the overall GSTP design could leave individual developing countries with as many as five or six layers in their tariffs, plus an even more complex layering of discrimination in the administration of quantitative controls. At one point, the UNCTAD planners even contemplated raising the MFN rate to give more room for fine tuning in the layers below.[2]

The concern shown for regional groupings in the GSTP planning exposes another factor that acts like a growth hormone. Even though discrimination appears costless at the outset, it often does cause unintended dislocations to friends and other deserving interests. This is not too serious, however, because the policy of discrimination which caused the problem can always supply a cost-free solution – more discrimination. It can be predicted, with a fair degree of certainty, that as soon as GSTP preferences begin to cause dislocation of some established expectations, there will be other proposals, advocating further forms of discrimination, to take care of them. The progressive evolution of the European Community's policy of discriminatory assistance, both its Mediterranean policy and its Lome Convention with ex-colonies in Africa, the Caribbean and the Pacific, is perhaps the most eloquent testimony there is of the inevitable march from one act of discrimination to the next.[3]

These self-inflicted refinements could, by themselves, bring the Enabling Clause system to an impasse. But the process does not end there. Developed countries who grant GSP preferences will also have refinements, for they, too, will have moral insights about when and where preferential treatment should be granted. Developing countries made a serious effort to limit such donor-imposed refinements when the GSP was first launched, but, in a system of benefits based on moral duty, it is an illusion to believe that the moral judgments of donor governments can ever be bound.[4]

In Part I, the range of donor-country refinements in the United States' GSP law of 1984 was described.[5] It was pointed out that the United States still insists on making its own decision about who is poor enough to be deserving; it claims the right unilaterally to graduate the most prosperous developing countries and to remove preferences in individual product categories when they are no longer "needed". It was also pointed out that poverty is not the only criterion of moral desert. The current legislation also judges the moral worth of developing countries according to whether they are cooperating to help prevent narcotics traffic, the counterfeiting of goods and the theft of intellectual property. Ultimately, of course, anything can become a condition of moral worthiness. The GSP legislation of 1984 comes full circle by authorizing the president to deny GSP treatment to developing countries that maintain immoral (that is, unduly restrictive) trade and investment policies.

These refinements introduced by developed countries sharply reduce the value of whatever market access GSP creates, for they deprive such access of the stability and predictability needed to induce new investment (the stated purpose of GSP) or to reap the value of investments already made. Moreover, they actually worsen the conditions of trade for the individual developing countries which are excluded by them. Being denied the benefits of GSP is not merely being returned to the status quo ante. The excluded country must now compete with other developing countries who, remaining inside the system, enjoy a discriminatory advantage that did not exist before. The threat of exclusion creates a rather forceful weapon that affects the freedom of every developing country.

Developed countries have also undermined the preferences policy in one other way. The main factor limiting further implementation of GSP preferences, as well as being a complicating factor in the GSTP scenario, has been the proliferation of other, narrower preference systems created by the developed countries. The European Community uses preferences as the cornerstone of important special relationships with Mediterranean and African developing countries and has limited its GSP program in various ways in order not to dilute the market advantages of these special preferences. More recently, the United States has begun to establish similar regional preferences. It has created the Caribbean Basin Initiative, a Community-type preferential system with Caribbean countries, and it has concluded a geographically absurd (albeit probably GATT-conforming) free trade area with Israel. In recent years, United States officials have also mentioned the possibility of some similar arrangement with Australasia and with the Association of South East Asian Nations (ASEAN). A grant of more meaningful GSP preferences would obviously dilute the perceived economic advantages of all these narrower preferential systems, a result that neither grantors nor present grantees wish to see.[6] It cannot be said that these preferential sub-systems have been an outgrowth of the developing countries' own policies of preferential treatment. Both the European Community and the United States had such preferential relationships long before the first UNCTAD preferences resolution in 1964. Yet a policy environment where discrimination is viewed as a proper solution to problems of economic development has certainly done nothing to discourage them.[7]

This, then, is the primary case against preferential treatment programs in terms of what might be called their legal costs. The premises that make discrimination so appealing to governments eventually lead those governments to produce too much of the product – so many layers, refinements, corrections and qualifications that eventually everyone is worse off than before. The inability to contain such policies should not be surprising. Nothing in political life is more appealing than the lure of solutions that shift the cost to someone else.

THE ALTERNATIVE POLICY: ENFORCING MFN OBLIGATIONS

If it is agreed that the legal costs of policies of preferential treatment exceed their economic benefits, it would follow that the only sensible policy alternative for developed and developing countries alike would be a policy aimed at securing maximum enforcement of MFN obligations. Given the lack of any better alternative, it is not really necessary to argue the value of such a policy for developing countries. There are, however, persistent misconceptions about MFN policies that tend to cloud rational analysis of this alternative – a tendency on the part of officials in developing countries to under-estimate the value of MFN discipline and a tendency on the part of critics to over-estimate the chances of restoring it.

The value of a genuinely effective MFN obligation for developing countries can best be illustrated by considering the difference between the way discriminatory trade restrictions are typically imposed and the way restrictions would have to be imposed under a strict MFN policy. In the former situation, the developed country typically singles out the few "disruptive" suppliers from developing countries and exports from these countries are restrained by direct discriminatory quota if necessary, but usually by voluntary export restraints (VERs). Exporters in third countries tend to benefit by the restrictions on their competitors and so they do not protest. Often, indeed, they lend silent encouragement. Even the exporters being restrained can be induced to support the restriction in many cases, for they will receive higher profits from higher prices caused by the quota (monopoly rents); they may also benefit if, as often happens, the quantitative controls limit entry into the export market by newer producers in their own countries. Discrimination thus permits the building of a nice coalition of interested parties, all in favor of restricting trade. The losers, of course, are the economies of the developing countries being restrained, especially the smaller new producers in those countries. But against this kind of coalition, protest by the losers is a rather small voice.

A requirement of MFN treatment would change the situation dramatically. The central idea of the MFN obligation is that all countries must be treated equally. Although GATT law recognizes several different ways to give equal treatment where quantitative restrictions are involved, the key requirement in all cases is that restrictions must be applied to all suppliers, including those from other developed countries. Needless to say, governments in developed countries think twice before imposing restrictions that injure their most powerful trading partners. A strict MFN regime would thus result in fewer restrictions being imposed in the first place and, under any of the MFN equal treatment formulas, it would ensure that whatever restrictions are imposed bear less heavily on the developing countries. While some established suppliers in developing countries might be worse off than under a cosy voluntary export restraint, there is no doubt that the developing countries as a group would benefit far more from an MFN approach.[8]

The preceding example is a good illustration of the old trade-policy proposition that the MFN obligation is, above all else, a legal substitute for economic power on behalf of smaller countries. By requiring that all governments be treated equally, it has the effect of marshalling the economic power of larger countries behind the claims of small countries. The strongest evidence of this effect is the relentless effort of developed countries to avoid it.

It is difficult to over-state the importance of these consequences of economic power for developing countries. As the previous chapter tried to demonstrate, the principal weakness of both the reciprocity and the non-reciprocity legal strategies is the fact that neither can provide developing countries with enough economic power to oppose claims for emergency protection. Restoration of an effective MFN discipline is the one legal policy that could supply an answer to this absolutely critical problem.[9]

In theory, the MFN obligation has many of the qualities needed to become an effective legal restraint – qualities that policies of preferential treatment do not have. Unlike the welfare obligations of rich to poor, the MFN principle states an obligation capable of being applied, effectively, to specific cases.[10] In addition, its substance gives it the widest possible appeal. First, new views of "equality" notwithstanding, the MFN principle still commands the broadest and strongest normative appeal as a general principle of government behavior. Second, the MFN obligation also has the broadest economic policy appeal, for, in addition to its significance for relations between developed and developing countries, it also serves as the preferred basis of relations among developed countries. Finally, the MFN obligation already has what is probably the longest and most respected legal tradition of any principle in trade policy.[11]

It is important to understand fully the potential value of the MFN obligation because the difficulty of actually implementing such a policy would make it hardly worthwhile to consider otherwise. In the author's view, the difficulties of restoring the MFN obligation are so great that it looks like an impossible task in the near future, no matter how it is approached.

An effective MFN legal discipline cannot be accomplished by partial or gradual reform. The reason that more or less universal observance is needed is that, unlike reciprocity, the MFN obligation makes little or no sense intuitively. It makes no sense to choose to provoke a large number of reciprocity claims when the number of claims can be made smaller through discrimination. It makes no sense either to require powerful friends to suffer as much as less powerful strangers. The only way to make such outcomes politically plausible is to make observance of the MFN obligation so pervasive that discrimination disappears as an option of day-to-day policy. With respect to domestic political relations, it is necessary to create the perception that the only choice is whether the local interest seeking protection is worth the cost of an MFN reciprocity backlash. Likewise, with respect to diplomatic reactions, the only way to eliminate adverse reactions is simply to remove the option of behaving in a more friendly manner. The option will not disappear if the landscape is littered with exceptions. The practice has to be reduced to such an extent that it disappears from view.[12]

Merely stating the requirement is perhaps enough to indicate its impossibility of execution. Nonetheless, a few aspects of the problem need further clarification.

As noted earlier, critics of the GATT's current legal policy sometimes argue that the growing number of preferential treatment regimes is to blame for the decline in MFN enforcement generally. This argument usually implies that improved enforcement would be possible if developing countries were to abandon the Enabling Clause. Neither the historical statement nor its suggestion of reform possibilities are correct. Developing countries in the GATT did not begin to press seriously for preferential treatment until the early 1960s. By that time, developed countries had already made major inroads in the MFN principle on their own initiative. Preferences for colonies and former colonies were built into the GATT's basic MFN obligation in 1947, and colonial-type preferences have continued to be a major element of the European Community's policy towards the countries of the Mediterranean and in Africa, the Caribbean and the Pacific. The original text of the General Agreement in 1947 also authorized the countries of Western Europe to discriminate against the rest of the world, including the poorest developing countries, in order to foster their own economic reconstruction. Later, in 1955, many developed countries in the GATT invoked Article XXXV in order to maintain discriminatory trade barriers against Japan and most continued to do so into the 1960s. And by 1958, the GATT had already begun to define the concept of "market disruption", the basic function of which was to justify the use of discriminatory import restrictions against textile exports from developing countries.[13]

As for the possibility that developing countries could change things by abandoning the Enabling Clause, developed countries have so far given no evidence of any interest in such a bargain. Nor is there much reason why they should be interested. Developed countries are not being harmed very much by the limited forms of discrimination being practiced under the Enabling Clause. On the other hand, governments in developed countries are deriving quite considerable political benefits from the easy solutions to their own trade problems that discrimination allows.

Another characteristic of the problem that is sometimes misunderstood is the position of the governments of developing countries. Even though developing countries are the clear losers in the present situation, many of them would have serious political difficulties in supporting genuine MFN reform. Economic interests in almost every developing country are deriving benefits from the existing pattern of discrimination, whether preferential access for themselves or market opportunities created by discriminatory burdens on their competitors. While the country as a whole may be harmed by the system, these beneficiaries will have the most tangible interests to defend and will tend to make the greatest noise. This is the pernicious thing about trade discrimination; once it achieves a certain mass, the political voice of the beneficiaries will usually drown out the voices of those being hurt. The number of interests benefitting from discrimination is already overwhelming. The network of preferential trade advantages surrounding the European Community includes more than half of the developing countries in the GATT. The United States, which for a long time was the loudest (if not necessarily the most consistent) voice in the GATT in favor of the MFN principle, has now also begun to form Community-type relationships with other developing countries. Indeed, even the much maligned Multi-fiber Arrangement has developed a class of "beneficiaries" in developing countries because the country-by-country quota allocations, calculated according to historical market share, are now giving the older suppliers market protection against more efficient newcomers in other developing countries. With all of these beneficiaries defending their interest in the way things are, it is difficult to believe that anything short of a major world economic crisis – something of the order of the 1930s – could tear the world loose from this vast spider's web.

The difficulties in bringing about MFN reform can in some respects be described as a lost opportunity. While it may be that there was never any hope of persuading governments to resist the temptation for easy solutions, there was a time in the early 1960s when a clear and consistent demand for better enforcement of the MFN obligation, made as a priority objective of developing countries, might have produced some results. The problem today is vastly more difficult because twenty-five years of investment in the other direction must now be overturned.

SUMMARY AND CONCLUSIONS

Political obstacles should not be allowed to obscure the problem. It remains true that GSP and allied preference schemes are a bad investment for developing countries; this is so whether or not there is any chance of MFN reform. It also remains true that the problem of market access for developing countries is primarily a function of their lack of economic power and that the best solution to that problem would be a stronger MFN policy. It will not improve things to pretend that the problem is something else. In a situation where correct solutions seem unattainable, a search must be made for policies that can attain more limited objectives – objectives such as not making things worse, laying the groundwork for future change and so forth. The following points seem worth making in this connection:

(a) Although GSP and GSTP are bad investments, it will not be easy to extricate the world from them. "Graduation" may be a good device for extricating individual developing countries from policies of excessive protection in their home markets, but it is not a good solution to problems of discrimination. An individual developing country graduating from GSP preferences will not be better off for doing so. On the assumption that its competitors remain inside the preferential system, the excluded country will be stepping into a worse-than-before position where (i) discrimination still clutters the channels of trade and (ii) it is now at a discriminatory disadvantage vis-a-vis its competitors. Advanced developing countries may be able to endure such a change and may be forced to do so if they reach an income-export level where welfare claims become politically unacceptable. But it will never be possible to persuade them that graduation from GSP is for their own economic benefit.

(b) Complete dismantling of GSP and GSTP preferences for all countries, even if it were politically possible, would not be a very good solution either. The problem is the large number of other preferential sub-systems that now exist, such as the Lome Convention or the Caribbean Basin Initiative. Abolition of GSP without also abolishing these agreements would actually increase the level of discrimination among developing countries. Given that the primary competitors for most developing countries are other developing countries, the economic harm from increasing such discrimination could be quite serious.

Indeed, even a truly global dismantling of all preference systems would pose problems. There is no recognized demarcation line between preferences and legitimate regional integration, such as the European Community. Half the preference schemes in the world today parade as customs unions or free trade areas under Article XXIV of the GATT. Article XXIV has been so badly abused over the past 25 years, especially with respect to developing-country unions, that there is probably no longer any way to sort out the ducks from the geese.

(c) The only way to dismantle the existing network of preferential measures is to concentrate on lowering the upper end of the discriminatory margin. Most of the major preference systems are based on tariffs. To the extent the MFN tariffs are reduced or eliminated, the preference will be reduced or eliminated as well. Most industrial tariffs in developed countries are already so low that there no longer appears to be any protective reason to keep them at all. While there will obviously be sectors where this is not so, it should be possible to eliminate or substantially dilute most preferences by this means.[14] The corollary to this tariff-cutting approach would be an agreement that no further expansion of GSP or its progeny should be granted or undertaken. The GSP schemes of developed countries appear to have already lost their forward momentum. Hopes that the GSTP program had smothered itself in its crib proved to be premature in view of the Brasilia Ministers' declaration in 1986. It is still likely, however, that the projected negotiations will be brought to an early standstill over the extremely complex tangle of interests which will need to be unravelled.

The desired outcome under this approach would be death by atrophy. It must be hoped that the absence of forward motion, the gradual erosion of preference margins and the eventual winding down of rhetoric will create a climate in which annoyance finally comes to exceed advantage by a wide enough margin to permit change. This is not a short-run strategy.

(d) As for MFN discipline in developed countries, the focal point of debate has been and will remain the issue of "selectivity" in the proposed Safeguards Code.[15] The issue for developing countries so far has been whether to agree to a formal exception to the MFN obligation, in exchange for a promise of closer GATT supervision over the economic justification for such measures. Realists argue that developed countries will never agree to a strict MFN obligation in this area and that developing countries will be better off with "some discipline" than with the present situation of "no discipline".

The perspective given by this study has persuaded the author that the proposed exchange of discrimination for discipline would be a bad deal for developing countries. The more the legal and economic situation of developing countries is understood, the clearer it becomes that the integrity of the MFN obligation is critical. In the author's view, the MFN obligation is the only solid foundation on which effective legal protection of the interests of developing countries can ever be built. Permission to discriminate on safeguard measures, no matter how tight the criteria, would be a gap in the wall exactly at the point where the pressure is greatest.

Although there seems little prospect that the Safeguards Code negotiations will come out the other way – that is, that all developed countries will agree to a strict MFN obligation – developing countries have little choice but to keep pressing this demand. Even if developing countries cannot muster the political support for giving up GSP or the Enabling Clause, they can at least shift negotiating priorities. The current expenditure of diplomatic capital on behalf of more Enabling Clause preferences is simply a waste of a scarce resources. Shifting the priority to MFN reform would at least focus the attention of developed countries on something that makes sense and thus at least has a chance to gain adherents and supporters over time. Again, this is decidedly not a short-term strategy.

NOTES AND REFERENCES

1. J. Michael Finger, "Ideas Count, Words Inform", loc. cit.
2. For fuller references to the GSTP proposals, see notes 14–23, Chapter 6.
3. In 1970, the Committee on External Relations of the European Parliament issued a report criticizing the Community's development of external commercial policy ("timidement et incompletement"), pointing to the apparently unplanned succession of preferential agreements in Africa (post-Yaounde) and in the Mediterranean. European Parliament Documents, 1970–1971, No. 64, pp. 3 and 12. For a general description of the succession of agreements involved, see Robert E. Hudec, *The GATT Legal System and World Trade Diplomacy*, op. cit., pp. 204–08.
4. A rather telling example of attitudes toward GSP benefits was a letter, dated 5 December 1985, signed by eleven United States Senators, asking that the Republic of Korea's GSP benefits be withdrawn for various trade-policy misdeeds. The Senators explained that, as a major beneficiary of GSP, Korea would have to be held to the "highest standards" in order to continue qualifying for benefits. *International Trade Reporter*, Vol. 2, 1985, p. 1550.
5. See notes 24–34, Chapter 6. For a fuller description of the GSP schemes in both the United States and the European Community, see sources cited in notes 18–19, Chapter 4.
6. For a description of how the European Community's system of regional preferences has limited its GSP scheme, see Rolf J. Langhammer and Andre Sapir, *Economic Impact of Generalized Tariff Preferences*, op. cit. For a criticism of the Community's preferential policy towards developing countries in general, see Martin Wolf, "An Unholy Alliance: the European Community and Developing Countries in the International Trading System", *Aussenwirtschaft*, Vol. 42, 1987, pp. 41–64, and in L.B.M. Mennes and Jacob Kot (eds), *European Trade Policies and the Developing World* (London: Groom Helm, 1987). For a more detailed description of (and commentary on) the emerging network of United States special arrangements of this kind, see Sidney Weintraub, "Selective Trade Liberalization and Restriction", in Ernest H. Preeg (ed.), *Hard Bargaining Ahead*, op. cit., pp. 167–84.
7. Article I of the GATT states the MFN obligation for tariffs and other border charges and for all taxes and regulations in internal commerce; the MFN obligation for quotas is stated in Article XIII. In addition to requiring that quotas must apply to trade from all sources, Article XIII requires one of three types of quota administration to assure equal treatment: A first-come-first-served quota gives every supplier an equal chance to race to the border before the quota closes. A distribution of quota shares by country, according to traditional market share, produces an equal cut-back for everyone. A distribution of global quota licenses to local importers or, better still, a distribution by government auction, allows all suppliers to compete for the reduced volume of sales.
8. MFN tariffs would, of course, be preferable to MFN quotas of any kind as a safeguard measure. Governments, however, do not often resort to tariffs for such purposes. One of the reasons is that it is easier to discriminate by using quantitative controls.
9. In recent years, the most articulate spokesman for the role of the MFN obligation was the late Jan Tumlir. In a book published posthumously, Tumlir made

perhaps his strongest case. He concluded by pointing out that the leading powers in the GATT have available to them one very simple measure that would halt the slide towards protectionism – a measure so simple that it could be agreed to between governments at the highest levels. The measure recommended is a firm and unqualified commitment to the MFN obligation, preferably made effective in the domestic law of each signatory so that it would be enforceable by their own courts. Jan Tumlir, *Protectionism: Trade Policy in Democratic Societies*, op. cit., pp. 62–70.

10. The difficulties of giving legal force to the welfare obligation are discussed in the text at notes 10–13, Chapter 10. There are problems of defining status, rights and duties for purposes of preferential treatment, and these problems make it impossible to go much beyond the sort of unilaterally declared grant of specific and selective rights as in the Lome Convention or the GSP. It is very difficult to imagine that any multilateral legal instrument, backed by a multilateral institution, could ever be negotiated.

11. The drafting and conclusion of legally binding most-favored-nation clauses on tariffs were already common practice in the seventeenth century. Drafting at a multilateral level has also been going on for some time. See *Recommendation of the Economic Committee Relating to Tariff Policy and MFN Clause*, League of Nations Document, Official No. E.805, 1933) II.B.1 (Geneva: League of Nations, 1935), a 300-word model text of an MFN clause, with commentary. See also the thirty-article draft created in the International Law Commission study cited in note 1, Chapter 6.

12. It will be noted that the original GATT, with all its MFN exceptions, never even required this degree of observance. The essence of the GATT's approach was to stake out MFN exceptions as carefully as possible and then to say, "This much, but not an inch more". That method has certainly not been crowned with success, but it might be worth another try if nothing better could be negotiated.

13. The classic study of discrimination in the early post-war years is Gardner Patterson, *Discrimination in International Trade: the Policy Issues 1945–1965* (Princeton: Princeton University Press, 1966).

14. In conversations with officials who participated in the United States' decision to accept the GSP, the author was told that officials placed little or no reliance on the supposed temporary character of GSP, but rather assumed that the only way to get rid of it would be to reduce MFN tariffs to zero. In the late 1960s, the officials said, it was believed that the zero tariff would be achieved, most likely by the end of the century. Early in the Uruguay Round negotiations that began in 1986, one delegation tabled a proposal to eliminate tariffs on industrial goods by the year 2000.

15. For an extensive description of the background and the negotiating history of the "selectivity" issue with respect to the Safeguards Code, see Marco C.E.J. Bronckers, *Selective Safeguard Measures in Multilateral Trade Relations: Issues of Protectionism in GATT, European Community and United States Law* (Deventer: Kluwer for the T.M.C. Asser Instituut, 1985). Bronckers recommends a compromise solution, discussed in Ernst-Ulrich Petersmann, "Economic, Legal and Political Functions of the Principle of Non-discrimination", *The World Economy*, March 1986, pp. 113–21.

12

First Steps Towards a Better Legal Policy

THE FIRST major conclusion of this study is that none of the legal strategies currently available to developing countries appears to offer much help in improving the behavior of developed countries towards them. Developed countries are already fairly well committed to policies calling for the continuance of the gradual liberalization efforts of the past twenty years and, subject to not very rigorous graduation demands, these affirmative policies appear likely to continue under just about any legal policy. On the other hand, developed countries also seem committed to the practice of imposing new restrictions that limit developing-country exports once they begin to cause discomfort, and none of the legal strategies currently being advocated appears capable of changing this situation.

The GATT's current legal policy towards developing countries cannot promise any significant improvement. The insistent demand for non-reciprocal trade liberalization has received more political support in developed countries than critics want to acknowledge. But neither the welfare obligation nor other general value preferences appear capable of generating the kind of political force needed to bring about major improvements. The companion policy calling for preferential treatment is also capable of generating political support for certain kinds of trade liberalization. Its long-range price, though, is the creation of so much additional discrimination that the overall trade environment is left in a worse condition than before.

The critics of the current policy do not have a better answer – not, at least, with respect to the market-access problem. Neither the granting of reciprocity nor the abandonment of preferences under the Enabling Clause can promise any significant gains over the present situation. Reciprocity given by developing countries simply does not generate the same kind of political support that reciprocity produces in other situations; it therefore adds little to the political support which already exists for liberal trade policies towards developing countries. Nor would abandoning the Enabling Clause have much impact on discrimination by developed countries, for its commercial significance is not nearly large enough to overcome the attractiveness of this quite deeply rooted evil. This study has suggested that the main factor limiting further improvements in market access is the relative lack of economic power of developing countries. It has been argued that the only effective cure for this problem would be agreement to a strong MFN obligation, in essence a self-inflicted limitation on the freedom of action of developed countries. Unfortunately, the moment to create a strong and effective MFN policy has been allowed to slip away, and the next opportunity will probably not arrive until the world's next major economic collapse.

Nonetheless, the author continues to believe that the MFN obligation is the only foundation on which can be built a legal policy that will be effective in promoting and protecting market access for developing countries. Consequently, the first major recommendation of this study is that developing countries should re-direct their long-term objectives to the strengthening of the GATT's MFN obligation in all respects. Developing countries should stop spending diplomatic capital trying to enlarge preferences under the Enabling Clause and, instead, should accept the progressive dilution of GSP and other preference systems through MFN tariff reduction and should allow the current GSTP initiative to languish. Developing countries should also continue to reject "selectivity" in a GATT safeguards code on emergency protection, even if it means continued impasse, and they should continue to challenge all other departures from MFN treatment as they occur.

The second major conclusion of this study is that developing countries are wrong to think of GATT legal policy primarily in terms of its impact on the behavior of developed countries and instead should start paying careful attention to its impact on their own trade-policy decisions. A government's own trade-policy decisions are really the most important determinant of its economic gains from trade, and this is where GATT legal policy has the greatest impact.

Under most economic assumptions, the current policy of non-reciprocity has been having a deleterious effect on the trade policy of developing countries. If it is assumed that trade intervention is generally harmful and that national economic interest is best served by the most liberal trade policy possible, the damage done by the GATT's current legal policy is quite clear. But even if it is assumed that trade intervention by governments is beneficial and ought to be practiced, governments still need assistance in restraining such policies, and GATT legal restraints would be an eminently suitable instrument to provide such assistance.

This conclusion points to the second major recommendation of this study – that GATT's legal policy towards developing countries should change and that the Contracting Parties should instead establish a regime of developing-country legal obligations that would provide support for governments of developing countries in opposing unwanted, protectionist policies at home. Such a change would involve setting aside both the principle of non-reciprocity and the principle of preferential treatment. It would involve accepting instead the proposition that developing countries should assume either equal legal obligations or, at least, an equal degree of legal control.

There is absolutely no chance that either of the major recommendations in this study can be accomplished in a single round of GATT negotiations. Part I of this study has described the painful word-by-word battle that diplomats from developing countries fought in order to establish the current legal policy. The diplomatic investment made in GATT affairs was only a small part of the total. The consequence is that the GATT's current policy towards developing countries now has the momentum of a fully laden supertanker underway at full speed. It will take many miles of ocean just to slow it down, much less to begin making a complete turn.

There are those who believe that the GATT has become so committed to the current policy that the only way to change it would be to start a new organization – a Super GATT, or a GATT of the Like-minded, as it is sometimes called. The author does not believe that such a strategy is called for. The GATT legal structure already contains several elements upon which a new policy could be launched – the graduation principle, the code mechanism and a negotiating tradition which has always affirmed, at bottom, the right to bargain for reciprocity. The GATT also has a basic legal code in force and, despite their reformist zeal on occasion, it is by no means certain that either the United States or the European Community would be able to re-enact as good a set of commitments in a new agreement. Finally, although the decks of the GATT are piled high with promises of special and differential treatment, the promises are essentially empty of any legal content and do not constitute an immovable barrier to change.

The main problem is one of political will, not institutional structure. As shown in Part I of this study, the GATT did not arrive at its present legal policy through mistakes in economics or ideology. The policy of non-reciprocity has flourished primarily because, for both sides, it has been the path of least resistance. It has been the easy way out for the governments of developing countries because it has given them a free hand to satisfy as many domestic political interests as possible. It has been the easy way out for the Group of 77 as a whole because it has offered an undemanding policy on which they can most easily achieve solidarity. It has also been the easy way out for diplomats from developing countries, for it has allowed them to maintain the posture of vigorous representation without ever having to ask home governments to take difficult decisions. Finally, and perhaps most important, it has been the easy way out for the governments of developed countries and for their diplomats. Relaxation of legal discipline has always been the cost-free answer – the concession that developed countries could make without having to go through the unpleasant business of asking legislatures for real trade liberalization. Like penny gin, it was an inexpensive way to keep the peace by pandering to the other side's worst instincts.

If there is going to be any possibility of change, governments on both sides will have to be prepared to spend some of the political courage they have been hoarding up all these years. This no doubt sounds simplistic. But it is fundamental.

Given the commitment of the developing countries to the current policy, it is clear that developed countries will have to take the lead in any effort to establish a different legal relationship. There appear to be two obstacles blocking such an action at present. One is the lack of agreement among developed countries themselves, particularly the European Community's unwillingness to support efforts by the United States to reform that policy. As noted in Chapter 5, this has been a long-standing conflict, rooted in differing perceptions of self-interest. The Community's support, even if not very active, is essential.

The other obstacle is a tendency, among all governments in developed countries, to lie back and simply watch as developing countries impale themselves on ineffective policies. This is perhaps an understandable reaction to years of being told to mind their own business. Yet, developed countries do have an obligation to the peoples of developing countries, and the policy of *laissez s'en sortir* is manifestly not discharging it. The main point of attack for any initiative from the developed countries will have to be the principle of non-reciprocity: Preferences can only be attacked indirectly, by MFN tariff reduction and by neglect, but the non-reciprocity doctrine will require that developed countries make demands for reciprocity in order to begin making inroads. Two elements will be needed in order to make such demands: (i) a justification for departing from the commitment of non-reciprocity and (ii) some structure or structures in which discrete demands can be put forward without producing a head-on confrontation with the Group of 77.

The major justification will no doubt be the graduation doctrine. But the graduation doctrine focusses only on the more powerful developing countries, and these are not the only developing countries that could benefit from GATT legal controls. Efforts should be made, therefore, to blur the negative message of the graduation doctrine (the free ride for smaller countries) and to look for ways in which the pressure for change can be applied more broadly.

The GATT already offers several structures that can be used in the way suggested. Conventional tariff negotiations are one possibility. In itself, a developing country's decision to "participate" in such negotiations has never been deemed a breach of solidarity. Any developing country wishing to separate itself from the policy of non-reciprocity could take this first step. Even though a single negotiation cannot revise an entire legal relationship, it can do a good deal. The demand for tariff concessions provides an occasion for bargaining confrontations in which the claimed "economic development" justification for protection can be tested across a broad range of products. Moreover, a basis for GATT legal control can be established simply by the relatively painless act of binding an existing tariff rate, or even a higher rate.

The code approach of the Tokyo Round negotiations is another structure that fits well into this strategy. Codes are, in a sense, mini-versions of a Super GATT. They create a new legal institution within the larger framework of the GATT in which like-minded governments can adopt rules containing more rigorous discipline. The GATT's MFN obligation prohibits code members from denying the benefits of any improved "treatment" to other members of the GATT, but it does not require signatories to admit other GATT members to membership or participation in the administration of the codes. Governments of developing countries seeking to justify participation in the arrangements can always argue that MFN entitlement to the new legal rights is hollow without the membership rights and thus that it is necessary to become a member.

A good deal of the potential value of the codes agreed during the Tokyo Round negotiations was lost because of last-minute concessions on "special and differential treatment" made to attract developing-country membership. These membership pressures will be wheeled out again for there will continue to be some developing countries who really do not want to accept greater discipline. Governments in developed countries seeking to change the current legal policy will have to recognize that they cannot satisfy both sides – those that want and those that do not want greater legal discipline. Nothing will change until developed countries are willing to see the latter group of developing countries walk away.

Another possible structure that should be considered is the existing procedure for reviewing balance-of-payments restrictions. These procedures have in general deteriorated into meaningless exchanges, in part because the whole idea has become an anomaly in a world of floating exchange rates. Nonetheless, these periodic reviews have a tradition of relatively faithful adherence by most developing countries (probably because of the IMF's involvement) and they do actually provide a legal hook that can be used to press for improvements – the power to withhold approval of restrictions. This structure would be particularly useful in dealing with the smaller and poorer developing countries.

Finally, and with some trepidation, the author would suggest that developed countries should at least make an effort to turn the work of the Trade and Development Committee of the GATT in this direction. Part IV of the GATT contains several exhortations concerning the trade policies of individual developing countries, provisions that could justify a review of such policies. To seek to inject discipline by this approach, however, would be to risk a head-on confrontation because the Trade and Development Committee has tended to regard itself as the high temple of special and differential treatment. For that reason, this is probably not an initiative to be considered immediately. But the Trade and Development Committee does have more credibility with developing countries than any other GATT body and, to the extent that it could be used, it would make acceptance of GATT discipline a lot easier for politicians in developing countries.

It is doubtful whether developed-country pressures for reciprocity will escape the attention of the Group of 77. Except for the Trade and Development Committee proposal, however, reciprocity demands put forward in the structures suggested above will not require affirmative approval in order to be implemented. They are all authorized by standing GATT law and practice.

The means by which legal change will occur, if it does occur, will be through decisions by individual developing countries to "cave-in" to pressure from developed countries. Such decisions, of course, will not be easy. Solidarity with other developing countries is a highly valued asset, and developed countries will have to press their demands with some intensity to provide a justification for breaking away. But it does seem that the time is coming when some break-away will be possible.[1]

The decisions made by individual developing countries will be the determining factor. If developing countries lash themselves to the current policy and refuse to consider any further change, developed countries are unlikely to have either the conviction or the tolerance for the political turmoil that would be needed to conduct real economic warfare over this issue. After all, it is the developing countries, not they, who are most harmed by such a policy.

It seems most likely, therefore, that the graduation demands and similar legal initiatives by developed countries will be carried only to the point of setting the stage for decisions that developing countries will have to take by themselves. Governments of developing countries will have to be persuaded that it is in their own national economic interest to respond with a fuller commitment to GATT law. That is why the present study is addressed primarily to them.

NOTE AND REFERENCES

1. There is evidence of a growing interest among some developing countries in adopting more GATT-consistent trade policies. This study itself was in part the product of such evidence. It was commissioned by the Trade Policy Research Centre following a series of meetings held by the Centre in the Asian-Pacific region at which the growing interest was evident. See Brian Scott et al., *Has The Cavalry Arrived? A Report on Trade Liberalisation and Economic Recovery*, Special Report No.6 (London: Trade Policy Research Centre, 1984). Other authors point to similar evidence. See C. Michael Aho and Jonathan D. Aronson, *Trade Talks: America Better Listen*, op. cit., pp. 110–11 (indications from various developing countries of conditional willingness to break with bloc positions); and Anne O. Krueger and Constantine Michalopoulos, "Developing-country Trade Policies and the International Economic System", loc. cit., p. 50.

List of References

THIS list contains only the more important references cited in the text. The reader should refer to the Notes and References at the end of each chapter for more complete bibliographical information.

KENNETH W. ABBOTT, "The Trading Nation's Dilemma: the Functions of the Law of International Trade", *Harvard International Law Journal*, Cambridge, Massachusetts, Vol. 26, No. 2, Spring 1985, pp. 501–32.

C. MICHAEL AHO and JONATHAN D. ARONSON, *Trade Talks: America Better Listen!* (New York: Council on Foreign Relations, 1985).

Arusha Programme for Collective Self-reliance and Framework for Negotiations, United Nations Document TD/236 (1979) p. 35, reprinted in Proceedings of the United Nations Conference on Trade and Development, Fifth Session (Manila), United Nations Document TD/269, Vol. 1, 1981.

BELA BALASSA, *The Newly Industrializing Countries in the World Economy* (New York: Pergamon Press, 1981).

ROBERT E. BALDWIN and TRACY MURRAY, "MFN Tariff Reductions and Developing Country Trade Benefits under the GSP", *Economic Journal*, Oxford, Vol. 87, March 1977, pp. 30–46.

ROBERT E. BALDWIN and ANNE O. KRUEGER (eds), *The Structure and Evolution of Recent US Trade Policy* (Chicago: University of Chicago Press, for the National Bureau of Economic Research, 1984).

ROBERT E. BALDWIN, *The Political Economy of US Import Policy* (Cambridge, Massachusetts: MIT Press, 1985).

ROMEO BAUTISTA, *Impediments to Trade Liberalization in the Philippines*, Thames Essay No. 54 (Aldershot, Brookfield and Sydney: Gower, for the Trade Policy Research Centre, 1987).

MOHAMMED BEDJAOUI, *Towards a New International Economic Order* (New York: Holmes & Meier, for the United Nations Educational, Scientific and Cultural Organization, 1979).

WOLFGANG BENEDEK, "Stabilization of Export Earnings of Developing Countries", in Progressive Development of the Principles and Norms of International Law Relating to the New International Economic Order: Analytical Papers and Analysis of Texts of Relevant Instruments, United Nations Document UNITAR/DS/5 (New York: United Nations Institute for Training and Research, 1982) pp. 219–90.

JAGDISH N. BHAGWATI, *Foreign Trade Regimes and Economic Development: Anatomy and Consequences of Exchange Control Regimes* (Cambridge, Massachusetts: Ballinger, for the National Bureau of Economic Research, 1979).

RICHARD BLACKHURST, NICOLAS MARIAN and JAN TUMLIR, *Trade Liberalization, Protectionism and Interdependence: GATT Studies in International Trade No. 5* (Geneva: GATT Secretariat, 1977).

RICHARD BLACKHURST, "Reciprocity in Trade Negotiations under Flexible Exchange Rates", in John P. Martin and Alasdair Smith (eds), *Trade and Payments Adjustment under Flexible Exchange Rates* (London: Macmillan, for the Trade Policy Research Centre, 1979) pp. 212–44.

AXEL BORRMANN et al., *The European Communities' General System of Preferences* (The Hague: Martinus Nijhoff, 1981).

MARCO G.E.J. BRONCKERS, *Selective Safeguard Measures in Multilateral Trade Relations: Issues of Protectionism in GATT, European Community and United States Law* (Deventer: Kluwer, for the T.M.C. Asser Instituut, 1985).

WILLIAM ADAMS BROWN, *The United States and the Restoration of World Trade: An Analysis and Appraisal of the ITO Charter and the General Agreement on Tariffs and Trade* (Washington: Brookings Institution, 1950).

MILAN BULAJIC, "Legal Aspects of a New International Order", in Kamal Hossain (ed.), *Legal Aspects of the New International Economic Order* (London: Frances Pinter, 1980) pp. 45–67.

SUBRATA ROY CHOWDBURY, "Legal Status of the Charter of Economic Rights and Duties of States", in Kamal Hossain (ed.), *Legal Aspects of the New International Economic Order* (London: Frances Pinter, 1980).

KENNETH W. CLEMENTS and LARRY A. SJAASTAD, *How Protection Taxes Exporters*, Thames Essay No. 39 (London: Trade Policy Research Centre, 1985).

T.G. CONGDON, *Economic Liberalism in the Cone of Latin America*, Thames Essay No. 40 (London: Trade Policy Research Centre, 1985).

W.M. CORDEN, *Trade Policy and Economic Welfare* (Oxford: Clarendon Press, 1974).

GERARD CURZON, *Multilateral Commercial Diplomacy: the General Agreement on Tariffs and Trade and its Impact on National Commercial Policies and Techniques* (London: Michael Joseph, 1965).

KENNETH W. DAM, "Regional Economic Arrangements and the GATT: The Legacy of a Misconception", *University of Chicago Law Review*, Chicago, Vol. 30, No. 4, Summer 1963, pp. 615–65.

KENNETH W. DAM, *The GATT – Law and International Economic Organization* (Chicago and London: University of Chicago Press, 1970).

KENNETH W. DAM, *The Rules of the Game: Reform and Evolution in the International Monetary System* (Chicago and London: University of Chicago Press, 1982).

WILLIAM DIEBOLD JR, *The End of the ITO*, Princeton Essays in International Finance No. 16 (Princeton: International Finance Section, Department of Economics, Princeton University, 1952).

GREGORY C. DORRIS, "The Very Specialized United States Generalized System of Preferences", *Georgia Journal of International and Comparative Law*, Athens, Georgia, Vol. 15, No. 1, Winter 1985, pp. 39–81.

RENE JEAN DUPUY (ed.), *The New International Economic Order: Commercial, Technological and Cultural Aspects* (The Hague: Martinus Nijhoff, 1981).

MARTHINUS GERHARDUS ERASMUS, *The New International Economic Order and International Organizations* (Frankfurt-Main: Haag und Herchen, 1979).

AUGUSTO-CAESAR ESPIRITU, "The Principle of the Right of Every State to Benefit from Science and Technology", in *Progressive Development of the Principles and Norms of International Law Relating to the New International Economic Order: Analytical Papers and Analysis of Texts of Relevant Instruments*, second volume, United Nations Document UNITAR/DS/6 (New York: United Nations Institute for Training and Research, 1983) pp. 1–153, European Parliament Documents, 1970–1971, No. 64.

JOHN W. EVANS, *The Kennedy Round in American Trade Policy: The Twilight of the GATT?* (Cambridge, Massachusetts: Harvard University Press, 1971).

ROQUE FERNANDEZ and CARLOS RODRIGUEZ, "Impediments to Trade Liberalization in Argentina", in Larry Sjaastad (ed.), *Impediments to Trade Liberalization in Latin America* (Aldershot, Brookfield and Sydney: Gower, for the Trade Policy Research Centre, forthcoming).

J. MICHAEL FINGER, H. KEITH HALL and DOUGLAS R. NELSON, "The Political Economy of Administered Protection", *American Economic Review*, Menasha, Wisconsin, Vol. 72, June 1982, pp. 452–66.

J. MICHAEL FINGER, "Ideas Count, Words Inform", in R.H. Snape (ed.), *Issues in World Trade Policy: GATT at the Crossroads* (London: Macmillan, 1986).

THOMAS M. FRANCK and MARK M. MUNANSANGU, *The New International Economic Order: International Law in the Making, Policy and Efficacy Studies*, No. 6 (New York: United Nations Institute for Training and Research, 1982).

RICHARD N. GARDNER, Sterling-Dollar Diplomacy (Oxford: Clarendon Press, 1956).

The Role of the GATT in Relation to Trade and Development (Geneva: GATT Secretariat, 1964).

The Tokyo Round of Multilateral Trade Negotiations, Report by the Director-General of the GATT (Geneva: GATT Secretariat, 1979) and The Tokyo Round of Multilateral Trade Negotiations, Supplementary Report by the Director-General of the GATT (Geneva: GATT Secretariat, 1980).

GATT Activities in 1985 (Geneva: GATT Secretariat, 1986).

GOH KENG-SWEE, "Public Administration and Economic Development in LDCs", Fourth Harry G. Johnson Memorial Lecture, *The World Economy*, London, Vol. 6, Issue 3, September 1983, pp. 229–43.

GOTTFRIED HABERLER et al., *Trends in International Trade: Report by a Panel of Experts* (Geneva: GATT Secretariat, 1958), known as the Haberler Report.

STEPHAN HAGGARD, "The Politics of Adjustment: Lessons from the 3MF Extended Fund Facility", *International Organization*, Madison, Wisconsin, Vol. 39, No. 3, Summer 1985, pp. 504–34.

KAMAI HOSSAIN (ed.), *Legal Aspects of the New International Economic Order* (London: Frances Pinter, 1980).

DAMIEN HUBBARD, "The International Law Commission and the New International Economic Order", *1979 German Yearbook of International Law*, Vol. 22 (Berlin: Duncker und Humblot) pp. 80–99.

ROBERT E. HUDEC, "GATT or GABB? The Future Design of the General Agreement on Tariffs and Trade", *Yale Law Journal*, New Haven, Connecticut, Vol. 80, No. 7, June 1971, pp. 1299–386.

ROBERT E. HUDEC, *The GATT Legal System and World Trade Diplomacy* (New York: Praeger, 1975).

ROBERT E. HUDEC, *Adjudication of International Trade Disputes*, Thames Essay No. 16 (London: Trade Policy Research Centre, 1978).

ROBERT E. HUDEC, "GATT Dispute Settlement after the Tokyo Round: An Unfinished Business", *Cornell International Law Journal*, Ithaca, Vol. 13, No. 2, Summer 1980, pp. 145–202.

HELEN HUGHES and ANNE O. KRUEGER, "Effects of Protection in Developed Countries on Developing Countries' Exports of Manufactures", in Robert E. Baldwin and Anne O. Krueger (eds), *The Structure and Evolution of Recent US Trade Policy* (Chicago: University of Chicago Press, for the National Bureau of Economic Research, 1984) pp. 389–418.

INTERNATIONAL LAW ASSOCIATION, "Third Report of the International Committee on Legal Aspects of a New International Economic Order", in *Report of the Sixty-first Conference* (London: International Law Association, 1985) pp. 107–53.

INTERNATIONAL TRADE 1984–85 (Geneva: GATT Secretariat, 1985).

JOHN H. JACKSON, *World Trade and the Law of GATT: A Legal Analysis of the General Agreement on Tariffs and Trade* (Indianapolis: Bobbs-Merrill, 1969).

JOHN H. JACKSON, JEAN-VICTOR LOUIS and MITSUO MATSUSHITA, *Implementing the Tokyo Round: National Constitutions and International Economic Rules* (Ann Arbor: University of Michigan Press, 1984).

HARRY G. JOHNSON, *The Canadian Quandary: Economic Problems and Policies* (Toronto: McGraw-Hill, 1963).

HARRY G. JOHNSON, "Optimal Trade Intervention in the Presence of Domestic Distortion", in Robert E. Baldwin (ed.), Trade, Growth and the Balance of Payments: Essays in Honor of Gottfried Haberler (Amsterdam: North Holland, 1965).

DONALD B. KEESING, "Manufactured Exports from Developing Countries", in Khadija Haq (ed.), *Equality of Opportunity within and among Nations* (New York: Praeger, 1977) pp. 98–103.

DONALD B. KEESING and MARTIN WOLF, *Textile Quotas against Developing Countries*, Thames Essay No. 23 (London: Trade Policy Research Centre, 1980).

KARIN KOCK, *International Trade Policy and the GATT 1947–1967* (Stockholm: Almqvist & Wiksell, 1969).

ANNE O. KRUEGER, *Foreign Trade Regimes and Economic Development: Liberalization Attempts and Consequences* (Cambridge, Massachusetts: Ballinger, for the National Bureau of Economic Research, 1978).

ANNE O. KRUEGER, "Trade Policies in Developing Countries", in Ronald W. Jones and Peter B. Kenen (eds), *Handbook of International Economics* (Amsterdam: North Holland, 1984) pp. 519–69.

ANNE O. KRUEGER and CONSTANTINE MICHALOPOULOS, "Developing-country Trade Policies and the International Economic System", in Ernest H. Preeg (ed.), *Hard Bargaining Ahead: US Trade Policy and Developing Countries* (New Brunswick, New Jersey: Transaction Books, for the Overseas Development Council, 1985) pp. 39–57.

DEEPAK LAL and SARATH RAJAPATIRANA, *Impediments to Trade Liberalization in Sri Lanka*, Thames Essay No. 51 (Aldershot, Brookfield and Sydney: Gower, for the Trade Policy Research Centre, 1987).

ROLF J. LANGHAMMER, *Ten Years of the EEC's Generalized System of Preferences for Developing Countries: Success or Failure?*, Kiel Working Paper No. 183 (Kiel: Institut fur Weltwirtschaft an der Universitat Kiel, 1983).

ROLF J. LANGHAMMER and ANDRE SAPIR, *Economic Impact of Generalized Tariff Preferences*, Thames Essay No. 49 (Aldershot, Brookfield and Sydney: Gower, for the Trade Policy Research Centre, 1987).

Recommendation of the Economic Committee Relating to Tariff Policy and MFN Clause, League of Nations Document Official No. E.805; 193 3, II. B.1 (Geneva: League of Nations, 1935).

STEPHANIE LENWAY, *The Politics of US International Trade* (Boston: Pitman Publishing, 1985).

FRITZ LEUTWILER et al., *Trade Policies for a Better Future: Proposals for Action*, the Leutwiler Report (Geneva: GATT Secretariat, 1985).

PETER H. LINDERT and CHARLES P. KINDLEBERGER, *International Economics*, 8th edition (Homewood, Illinois: Richard D. Irwin, 1982).

I.M.D. LITTLE, TIBOR S.C. ITOVSKY and M.F.G. SCOTT, *Industry and Trade in Some Developing Countries: A Comparative Study* (London: Oxford University Press, for the Organization for Economic Cooperation and Development, 1970).

I.M.D. LITTLE, *Economic Development: Theory, Policy and International Relations* (New York: Basic Books, for the Twentieth Century Fund, 1982).

OLIVIER LONG, *Law and its Limitations in the GATT Multilateral Trade System* (Dordrecht: Martinus Nijhoff, 1985).

HIDEKO MAKIYAMA (ed.), *A New International Economic Order: Selected Documents 1976*, United Nations Document UNITAR/DS/2 (New York: United Nations Institute for Training and Research, 1980).

HIDEKO MAKIYAMA (ed.), *A New International Economic Order: Selected Documents 1977*, United Nations Document UNITAR/DS/3. (New York: United Nations Institute for Training and Research, 1982).

EDMOND MCGOVERN, *International Trade Regulation: GATT, the United States and the European Community*, 2nd edition (Exeter: Globefield Press, 1986).

RACHEL MCCULLOCH, "United States Preferences: the Proposed System", *Journal of World Trade Law*, Geneva, Vol. 8, No. 2, March-April 1974, pp. 216–26.

ROBERT F. MEAGHER, *An International Redistribution of Wealth and Power: A Study of the Charter of Economic Rights and Duties of States* (New York: Pergamon Press, 1979).

L.B.M. MENNES and JACOB KOT (eds), *European Trade Policies and the Developing World* (London: Croom Helm, forthcoming).

ALFRED GEORGE MOSS and HARRY N.M. WINTER (eds), *A New International Economic Order: Selected Documents 1945–1975*, in two volumes, United Nations Document UNITAR/DS/1 (New York: United Nations Institute for Training and Research, no date).

GERALD M. MEIER, *International Trade and Development*, 2nd edition (New York: Harper & Row, 1968).

TRACY MURRAY, Evaluation of the Trade Benefits under the United States Scheme of Generalized Preferences, United Nations Document TD/BIG. 5/66 (1980).

A. PETER MUTHARIKA, "The Principle of Entitlement of Developing Countries to Development Assistance", in *Progressive Development of the Principles and Norms of International Law Relating to the New International Economic Order: Analytical Papers and Analysis of Texts of Relevant Instruments*, second volume, United Nations Document UNITAR/DS/6 (New York: United Nations Institute for Training and Research, 1983) pp. 154–351.

GUNNAR MYRDAL, *An International Economy: Problems and Prospects* (New York: Harper & Row, 1956).

HENRY R. NAU, "The NICs in a New Trade Round", in Ernest H. Preeg (ed.), *Hard Bargaining Ahead: US Trade Policy and Developing Countries* (New Brunswick, New Jersey: Transaction Books, for the Overseas Development Council, 1985) pp. 63–84.

BARRY H. NEMMERS and TED ROWLAND, "The US Generalized System of Preferences: Too Much System, Too Little Preference", *Law and Policy in International Business*, Washington, Vol. 9, No. 3, 1977, pp. 855–911.

MANCUR OLSON, *The Logic of Collective Action* (Cambridge, Massachusetts: Harvard University Press, 1965).

GARDNER PATTERSON, *Discrimination in International Trade: The Policy Issues 1945–1965* (Princeton: Princeton University Press, 1966).

JAN PEN, *A Primer on International Trade* (New York: Random House, 1967).

ERNEST F. PENROSE, *Economic Planning for the Peace* (Princeton: Princeton University Press, 1953).

ERNST-ULRICH PETERSMANN, "International Trade and International Trade Law", Discussion Paper for the International Law Association's International Committee on Legal Aspects of the New International Economic Order, 1986.

RAUL PREBISCH, *The Economic Development of Latin America and Some of its Problems* (New York: United Nations Economic Commission for Latin America, 1949).

ERNEST H. PREEG, *Traders and Diplomats: An Analysis of the Kennedy Round of Negotiations under the General Agreement on Tariffs and Trade* (Washington: Brookings Institution, 1970).

ERNEST H. PREEG (ed.), *Hard Bargaining Ahead: US Trade Policy and Developing Countries* (New Brunswick, New Jersey: Transaction Books, for the Overseas Development Council, 1985).

B.G. RAMCHARAN, "Equality and Discrimination in International Economic Law (XII): The Proposed Global System of Trade Preferences among Developing Countries", in *The Yearbook of World Affairs 1984* (London: Stevens, for the London Institute of World Affairs, 1984) pp. 199–215.

OSWALDO DE RIVERO, *New Economic Order and International Development Law* (New York: Pergamon Press, 1980).

FRIEDER ROESSLER, "The Rationale for Reciprocity in Trade Negotiations under Floating Currencies", *Kyklos*, Basel, Vol. 31, No. 2, 1978, pp. 258–74.

FRIEDER ROESSLER, "The GATT Declaration on Trade Measures taken for Balance-of-payments Purposes: A Commentary", *Case Western Reserve Journal of International Law*, Cleveland, Ohio, Vol. 12, No. 2, 1980, pp. 383–403.

FRIEDER ROESSLER, "The Scope, Limits and Function of the GATT Legal System", *The World Economy*, London, Vol. 8, No. 3, September 1985, pp. 287–98.

MILAN SAHOVIC, "The Principle of Participatory Equality of Developing Countries in International Economic Relations: Analytical Paper", United Nations Document UNITAR/DSI6/Add.1 (New York: United Nations Institute for Training and Research, 1984) pp. 1–54.

ANDRE SAPIR and LARS LUNDBERG, "The US Generalized System of Preferences and its Impacts", in Robert E. Baldwin and Anne O. Krueger (eds), *The Structure and Evolution of Recent US Trade Policy* (Chicago: University of Chicago Press, for the National Bureau of Economic Research, 1984) pp. 195–236.

KARL P. SAUVANT, *The Group of 77: Evolution, Structure, Organization* (New York: Oceana Publications, 1981).

BRIAN SCOTT et al., *Has the Cavalry Arrived? A Report on Trade Liberalisation and Economic Recovery*, Special Report No. 6 (London: Trade Policy Research Centre, 1984).

PIETER VERLOREN VAN THEMAAT, *The Changing Structure of International Economic Law* (The Hague: Martinus Nijhoff, 1981).

ROBERT D. TOLLISON, "Rent Seeking: a Survey", *Kyklos*, Basel, Vol. 35, No. 4, 1982, pp. 575–602.

JAN TUMLIR, *Protectionism: Trade Policy in Democratic Societies* (Washington: American Enterprise Institute, 1985).

JAN TUMLIR, Economic Policy as a Constitutional Problem, Fifteenth Wincott Memorial Lecture, Occasional Paper No. 70 (London: Institute of Economic Affairs, 1984).

The History of UNCTAD 1964–1984, United Nations Document UNCTAD/OSG/286 (New York: United Nations, 1985).

Towards a Global Strategy of Development, Report by the Secretary-General, United Nations Document TD/3/Rev. I (Geneva: UNCTAD Secretariat, 1964).

The Kennedy Round: Estimated Effects on Tariff Barriers, Report by the Secretary-General, United Nations Document TD/6/Rev. 1 (Geneva: UNCTAD Secretariat, 1968).

Assessment of the Results of the Multilateral Trade Negotiations, United Nations Document TD/B/778/Rev. 1 (Geneva: UNGTAD Secretariat, 1982).

Protectionism and Structural Adjustment in the World Economy, United Nations Document TD/B/888/Rev. 1 (Geneva: UNCTAD Secretariat, 1982).

"Permanent Sovereignty over Natural Resources", UNITAR staff paper, in *Progressive Development of the Principles and Norms of International Law Relating to the New International Order: Analytical Papers and Analysis of Texts of Relevant Instruments*, United Nations Document UNITAR/DS/5 (New York: United Nations Institute for Training and Research, 1982) pp. 291–465.

"The Principle of Participatory Equality of Developing Countries in International Economic Relations: Analysis of Texts", UNITAR staff paper, in *Progressive Development of the Principles and Norms of International Law Relating to the New International Economic Order: Analytical Papers and Analysis of Texts of Relevant Instruments*, second volume, United Nations Document UNITAR/DS/6 (New York: United Nations Institute for Training and Research, 1983) pp. 353–436.

Progressive Development of the Principles and Norms of International Law Relating to the New International Economic Order, Report by the Secretary-General, United Nations Document A/39/504/Add.l (New York: United Nations, 1984).

An Evaluation of US Imports under the Generalized System of Preferences, Publication No. 1379 (Washington: United States International Trade Commission, 1983).

Review of the Effectiveness of Trade Dispute Settlement under the GATT and the Tokyo Round Agreements, Publication No. 1793 (Washington: United States International Trade Commission, 1985).

WIL D. VERWEY, "The Principle of Preferential Treatment for Developing Countries", in *Progressive Development of the Principles and Norms of International Law Relating to the New International Economic Order: Analytical Papers and Analysis of Texts of Relevant Instruments*, United Nations Document UNITAR/DS/5 (New York: United Nations Institute for Training and Research, 1982) pp. 6–218.

SIDNEY WEINTRAUB, "Selective Trade Liberalization and Restriction", in Ernest H. Preeg (ed.), *Hard Bargaining Ahead: US Trade Policy and Developing Countries* (New Brunswick, New Jersey: Transaction Books, for the Overseas Development Council, 1985) pp. 167–84.

CLAIR WILCOX, *A Charter for World Trade* (New York: Macmillan, 1949).

MARTIN WOLF, "Two-Edged Sword: Demands of Developing Countries and the Trading System", in Jagdish N. Bhagwati and John Gerard Ruggie (eds), *Power, Passions and Purpose: Prospects for North-South Negotiations* (Cambridge, Massachusetts: MIT Press, 1984) pp. 201–29.

MARTIN WOLF, "An Unholy Alliance: The European Community and Developing Countries in the International Trading System", in L.B.M. Mennes and Jacob Kol (eds), *European Trade Policies and the Developing Countries* (London: Croom Helm, forthcoming).

MARTIN WOLF, "Timing and Sequencing of Trade Liberalization", *Asian Development Review*, Manila, Asian Development Bank, Vol. 4, No. 2, 1986.

HARRY WOLFRUM, "The Principle of the Common Heritage of Mankind", in *Progressive Development of the Principles and Norms of International Law Relating to the New International Economic Order: Analytical Papers and Analysis of Texts of Relevant Instruments*, second volume, United Nations Document UNITAR/DS/6 (New York: United Nations Institute for Training and Research, 1983) pp. 437–564.

ALEXANDER J. YEATS, *Trade Barriers Facing Developing Countries* (London: Macmillan, 1979).

ABDULQAWI YUSUF, *Legal Aspects of Trade Preferences for Developing States* (The Hague: Martinus Nijhoffs, 1982).

Index